D1286839

REMAKING U.S. TRADE POLICY

REMAKING
U.S. TRADE POLICY

From Protectionism to Globalization

NITSAN CHOREV

Cornell University Press
Ithaca and London

First published 2007 by Cornell University Press

Printed in the United States of America

Library of Congress Cataloging-in-Publication Data

Chorev, Nitsan.
    Remaking U.S. trade policy : from protectionism to
globalization / Nitsan Chorev.
        p.   cm.
    Includes bibliographical references and index.
    ISBN 978-0-8014-4575-0 (cloth : alk. paper)
    1. Protectionism—United States.   2. Free trade—United
States.   3. Globalization—Economic aspects—United States.   4.
United States—Commercial policy.   I. Title.   II. Title:
Remaking US trade policy.
    HF1455.C556 2007
    382'.30973—dc22   2007018955

Cloth printing   10 9 8 7 6 5 4 3 2 1

To my family

CONTENTS

Preface

Globalization is an economic event, one that is pushing capitalism to its technological, geographical, and cultural extremes. The premise of this book, however, is that economic transformations require a political infrastructure. To make the "free flow" of commodities, capital, money, or professionals possible, governments first have to lower high duties, change laws that prohibit capital transfer, and modify naturalization regulations. These are political obstacles, not economic or technological ones. While the literature on globalization has offered rich and thoughtful accounts of global economic transformations, the goal of this book is to complement these studies by looking at the *political* origins of economic globalization. It therefore offers an inquiry into the political conditions that have allowed economic globalization to emerge.

The book focuses on the particular experience of trade liberalization in the United States from the 1930s to the present. The ability of the U.S. government to impose its preferences on other governments is a necessary part of the narrative, but more central to my analysis is understanding of why the U.S. government supported trade liberalization in the first place. The explanation lies in domestic political struggles. In order for the U.S. government to support trade liberalization, economic actors advocating free trade principles had to prevail over protectionist industries and workers.

Globalization, then, started as a domestic affair. Interestingly, these political struggles focused not on substantive laws—for example, reducing the level of particular duties—but on procedural and organizational matters. In other words, advocates of free trade prevailed in the struggle with protectionists by manipulating the institutional arrangements governing trade policy formation and implementation, replacing institutional arrangements that favored protectionism with new ones that favored a more internationalist orientation. Concretely, internationalist business managed to transfer authority from a protectionist-oriented Congress to agencies in the administration supporting free trade; and they later managed to transfer authority from the administration to the liberal World Trade Organization.

The institutional arrangements introduced by supporters of free trade are of a particular nature. The shift of authority from Congress to the executive and the World Trade Organization entailed a move from a politicized location, in which direct struggles, negotiations, and debates dominate the process of decision-making, to bureaucratic and judicial sites, where political debates are effectively filtered out and replaced by third-party adjudication. In this way, the globalization project has done more than merely replace one site of authority with another. It has fundamentally transformed the democratic nature of policymaking.

An earlier version of chapter 4 appeared as "Making and Remaking State Institutional Arrangements: The Case of U.S. Trade Policy in the 1970s," *Journal of Historical Sociology* (2005); parts of chapter 6 appeared as "The Institutional Project of Neo-Liberal Globalism: The Case of the WTO," *Theory and Society* (2005). I thank Blackwell Publishing and Springer, respectively, for permitting the inclusion of the materials in this book.

The arguments in the book are supported with detailed evidence drawn from original archival materials and numerous interviews. I would not have been able to construct the historical narrative without the great help of resourceful archivists at the U.S. National Archives in Washington, D.C., where the Nixon presidential materials are also located, at the Ford Presidential Library, at the Carter Presidential Library, and at the World Trade Organization Library. I would also like to thank the many individuals who agreed to be interviewed, including former and current officials at the U.S. Trade Representative office, congressional staff, lobbyists for the steel, apparel, and textile industries, trade union representatives, and WTO officials. Their insightful comments and clarifications were fundamental for my understanding of the politics of trade. I was able to conduct this research thanks to financial support provided by New York University and by a Dissertation Improvement Award from the National Science Foundation (2001). I also thank the Ford Presidential Library for a Research Travel Grant.

The photocopies of archival materials, tapes of interviews, and scores of books have traveled many miles from the day I started exploring trade policy formation until today. This endeavor began when I was a graduate student in the Sociology Department at New York University. There, I was taken care of and challenged by a wonderful group of faculty members. Craig Calhoun has taught me a deep appreciation for social theory and critical thinking. Craig's ability to turn raw graduate student papers into coherent scholarly work exemplifies for me the art of sociological thinking, and I thank him for this experience. Neil Brenner, Vivek Chibber, Doug Guthrie, and Steven Lukes were all deeply involved in the process of shaping my thoughts. Vivek spent hours discussing Marxist analysis with me and many other students and pushing my thoughts forward. Neil introduced me to the multidisciplinary literature on globalization and read an endless number of my rough drafts. Doug generously provided intellectual guidance and invaluable professional advice. Finally, Steven Lukes patiently discussed with me various aspects of politics and globalization but also managed to remind me, over engaging lunches, that trade law is not the only fascinating issue around. I am grateful not only for their mentoring but also for their friendship, on which I could always rely. I would also like to thank Troy Duster, Tom Ertman, Ruth Horowitz, and especially Dalton Conley, who was extremely kind and helpful as I prepared the final manuscript.

In Hungary, where I spent two lovely years as an assistant professor in the Department of Sociology and Anthropology at Central European University, I encountered another committed group of readers, including sociologists, anthropologists, political scientists, and philosophers. I am grateful to Dorothee Bohle, Ayse Caglar, Mike Griffin, Erin Jenne, Don Kalb, and Balázs Vedres. For their intellectual support and friendship, I extend special thanks to Gábor Betegh, Judit Bodnar, and Nicole Lindstrom.

I left Budapest for a fellowship at the University of California, Los Angeles. As a Global Fellow at the UCLA International Institute, I was given the opportunity to start a new project, but also to spend some more time on trade issues. I thank Ronald Rogowski and Françoise Lionnet for their support. During my time in Los Angeles, Eric Hayot, Nathan Jensen, Greta Krippner, and Gerardo Munck volunteered to be my local audience, and I am grateful for their constructive comments and advice.

I completed work on this book in the Department of Sociology at Brown University, where I was fortunate to find a group of supportive colleagues.

Nancy Luke, Simone Pulver, and Katherine White have gotten involved not only in the substance of trade issues, but also in the more entertaining tasks of choosing a title and a cover for the book. I owe special thanks to Peter Wissoker, at Cornell University Press, for his support and guidance. At CUP, Susan Specter, Teresa Jesionowski, Jack Rummel, Do Mi Stauber, and the book reviewers, also deserve by sincerest gratitude.

I have collected many other debts along the way. Ronen Shamir, years ago in Tel Aviv University, introduced me to sociology and thereby transformed my professional trajectory. At NYU, Karen Albright, Samera Esmeir, Dorith Geva, Samantha McBride, Emma Naughton, Suzanne Risely, Vanessa Barker, Alexandra Kowalski, and Olga Sezneva shared with me the daunting task of being a graduate student. Also part of my New York and post–New York life were Amir Gotlib, Josh Guetzkow, Jim Jasper, Victoria Johnson, Alexandra Kalev, Dori Kimel, Michael Laskawy, Julia Loktev, Ruti Palmon, Jim Ron, and Yehouda Shenhav. They are the proof that writing is not an isolated task after all. It was thanks to this contentious, demanding, and at times, impossible bunch that, against all odds, these were enjoyable times.

And, finally, there is my family, watching over me from afar. I know they wish I had planned my life somewhat differently, but this has never stopped them from wholeheartedly supporting me. I dedicate this book to my sister Liran and my brother Yariv, whom I love dearly; to my mother, who taught me the theory and practice of independence; and to my father, who respected this independence but always supported me when I needed him.

NITSAN CHOREV

Providence, Rhode Island

Abbreviations for Archival Documents

BE	Business-Economics
CF	Confidential Files
DPS	Domestic Policy Staff
GFL	Gerald R. Ford Library
JCL	Jimmy Carter Library
NPMP	Nixon Presidential Materials Project
NSC	National Security Council
STR	Office of Special Trade Representative
SF	Subject File
TA	Trade
WHCF	White House Central Files
WHCFSF	White House Central Files Special Files
WHSF	White House Special Files

CHAPTER ONE

THE POLITICS OF GLOBALIZATION

One of the initial and persistent images of the current process of globalization has been the free flow of commodities across borders.[1] Rather than
national producers providing for domestic consumers, economic globalization entails a radical increase in the consumption of commodities produced elsewhere. In the year 2000, Americans consumed $9.3 billion worth
of imported vegetables and fruits, $14.9 billion worth of imported shoes,
and $161.7 billion worth of imported cars. In the same year, American man-
ufacturers exported $11.1 billion worth of cereals and $10.9 billion worth of
paper. Americans consumed $14.7 billion worth of imported pharmaceuti-
cal products at the same time that American pharmaceutical companies exported medicines worth $13.1 billion.[2] The total value of U.S. imports in
2000 was $1.476 trillion, and the total value of exports was $1.096 trillion.[3]

[1] For studies that use trends in trade to "measure" globalization, see Dicken 1998; Hirst
and Thompson 1999; Held et al. 1999; Chase-Dunn, Kawano, and Brewer 2000.
[2] U.S. International Trade Administration data, Table 23 (U.S. Total Exports, 1998–2003),
available at http://www.ita.doc.gov/td/industry/otea/usfth/aggregate/Ho3t23.html, and Table
24 (U.S. Total Imports, 1998–2003), available at http://www.ita.doc.gov/td/industry/otea/us-
fth/aggregate/Ho3T24.html.
[3] U.S. Department of Commerce, Bureau of Economic Analysis, National Income and
Product Accounts Tables, Table 1.1.6. Real Gross Domestic Product, Chained (2000) Dollars.
Available at http://bea.gov/bea/dn/nipaweb/index.asp.

The economic features of globalization that this frenzied flow of commodities captures cannot be dissociated from parallel political developments. As Karl Polanyi (1957 [1944], 37) compellingly insisted, "A belief in spontaneous progress must make us blind to the role of government in economic life. This role consists often in altering the rate of change, speeding it up or slowing it down as the case may be." The process of trade liberalization would not have been possible without corresponding policy changes, which regulated its scope and pace. For the production, sale, and investment in foreign markets to be legally possible and financially profitable, domestic and international laws had to be drastically transformed (Vogel 1996). The "free" (ostensibly without limits on quantity and without duties or other costs) flow of commodities from one domestic market to another depended on and was tightly monitored by national governments, which had to agree to cut existing tariffs, limit import quotas, reduce export subsidies, and restrict other nontariff barriers (NTBs) to trade, such as buy-national procurement regulations or product standards. In short, governmental restriction of the so-called "protectionist" measures was necessary for the increased volume of commodities flowing into and out of domestic markets. Indeed, in the United States, the increase in the flow of commodities across the border, which started as early as the mid 1930s,[4] was accompanied by increasingly liberal trade policies. Duties were lowered from a high of 52.8 percent in 1930 to 9.9 percent in 1967 and 5.2 percent by 1982 (Keech and Pak 1995; Hansen and Prusa 1997); import quotas have been gradually eliminated; and nontariff barriers, while still common, have been used in an increasingly restrained manner. "The contemporary open global . . . order," Helleiner (1994, vii) rightly asserts, "could never have emerged without the support and blessing of states as well."

Yet remarkably little attention has been drawn to the political *foundations* of recent economic transformations. The most prevalent descriptions of globalization still see it as the product of economic or technological developments, and narrow its political dimension to a *reaction* by states to processes occurring outside their domain. In typical accounts of the trajectory of globalization, a set of technological changes, in particular those advancing communication and transportation, and/or new economic

[4] In 1932, the total value of imports was $27.9 billion. It increased from then on, with the exception of the years of the Second World War, to $59.3 billion total of imports in 1950 and $213.4 billion in 1970. Twenty years later, in 1990, the total value of imports rose to $607.1 billion, and by the year 2000 it reached $1.4758 trillion. U.S. Department of Commerce, Bureau of Economic Analysis, National Income and Product Accounts Tables, Table 1.1.6. Real Gross Domestic Product, Chained (2000) Dollars. Available at http://bea.gov/bea/dn/nipaweb/index.asp.

conditions that forced manufacturing and finance capital into cross-national expansion, brought about the economic characteristics of today's globalization. The resulting mobility of capital put an inescapable structural pressure, to which national governments *then* had to succumb, by introducing globalization-inducing policies.[5]

These economic or technological accounts suggest that the global economic changes have *preceded* the political ones. However, classical sociological analyses have long ago insisted on the necessity of political and institutional conditions for radical economic transformations. Max Weber emphasized the role of formal-rational legal systems and bureaucratic states in bringing about capitalism in Europe (Weber 1968 [1922]). Even Karl Marx conceded the necessity of private property—a legal construction—for the emergence of capitalism (Marx and Engels 1978 [1845]; Marx 1978 [1859]). As Martin Shaw asserts, therefore, "It is simply implausible that there could have been significant technical, commercial or cultural change without important political antecedents and concomitants, as well as effects. . . . It literally does not make sense to propose that economic or cultural globalization could by itself undermine the nation-state, without specifically political transformations actively influencing the process" (Shaw 2000, 13). Capital could not become mobile and financial markets could not internationalize without *corresponding* legal and political transformations. Furthermore, as Philip McMichael rightly observes, the argument that the political reorganization of world capitalism lags behind its economic reorganization "discounts the political moment, obscuring the political *struggles* that define the relations of globalization" (McMichael 2001, 203, italics added). In the United States, advocates of policies advancing global economic developments—among them internationally competitive corporations, local industries using imported goods, commercial and investment banks, as well as private policy-discussion groups and various state officials—had to prevail over protectionist demands made by various domestic industries and their workers, and supported by economic nationalists and American isolationists. Similar struggles between supporters of free trade on the one hand and protectionists on the other have emerged in other countries where liberal trade policies were considered. The contours of today's globalization are the result of these struggles. In short, because they assume an unmediated link between

---

[5] On technological changes and their effect on state power, see Strange 1996; Dicken 1998; on capitalist mobility and expansion, see Sklair 1991; Camilleri and Falk 1992; Bonacich et al. 1994; Sassen 1996; on international financial markets, see Arrighi 1994; Block 1996; Strange 1996; Mann 1997.

economic conditions and states' reaction to them, those holding a structuralist perception of globalization have failed to study the political debates, negotiations, and compromises that strongly shaped the process of globalization, its scope, and its pace.

Appropriately, political struggles over the global expansion of capital have occurred both at the domestic and the interstate level. While analytically it is useful to differentiate between the two levels, in practice political struggles over globalization often happened at the same time in both spheres, with internationalist business pushing for the imposition of neoliberal and globalizing policies at home and abroad. In the case of trade, internationalist business was primarily concerned with bringing down tariffs and nontariff barriers to trade in *other* countries, in order to improve their access to foreign markets. But a logic of reciprocity in interstate trade negotiations meant that they first had to defeat protectionist demands at home. Obviously, the two struggles were interrelated—government support at the international level depended on political success at the domestic level, and political success at the domestic level was partly influenced by international pressures.

So far, however, the few studies on the political making of globalization have focused on political processes and struggles almost solely at the international level. In particular, scholars have most often studied how the United States imposed neoliberal laws and globalizing practices on others (Gilpin 1975; Helleiner 1994; Gowan 1999). This emphasis on interstate relations has come at the expense of an analysis of domestic processes. While documenting the active role of states in enabling capital's global expansion and in imposing globalizing practices on other countries, these scholars say little about domestic political debates, negotiations, and compromises that shaped the global-oriented practices of the "pioneering" governments.[6] Interstate negotiations and international rules are fundamental to the diffusion of global practices such as open trade (Henisz, Zelner, and Guillén 2005; Polillo and Guillén 2005; Simmons, Dobbin, and Garrett 2006) and will be an integral part of the analysis here, but we also need to explore political processes at the domestic level. In particular, we need to study the *domestic* origins of governments' support of globalization: how could internationalist business curb opposition and impose global rules *at home*? This is particularly necessary for the study of dominant or core states, which created the rules at the international level rather than being pressed to

---

[6] Kapstein (1994), who employs Putnam's two-level game approach to study the response of states to the challenges posed by financial globalization, is an exception in this regard.

comply with them. In the case of trade, before supporters of internationalist policies in the United States could bring down barriers to trade, they first had to defeat the protectionist opposition led by domestic industries that were not internationally competitive and therefore expected to be hurt by a process of trade liberalization. The U.S. textile, apparel, and footwear industries, the steel industry, and latecomers such as automobile manufacturers and the semiconductor industry invested extensive political resources in an effort to block the entry of competing commodities into the domestic market. Initially, their political influence exceeded that of the internationalists. To understand the possibility of trade liberalization in the United States, therefore, we need to explain how internationally competitive corporations, bankers, foreign investors, and importers could overcome the persistent opposition of domestic protectionists.

Assertions of the importance of studying domestic processes for understanding the politics of globalization have, of course, been made before. In response to the prevailing view that describes the state as a victim of the globalization process, scholars who study domestic transformations have insisted that certain states, if not all, may be able to adapt to (Weiss 1998), resist (Garrett 1995), or take advantage of (Evans 1995) the structural conditions imposed from above (see also Thomson and Krasner 1989; Krasner 1995). Central to this approach is an emphasis on the variation in the reaction of nations to external economic pressures. This variation, many scholars have argued, has been an outcome of conditions not at the international level but at the domestic one. Specifically, many have maintained that the institutional features of the state, such as the inclusiveness of electoral institutions or the structure of welfare programs, determine the extent to which economic pressures associated with globalization would bring domestic changes (Swank 2002; see also Keohane and Milner 1996; Weiss 1998; Weiss 2003; Kahler and Lake 2003; Campbell 2003).

Such studies offer an important contribution for our understanding of how state institutions mediate between global economic developments and domestic reactions. Yet in these accounts the state is again merely reactive. Global processes are considered as given, and this position's only dispute with the "globalist" approach is that the "challenges of openness" are not resolved automatically or deterministically, but are mediated by the domestic institutions of governance (Weiss 1998). However, globalizing policies at the domestic level have not always reflected a passive reaction to economic or technological developments, but, at times, preceded these developments. By assigning only a reactive role to the state, these studies fail to see that state institutions, as well as domestic political struggles over them, are an integral, rather than responsive, part of the globalization process.[7]

In short, the literature on globalization and the state tends to concentrate either on *international* pressures or on domestic *reaction* to global processes already there, and therefore offers little by way of explaining how domestic political processes contributed to economic developments, such as trade liberalization, in the first place. The aim of this book is to fill this lacuna, by highlighting the domestic aspects of globalization politics, as well as linking together, empirically and theoretically, the domestic and the international dimensions of the political game.

The starting point of my argument, as already discussed, is that corporations seeking to expand beyond the boundaries of their domestic markets could not just create a global economy without the support of their governments. For capital expansion to be possible, governments had first to reach interstate agreements for the reduction of barriers to commodities, money, and services. The reciprocal nature of such agreements—governments could not expect others to reduce barriers to their markets without offering equivalent concessions—placed their champions in direct conflict with protectionist interests. Hence, gaining the support of states for such policies necessitated, more than globalization scholars usually appreciate, a taxing struggle against domestic opposition, which came from economic actors concerned with international competition and, more recently, social movements concerned with the implications free trade has on domestic social standards. The success of internationalists was not a trivial or predictable matter. In the United States, protectionists had prevailed in the struggle for the previous century and a half. Businesses interested in liberal trade had rarely gained any concessions, and these concessions were often quickly overturned (see chapter 3 of this book). In 1934, trade policy was turned on its head even though protectionist industries still occupied a major part of the economy and had great political influence in Congress. How could internationalists, all of a sudden, gain the upper hand? Struggles often revolved around particular policies—whether or not, for example, to increase import quotas on textiles. But to understand the success of U.S.

---

[7] For an important exception, see Panitch (1994; 1996), who has strongly asserted the active role of the state in bringing about globalization. His analysis of NAFTA assigns an active role to the Mexican and Canadian governments, who represented the interests of their bourgeoisies and bureaucracies (as these have already been penetrated by American capital and administration). See also Kapstein 1994; Weiss 1998, 208. See Sell 2003; Drahos and Braithwaite 2003, for two studies that document the role of U.S. industries in pushing the regulation of intellectual property rights at the international level.

internationalists, and the durability of their globalizing project, it is more important to look elsewhere. I will show that the more consequential political struggles focused not on substantive policies, but rather on changing the institutional arrangements in place, that is, the rules and procedures that govern how future policies would be formulated and implemented. Over time, free trade forces succeeded in changing the playing field in ways that rendered protectionists' old strategies futile, and that effectively disorganized protectionists and deprived them of the political clout and unity they needed to chart an alternative course. In particular, internationalists put in place institutional arrangements that limited the political influence of protectionists and their supporters in Congress, and enhanced the influence of officials supportive of the globalization project in U.S. administrations and the international organization governing trade relations. It was this "structural internationalization" of the state and international organizations, I argue, that assured the prevalence of trade liberalization.

Rethinking Institutions

The emergence of new state and international structures in tandem with globalizing practices is readily noticeable, as a long list of examples can illustrate. In some cases, this involves an internal reorganization of the state, so that "power within the state becomes concentrated in those agencies in closest touch with the global economy" (Cox 1996, 302; cf. McMichael 1996). One particularly suitable example is the transformation of central banks. During the postwar era, finance ministers were often the key decision makers, while most central banks had little discretionary power. Globalization and neoliberalism, however, are more compatible with the recentering of power in the hands of economic technocrats and financial interests. Central banks free from political contingencies were expected to be in a position to pursue the goals of fiscal discipline and monetary stability, to impose austerity and stability on the economy, and to guarantee foreign investors that the value of their holdings would not be undermined (Polillo and Guillén 2005). From the late 1980s on, a great number of governments in Western Europe, but also in Latin America, Eastern Europe, and elsewhere, made their central banks legally independent (Carruthers, Babb, and Halliday 2001; Polillo and Guillén 2005).

While the example of central banks describes an institutional innovation shared by many, countries have also gone through unique institutional transformations that then affected the scope and pace of their integration into the global economy. Mexico, China, and Hungary offer interesting cases. In Mexico, globalization and neoliberal practices—including reforming the central bank, and liberalizing its financial market and trade policies—have been a result of IMF pressure *combined with* particular institutional and political transformations at the state level (Babb 2001). Babb describes how a culmination of a historical process whereby elected officials systematically lost ground to other groups within the ruling party put U.S.-educated professional economists in positions of authority, from which they could passionately defend and actively advance the economic reforms prescribed by the IMF (Babb 2001, 175–77). In China, too, fundamental changes in the economy were preceded by institutional transformations, in this case a reorganization of previous administrative hierarchies. According to Guthrie, the decision to delegate production decisions, development plans, and investment strategies down the hierarchy of the command economy meant that many factories have been forced to handle these responsibilities on their own. This dramatically changed the constraints, interests, and incentives in the process of decision making, and led to a radical transformation in the economic practices of Chinese corporations (Guthrie 2001, 25–31). The role of institutional transformations in shaping the degree and form of economic globalization is even more apparent in societies "in transition." As David Stark and Laszlo Bruszt show, the *economic* paths that different Central European countries have taken have been largely affected by the *political* institutions that had been put in place. Thus, whereas in Hungary concentrated authority gave policymakers free rein to lurch from one set of extreme policies to another, each provoking new rounds of economic crises, in the Czech Republic limitations on executive authority produced more moderated, sustainable reforms (Stark and Bruszt 1998, 10–11). Ekiert (2003) similarly shows that the economic trajectory of postcommunist Poland is best explained by reforms to its state structure.[8]

In other cases, the institutional transformation of the state has not entailed an internal reorganization of the state but rather a redistribution of functions between the state and other political entities, with "old and new state capacities being reorganized . . . on sub-national, national, supranational and

---

[8] Relative to other countries "in transition," Russia has had grave difficulties integrating into the global market. It is possible that Russia's difficulties stem from the failure to establish monetary consolidation at the national level to replace the prevalent barter economy. This failure has itself been the outcome of dispute over the location of authority; the central state failed to make an exclusive claim to monetary sovereignty in face of the challenge made by Russian provincial governments (Woodruff 1999).

trans-local levels" (Jessop 1997, 573–74). On the subnational level, there has been a greater engagement of private bodies. This has often involved the creation of "networks" (Castells 1996; O'Riain 2000) or "partnerships" among public institutions and private organizations. These partnerships allowed direct collaborations between state agencies and private interests, with the state often taking the position of an equal partner rather than that of a regulating force. Such cooperation involved entrepreneurial activity,[9] the provision of services, or even the formation of rules and regulations.[10]

Added to that was a visible movement "upwards" (Jessop 1997, 574), that is, the delegation of authority to supranational authorities. Most noticeable is the political and institutional integration of Europe, which has radically changed the economic policies and practices of member-states. For example, the European Council wrote quite a radical directive, which obliged members to liberalize all capital movements (Abdelal 2007). Similarly, the rules governing intra-European trade liberalization—some of which enforced by the European Court of Justice (Alter and Meunier-Autsahalia 1994; Mattli and Slaughter 1995; Mattli and Slaughter 1998)—led to complete liberalization, not necessarily to the liking of all states. Case studies illustrate that the institutional arrangements in place, including the internal voting rules and the nature of delegation to the negotiating agent, lessen the ability of EU members to successfully pass protectionist measures aimed at non-European trading partners (Hanson 1998, 56) and have a great impact on the EU's position in international trade negotiations (Meunier 2000; Meunier 2005).

In line with theoretical approaches that emphasize the role of institutions in policy outcomes (Skocpol 1985; Hall 1986; Jessop 1990; Thelen and Steinmo 1992; Thelen 2004), these examples illustrate an elective affinity between new political institutions and global economic activities. They thereby invite a more thorough examination of the institutional dimension of globalization, including a study of the political struggles that allowed the emergence of these new institutional arrangements in the first place. In this book, I offer such an examination. I look at the politics of globalization—particularly, the

---

[9] In the United Kingdom, for example, Private Finance Initiatives were formed for the purpose of building infrastructural facilities. Rather than the government buying such facilities from the private companies that have built them, these facilities are now built and *owned* by private companies that then charge the government rent for using those sites.

[10] In 1997, in reaction to a public cry against U.S. clothing companies outsourcing to sweatshops in poor countries, the Clinton administration initiated an Apparel Industry Partnership—a task force of clothing companies and human rights organizations, to draft a voluntary "No Sweatshop" Code of Conduct for U.S. apparel and footwear companies.

political struggles over institutional transformations—by presenting a detailed historical analysis of one case study, that of trade liberalization in the United States.

I show that in the United States, supporters of trade liberalization managed to defeat domestic (as well as international) opposition, not by simply changing the substance of trade-related policies, such as lowering high tariffs or abolishing import quotas, but rather by changing the domestic and international institutions that governed how particular trade policies were formed and implemented. It was only within the context of the new institutions that liberal laws could pass and objectionable protectionist measures were abandoned. And it was only once protectionism was sufficiently restrained that globalization in its contemporary features could develop.

My book identifies three major institutional shifts in the United States since the initial formal support of liberal trade policies in the 1930s. Each institutional shift brought about a trade regime characterized by policies more liberal than the previous ones. The first turning point combined two institutional moments, one domestic and one international. In 1934, Congress delegated, for the first time in American history, authority to raise and lower tariffs to the executive branch. In 1947, the Truman administration signed the multilateral General Agreement on Tariffs and Trade (GATT), which functioned as a legal and organizational framework for reaching interstate trade-liberalizing agreements. Together, the 1934 and 1947 arrangements provided the institutional skeleton of a trade policy regime I call *selective protectionism*. This institutional framework permitted successive administrations to pursue the liberal agenda of reducing tariffs, but it also allowed Congress, which was attentive to protectionist sentiments, to keep addressing the concerns of declining industries. The second institutional turning point occurred in 1974, when Congress increased the administration's authority over protectionist measures other than tariffs, by strengthening trade remedy laws under the jurisdiction of the executive branch. I call the regime that emerged in 1974 *conditional protectionism*. I show that the concentration of authority over protectionist measures in the hands of quasi-judicial executive agencies made it more difficult for protectionist industries to get the measures they asked for, and less disruptive for the general liberalization agenda even when they did. At the third institutional turning point, in 1994, Congress approved a strengthened disciplinary authority for the newly established World Trade Organization (WTO), effectively delegating authority from the U.S. government to panelists at the international level. This brought about the regime I call *legalized multilateralism*. Thanks to the new dispute settlement mechanisms,

U.S. administrations improved their ability to impose trade liberalizing practices on others, but the legalization of the WTO also weakened the executive branch's ability to maintain its own protectionist measures when challenged by other countries.

None of the institutional arrangements put in place since the 1930s could completely eliminate protectionist practices. At the same time, I show that while always providing some space for protectionist exceptions, each new set of institutional arrangements filtered out those protectionist interventions that were considered by internationalists the most disruptive to the general process of trade liberalization.[11] Under *selective protectionism*, all-encompassing high tariffs were eliminated, replaced with "selective cases." Under *conditional protectionism*, this unilateral legislation was largely replaced with measures based on trade remedy laws. Under *legalized multilateralism*, these remedies had to be compatible with international obligations. In short, the institutional arrangements in place forced the gradual, partial elimination of the "worst" kinds of protectionism, but allowed, partly thanks to the adaptive strategies of protectionists, the creation of new (albeit more "disciplined") measures. As a result, today's protectionist sentiments pose little threat to the durability of economic globalization and the future expansion of economic practices.

Globalization, Power, and Democracy

The institutional transformations of 1934, 1974, and 1994 share, in spite of significant differences, important common characteristics. First, the delegation of authority from Congress to the executive branch (in 1934 and 1974) and then to the WTO (in 1994) gradually restricted the political influence of protectionist industries—which they had on Congress, less so on quasi-judicial bodies in the administration, and hardly at all on WTO panelists. In other words, each new institutional regime led to the further exclusion of protectionist voices from the process of decision making. However, it was not simply that internationalists improved their political

[11] The relations between protectionism and trade liberalization should not be viewed as a zero-sum game, where more trade liberalization necessitates less protectionism and vice versa. Protectionist practices do not *necessarily* impede the process of trade liberalization. Instead, as I argue in detail in the empirical chapters, protectionist practices of different kinds would have a different effect on trade trends. Some protectionist practices (e.g., import quotas) are considered more harmful for international trade than others (e.g., adjustment assistance for workers, or even high tariffs).

influence at the expense of protectionists. Rather, with the shift of authority from Congress to the executive, and then to the WTO, the political influence of *all* nonstate actors has generally decreased and the autonomy
and influence of administration officials and WTO panelists increased.

Hence, the political project of putting in place institutional arrangements that are favorable to globalizing policies has not merely changed the
relative political influence of competing interest groups. Rather, it transformed the very nature of politics. At the domestic level, the new institutional arrangements channeled policymaking authority away from direct
political struggles in Congress to bureaucratic and quasi-judicial bodies in
the administration. At the international level, the new institutional arrangements channeled debates away from diplomatic negotiations, where
member-states could deliberate, challenge and renegotiate international
agreements, to WTO judicial panels, where exogenous voices and political
deliberations are effectively filtered out and third parties impose interpretations and require the implementation of existing agreements. Together,
these institutional transformations have constituted a shift of authority away
from locations that are more inherently political, to bureaucratic or judicial
sites. The institutional project of globalization entails a process of *depoliticization*, where bureaucratic orientation and structural constraints dominate the process of decision making, at the expense of public debates and
political deliberations.

This feature of the institutional transformation of states and international organizations also provides new conceptual tools that can be employed to reconsider common arguments regarding the weakening of the
state and the possible loss of sovereignty. As for state power, I agree with
Strange (1996) and many others that the U.S. state's capacity to manage or
resist internationalized capital has been weakened but suggest an alternative reason for this weakening. This was not a direct or automatic outcome
of capital's economic manifestations of power, as it is usually portrayed in
the literature. On the contrary, I argue that the bureaucratization and legalization of the state made state officials less exposed to direct political pressures, of both protectionists *and* internationalists. At the same time,
bureaucratization led to the inability of states—due to the exclusion of alternative voices and hence lack of effective opposition—to resist *structural*
constraints. It is because of these structural constraints—themselves an
outcome of the institutional transformation of the state—that the U.S.
state adheres to internationalized capital. Regarding state sovereignty, I argue that while the existence of international organizations as such does not
necessarily impede the sovereignty of dominant states, the bureaucratiza-

tion and legalization of an international organization—with decisions reflecting the internal logic of the organization more than the interests of particular member-states—do lead to the weakening of states' political influence.

An Outline of the Book

The book offers a detailed empirical investigation of trade policy formation in the United States from 1934, when the slow process of U.S. trade liberalization started, to 2004. It identifies the political struggles that led to institutional transformations of the U.S. state and of the international organization governing trade relations, and explains the substantive outcomes that emerged as a result of those institutional changes. To the best of my knowledge, this is the first political history of global trade liberalization to be produced.[12] Additionally, the trajectory of trade liberalization in the United States serves here as a case study of the politics of globalization—not of U.S. politics as a driver of that process. Hence, it can offer conceptual and historical insights into political struggles and institutional transformations in non-U.S. cases as well, as the examples above demonstrate. This book's inquiry into domestic struggles over trade policies challenges the common logic of most studies on globalization in three important ways. First, it examines the *political* dimension of globalization not as a reaction to economic processes, but as a parallel and necessary condition for those very processes. Second, it examines *domestic* processes not as epiphenomenal to international occurrences, but as an alternative starting point, and then goes on to analyze the interplay between those domestic and international processes. Finally, it focuses on the *interplay* between political struggles and institutional arrangements. In contrast to most analyses, which highlight one factor—political struggles *or* institutional arrangements—while holding the other constant, in this book I show the dynamic interaction between the two factors.

In chapter 2 I provide the methodological and theoretical foundations for my empirical claims. In this chapter I offer a historical institutionalist approach for analyzing domestic as well as international political developments. I first describe how institutional arrangements shape policy outcomes. I argue that institutional arrangements—in particular, those

---

[12] Most of the studies on the politics of globalization focus on the case of money and finance (Kapstein 1994; Helleiner 1994; Krippner 2003; Abdelal 2007).

determining the distribution of authority among alternative sites, the level of discretion provided to those making decisions, and the degree of access provided to others—directly and substantively affect the political influence of interested actors. The interested actors considered here are nonstate actors as well as state and international organization (IO) officials. I differentiate between three types of relationships that institutional arrangements affect: the relative influence of competing (nonstate and non-IO) actors; the level of relative autonomy state and IO officials enjoy; and the relative authority and influence of competing state/IO agencies.

While my book draws on historical institutionalist analysis, I emphasize the interplay between institutions and strategic actors more than most current formulations. This, I argue, allows for a better understanding of the possibility of institutional change, as well as of policy outcomes within a given set of institutions. I argue that institutional change is a result of deliberate political action of strategic players (those include either nonstate actors or state officials, and often a collaboration of the two). Institutions that originate in such political struggles are then biased in favor of those who designed them. As a result, future policies often reflect the designers' interests. But biased institutional arrangements can never completely silence or co-opt competing political actors, who often develop strategies better suited to the new institutional context. When successful, these counter-strategies improve the position of the contenders, and allow them to gain important concessions.

In the ensuing chapters I describe the political struggles leading to the establishment of new institutional regimes in 1934/1947, 1974, and 1994, and carefully analyze the impact each institutional transformation had on subsequent trade policies, and on the globalization project as it unfolded over time. Each chapter also emphasizes one of the theoretical points established in chapter 2. Chapter 3, about the institutional changes in 1934 and 1947 and the substantive outcomes that followed those changes, provides evidence to the basic claim that institutions "mattered" in the making of liberal trade policies. Chapter 4 focuses on the question of institutional change by describing and analyzing the political struggles leading to the institutional turn in 1974. While chapter 4 shows that the globalizing institutions have been intentionally designed by internationally oriented business and state officials, chapter 5, about the period between 1974 and 1994, provides evidence that the expectations from those institutions have been met. At the same time, I also demonstrate how "unexpected consequences" are the outcome of ongoing political struggles. Finally, in chapter 6, an examination of the establishment of the World Trade Organization in 1994 shows the utility in applying this historical institutionalist analysis to the international level. Together, the chapters offer extensive empirical evidence of the political struggles, institutional transformations, and policy outcomes that resulted in a comprehensive, and surprisingly efficient, set of domestic and international rules governing the liberalization of international trade.

Chapter 3 first describes the legal and procedural framework that governed trade policy formation before 1934. During that period, Congress used its constitutional authority over tariff setting to keep tariffs consistently high, thereby limiting the flow of commodities into the domestic market. This tradition climaxed in 1930, when members of Congress responded to a wave of demands from industries hurt by the Great Depression by passing the infamous Smoot-Hawley Tariff, which increased the average tariff rate to one of the highest in American history. The Smoot-Hawley Tariff, and the subsequent wave of protectionist responses among trading partners of the United States, encouraged U.S. businesses— including technologically advanced manufacturers, extractive industries, and major commercial and investment banks—that benefited from lower tariffs, in cooperation with internationalists in the State Department, to finally change the rules of the political game. To allow for the possibility of bilateral trade-reducing agreements, the Reciprocal Trade Agreements Act (RTAA) of 1934 shifted the authority to raise and lower tariffs from Congress to the administration. At the international level, and as part of the postwar reconstruction, the U.S. government established the General Agreement on Tariffs and Trade (GATT), which became the organizational framework for *multi*lateral trade agreements.

Together, the RTAA and the GATT provided the institutional framework for the regime of *selective protectionism*. Under this regime, successive U.S. administrations used their novel authority to bring about a historically unprecedented drop in U.S. tariffs. At the same time, however, protectionist measures other than high tariffs were still under the jurisdiction of Congress, which willfully arranged "pockets" of special protection for certain industries. The main beneficiaries were large, labor-intensive, and geographically dispersed industries, such as textile and apparel. The institutional arrangements of the GATT allowed rich member-states to control the agenda, and the GATT was therefore ineffectual against Congress's violation of its international obligations.

In retrospect, it turned out that the compromise between internationalist interests and protectionist ones depended more on the good will of the protectionists than the internationalists were willing to admit. The institutional arrangements in place provided some room for protectionist "abuse" that declining industries took advantage of as soon as the economic recession of the early 1970s surfaced. Successful attempts by a number of protectionist industries, most particularly the textile industry, to mobilize Congress on their behalf, clashed with the internationalists' preferred response to the economic recession. Internationalists then again sought to transform the institutional arrangements in place. In chapter 4, I describe in detail the political struggles leading to the Trade Act of 1974, where institutional arrangements that further narrowed the control of Congress over protectionist claims were introduced. I describe how supporters of open trade in the Nixon administration, with the backing of internationalist-oriented business associations, such as the Committee for a National Trade Policy (CNTP) and the Emergency Committee on American Trade (ECAT), concluded that the best way to direct protectionist complaints away from Congress, where such complaints could have resulted in legislated import quotas, was to strengthen the so-called trade remedy laws. These were laws in the books—including trade adjustment assistance, escape clause, antidumping law, and countervailing duty law—that provided some authority for the administration to deal with trade-related complaints. Before 1974, however, the conditions for providing relief were so strenuous that protectionist industries only rarely referred to them. One of the major sections of the Trade Act of 1974, therefore, included provisions to make these remedies more lenient. The case of the Trade Act of 1974 provides ample evidence that the institutional transformations in the history of American trade policy were designed by supporters of trade liberalization precisely to curb protectionist influence over international trade policy. It also explains why it was the case that while protectionists had sufficient political leverage in Congress to pass protectionist legislation, they often failed to block damaging legislation that dealt with institutional matters. I show how internationalists managed to divide the protectionist coalition by "buying out" the most politically influential industries, and analyze how, somewhat paradoxically, it was easier for protectionist industries to form stable coalitions for supporting particularistic policies (e.g., import quotas for the textile industry) than to oppose general policies.

The enhanced authority of the executive branch to act unilaterally on trade issues was at the core of the regime of *conditional protectionism*. Under this new regime, Congress no longer provided selective treatment to politically influential industries. Instead, members of Congress focused only on making the trade remedy laws as lenient as possible and overseeing the administration's implementation of these laws. The most that protectionist industries could ask of the executive were measures against demonstrated injury or unfair trade practices of international competitors. While the political maneuvering of protectionist industries was quite severely restricted as a result, protectionists did adapt to the new constraints with innovative political strategies, which enabled the more concentrated, capital-intensive, and potentially more internationally competitive industries, such as steel, to gain significant benefits. The analysis of the regime of *conditional protectionism*, including an explanation for the variation in the ability of protectionists to gain supportive intervention from different administration agencies, is the subject of chapter 5.

In the 1990s, struggles over institutional arrangements shifted to the international realm. In an attempt to strengthen American control over trade practices in other countries, particularly in regard to nontraditional issues such as services, investment, and intellectual property, the U.S. administration fought for strengthening the disciplinary authority of the international organization governing trade. In the 1994 agreement concluding the Uruguay Round of multilateral trade negotiations, member-states gave the newly established World Trade Organization (WTO) more effective judicial powers. Consequently, under the new regime of *legalized multilateralism*, national measures for protecting domestic industries that violated international obligations could be effectively challenged by other countries. The WTO's intensified involvement in domestic trade laws and practices led to further liberalization of trade. In particular, the new dispute settlement mechanisms strengthened the ability of the United States to control domestic legislation and economic practices of other countries, but it also constrained its ability to apply protectionist practices at home. The primary beneficiaries among protectionists were those industries interested in improving access to foreign markets, such as the semiconductor industry. This is analyzed in chapter 6, which brings to the forefront the analysis of the international dimension of trade policymaking.

In the conclusion I draw on the case of trade liberalization in the United States to make some general claims concerning the institutional nature of the globalization project, the transformation in state-capital relations, and the alleged decline in states' sovereignty. I reiterate my argument that globalization should be viewed as a deliberate political project of putting in place institutional arrangements that are favorable to globalizing policies. This institutional project, I then argue in more detail, has entailed a shift of authority away from locations that are more inherently political, to *bureaucratic* or *judicial* sites. In these sites, the bureaucratic orientation of state and IO officials and structural constraints dominate the process of decision making at the expense of public debates and political deliberations. I argue that this bureaucratization/judicialization of political processes and the ensuing political weakening of the opposition, rather than global capital's economic activities, is responsible for the weakening of states' capacity to manage or resist internationalized capital. In a parallel development, the judicialization of the WTO weakened the political influence of member-states, including the United States, at the international level. The book concludes with some suggestions for future research and the irresistible attempt to discuss possible future developments.

CHAPTER TWO

INSTITUTIONS IN DOMESTIC AND INTERNATIONAL POLITICS

Globalization is (also) a political project. The formation and development of the global economy have entailed political struggles over the rules governing global economic activity. Of great importance were political struggles over the institutional reorganization of states and international organizations. I show that internationalist businesses have won liberal trade policies by introducing institutional arrangements biased in their favor. The institutions that emerged are of a particular kind: policymaking at both the domestic and international levels have become increasingly bureaucratized and legalized.

To appreciate the role of institutions in bringing globalization about, in this chapter I offer a general theory of political institutions. I address two fundamental questions in institutional theory: why institutions matter, and how they change. Interwoven into the discussion is an exploration of the role of institutions at the international level, which is essential to our understanding of the political trajectory of the process of globalization.

At the core of my institutionalist approach is an *ongoing* interplay between institutions and strategic actors. Institutions, I argue, shape actors' political influence. As institutions are often biased, they enable some interest groups to shape laws and policies in their favor, while denying influence from others. I do not suggest, however, that the political preferences, strategies, and successes of political actors are entirely determined by the institutions in place. Within any *given* institutional context, political strategies still matter for the final outcome. Political actors, in other words, always maintain the capacity to slightly manipulate the institutional context, so that political decisions are the outcome of a constant interplay between the institutions in place and the political resources and strategies employed (often in reaction to the institutional context). As I show here, protectionist industries were at times able to utilize institutional opportunities in a way unforeseen by internationalists. My analysis, however, provides an even more important role for political strategies. I argue that the biased institutional arrangements themselves are an outcome of intended political action. Intended, that is, precisely to favor those who put the institutions in place. There is a dynamic process in which the rules and procedures of institutions are under constant negotiation even as these same institutions have the capacity to shape the outcome of those very negotiations.

My analysis draws most directly on the historical institutionalist approach, from which I take the arguments that institutions shape the outcome of political struggles and that institutional arrangements provide advantage to some competing social groups at the expense of others (Weir 1992a; Hall and Taylor 1996, 937–41; Thelen 1999, 395; see also Jessop 1990). At the same time, my analysis also draws, when appropriate, on alternative institutionalist approaches.[1] While I disagree with the functional view of rational choice institutionalists, according to which institutions are put in place to reduce transaction costs and achieve other *joint* gains (Shepsle 1989; Koremenos, Lipson, and Snidal 2001; Rosendorff and Milner 2001; cf. Thelen 1999),[2] I share with them the view that competing actors are both

---

[1] Following Hall and Taylor (1996), I see the rational choice, historical, and sociological variants of institutionalist analysis as potentially compatible. See also Thelen (1999) for a review of a tendency toward convergence among the competing approaches. See Hay and Wincott (1998) for a counterargument.

[2] Rosendorff and Milner (2001), for example, argue that safeguards in international agreements, which allow governments to withdraw previous concessions, are a rational response of governments to domestic political uncertainties. This is undoubtedly true, but it is also true that these safeguards are not equally rational (that is, beneficial) to all governments. Particularly, the United States and other developed countries have used the safeguard provisions often, usually withdrawing concessions of most value for developing countries. As a result, the United States kept pushing for maintaining lenience in the provisions, whereas developing countries wanted to limit the flexibility inscribed in the agreement. It should be mentioned that there are scholars who adhere to rational choice institutionalism while following a nonfunctionalist view of institutions (see North 1990; Knight 1992; Pierson 1996; cf. Thelen 1999).

rational and strategic, involved in "material-based" (rather than "norm-based") actions.[3] For the analysis of conflicts over trade policy, there is little gain in thinking of institutions as constituting actors' *interests*, rather than mainly shaping their preferences and strategies. Institutions rarely "socialize" but often make some political strategies more rational to pursue than others, and then "lock" actors in those paths.[4] From the other side of the institutionalist map, I take from Bob Jessop's strategic-relational approach to the state the emphasis on political struggles as the major source of institutional dynamism (Jessop 1990; Jessop 2001).[5] It is this somewhat eclectic view of institutions, I argue, that best captures the institutional trajectory of trade policy formation in the United States.[6]

[3] See Thelen's cautious suggestion that the divide between rational choice and historical institutionalism is possibly giving way to a divide between materialist-oriented analysis and norm-oriented analysis (Thelen 1999, 380n).

[4] One of the core claims of historical institutionalism is that "the definition of interests and objectives is created in institutional contexts and is not separable from them" (Zysman 1994, 244; cited in Thelen 1999, 375; cf. Thelen 1999, 374–77; Orren and Skowronek 2002, 739). At the same time, as Ellen Immergut argued, "most institutionalists focus on how institutions may foster the emergence of particular definitions of mutual interest, or advantage particular political choices, without necessarily re-socializing citizens in a fundamental way" (Immergut 1997, 339–40; cited in Thelen 1999, 375n).

[5] The strategic-relational approach to the state conceptualizes the state as a form-determined condensation of the balance of political forces. According to Jessop, "This approach puts the form of the state at the heart of any analysis of . . . state intervention in so far as the *complex form of the state as an institutional ensemble shapes and conditions the whole political process*. But it also directs attention to the differential constitution of the *various forces engaged in struggle within, as well as without, the state* and to the diverse structural and conjunctural factors that determine their relative weight" (Jessop 1990, 149, italics added).

[6] The major goal of this chapter is to introduce institutionalist analysis to the study of the making of globalization. It is still worthwhile to make explicit my position in relation to institutionalist theories of trade. Following general trends in international relations and comparative politics, institutionalist analysis has been, especially recently, prevalent in the studies of trade policy. At the international level, institutionalists successfully argued against the neorealist hegemonic stability theory (Kindleberger 1973; Krasner 1976; Gilpin 1981; Lake 1988) and showed that international organizations and regimes, and not (only) geopolitical balance of power, explain trends in trade liberalization (Finlayson and Zacher 1981; Ruggie 1982). At the domestic level, institutionalists have argued, mainly in a debate with pluralists or other interest-based approaches (Schattschneider 1935; Gourevitch 1977; Frieden 1988), that the institutional setting in which struggles over trade policies take place has an important impact on the final outcome (Ikenberry 1988; Keohane and Milner 1996; Milner 1997). I rely on these studies' theoretical insights and empirical findings throughout my analysis. My disagreements with institutionalist theories of trade, in turn, mostly echo my disagreements with rational choice institutionalism, from which most theories of trade policymaking draw. While my historical institutionalist analysis shares a lot with competing institutionalist analyses of trade, I emphasize the political struggles and conflicts preceding the establishment of the

Domestic Politics and Institutions in the Literature on Globalization

In the literature on globalization, the adoption of globalizing policies has been most often explained as an outcome of changing power relations between state and capital. Capital mobility and the consequent ability of businesses to threaten to move their investments elsewhere, improved businesses' bargaining position and made the state incapable of rejecting their demands (Ohmae 1990; Ohmae 1995; Reich 1992; Camilleri and Falk 1992; *Daedalus* 1995; Strange 1996; Albrow 1996; Falk 1997; Greider 1997). This view of the state as a passive victim of capitalist expansion across national borders, however, has been at least partly challenged by institutionalists who rightly assert that this argument grants states little leverage to resist, and therefore cannot explain variation in the reactions of nations to their common structural predicament (Weiss 1998; Weiss 2003; Swank 2002; Kahler and Lake 2003; Campbell 2003). Institutionalist literature on globalization hence enriches the discussion by assigning a mediating role to domestic institutions; at least under certain institutional conditions, states have been able to resist these pressures. As I argue in the introductory chapter, however, the literature on the domestic politics of globalization fails to assign to states the active role they deserve. In particular, and fundamental to the discussion in this chapter, the institutionalist literature on the politics of globalization treats state institutional arrangements as exogenous to the analysis and as being constant over time. As a result, it overlooks the crucial fact that state institutional arrangements have themselves been *negotiated* and *transformed* to facilitate the project of globalization (Cox 1987; Cox 1992; McMichael 1996; Jessop 1997). Precisely because of changes *made to* domestic and international institutions, U.S. trade policies have been able to support and advance the processes of trade liberalization and globalization in spite of the persistent opposition of import-sensitive industries. By making the political influence of protectionists less effective, the institutional arrangements have *later* made possible substantive changes. In the remainder of this chapter I will make the claim that the historical institutionalist approach is the most adequate to capture the logic of such institutional transformations and their impacts at the domestic and the international levels.

---

institutions and maintain that institutions reflect these struggles, rather than mutual interests (Rosendorff and Milner 2001) or the prominent ideas of the time of their construction (Goldstein 1993). I return to these theoretical disagreements, as well as some empirical divergences, in the empirical chapters of the book.

How Do Institutional Arrangements Matter?

My analysis of the place of institutions in policymaking starts with the ultimate beneficiaries, and therefore with political struggles.[7] Policies and laws, I contend, are the outcome of political action of strategic players, who attempt to advance their interests by bringing about a favorable legal environment. But competing actors do not have an equal ability to attain their goals. Instead, the ability to attain favorable results in the face of opposition depends on the relative situational and structural positions of the competing forces. Actors' *situational* position depends on their available resources (material and otherwise) and on the political strategies they employ. All else being equal, actors who have resources to spend on their political cause are better off than actors without these resources; actors with a capacity to mobilize supporters are better off than actors without such capacity; and so on. Actors' *structural* position reflects the extent to which state officials are structurally dependent on those actors' decisions and practices to assure national security or economic growth.[8] All else being equal, actors are better off if supporting them would contribute to the economy at large, or to national security.

Institutionalist analyses contribute to our understanding of policymaking by noting that actors' situational and structural positions are not determined exogenously or independently of the institutional context. The possession of resources, the choice of strategies, and favorable structural positions depend on, and are altered by, the institutional arrangements in place. The institutional frame within which the political struggles take place would also determine how effective particular resources, strategies, and positions are (Skocpol 1992; Thelen and Steinmo 1992, 2–3; Steinmo 1993; Hall and Taylor 1996, 948; Immergut 1998; Pierson and Skocpol 2002).

To understand *how* institutions matter, we need to analyze how institutions affect the situational and structural positions of strategic actors. Analytically, it is useful to differentiate three types of relationships that are shaped by the institutional arrangements in place: the relations between the

---

[7] While it makes chronological sense to first describe how institutions originate, then describe how they matter once in place, and how they transform, analytically it is necessary to start with how institutions matter, and only then describe how they originate and change.

[8] Pluralist and instrumentalist analyses of the state emphasize the determining role of competing groups' situational position (Mills 1956; Dahl 1961; Miliband 1969; Manley 1983; Domhoff 1990). Structuralist analyses of the state emphasize groups' structural position (Offe 1974; Block 1977b; Block 1980a).

competing interest groups; the relations between nonstate actors and state agencies; and the relations between the various state agencies.

1. Institutional arrangements affect the relative *situational* position of competing interest groups (or other nonstate actors). By providing differentiated access to the sites of decision making, institutional arrangements can grant a disproportionate advantage to some actors, at the expense of others (Weir 1992a; Steinmo 1993; Hall and Taylor 1996, 941).[9] The form of representation in the U.S. Congress, for example, provides better access to regionally concentrated interest groups than to regionally dispersed groups of similar size (Pincus 1975; Rogowski 2002). Institutions shape the relative political position of interested actors in other ways as well. By structuring the incentives, options, and constraints faced by political participants (Hansen 1991), they shape their strategies, alliances, and coalition possibilities (Hall 1986; Jessop 1990; Weir 1992b; Immergut 1992, 83; Swank 2003), which inevitably affect the content of the final outcome. The strengthening of the trade remedy laws in 1974, for example, encouraged protectionist industries to shift the site of their demands from Congress to the U.S. administration, which altered the type of protectionist measures they could obtain.

2. State institutional arrangements affect not only the relative position and influence of nonstate actors, however, but also the position of state officials. To appreciate the impact institutional arrangements have on officials' ability to shape policies, we first need to recognize that state officials are active participants in the struggle over favorable outcomes, and view their preferences as *potentially* different from the preferences of dominant nonstate actors. The state is not a neutral body, merely responding to domestic (or international) pressures, for government officials have interests and affiliations that affect how they *react* to such constraints.[10] We must also reject the view of the state as a unified entity and recognize that the state (or any other political body) is a fragmented set of positions and voices. Tasks and authorities are divided among different entities and agencies, each potentially having a distinct position on policy matters (Levi 1988; Migdal 1988; Waldner 1999; Grzymala-Busse

---

[9] For classical studies on the mobilization of bias, see Schattschneider 1960; Bachrach and Baratz 1962; Bachrach and Baratz 1970. See also Offe (1974) on structural selectivity and Jessop (1990) on strategic selectivity.

[10] See Evans, Rueschemeyer, and Skocpol 1985; Block 1977b. Structural Marxism is often categorized as a "society-centered" approach, but Block and others have explicitly analyzed the independent interests of state officials and their autonomy from direct pressures of interest groups, including capitalist interests.

and Luong 2002). A state *agency's* position would depend on a combination of direct pressure from interested groups, structural constraints (Block 1977b; Block 1980a), and the bureaucratic responsibilities assigned to the particular agency.

Since state agencies do not *necessarily* succumb to interest group pressures, the second way in which institutional arrangements matter is by affecting the relations of power between state agencies and nonstate actors, largely by determining the level of autonomy (or insulation) enjoyed by state officials.[11] When not insulated, state officials make decisions that reflect the interests of those nonstate actors with greater situational influence. When insulated from direct pressures, however, state officials make decisions that reflect instead the preferences already inscribed in the agencies themselves. These inscribed preferences reflect, as I mentioned above, structural constraints and/or bureaucratic assignments.[12] Structural constraints and bureaucratic assignments are usually compatible: an agency's responsibilities already take into account structural pressures. At the same time, an agency's responsibilities may affect its relative sensitivity to competing structural pressures: depending on their bureaucratic responsibilities, state officials are inclined to prioritize some structural necessities, such as national security, over others, such as economic growth. Institutional arrangements, such as an agency's degree of discretion, can also affect how tensions between structural constraints and bureaucratic responsibilities are resolved. A low level of discretion entails greater adherence to an agency's bureaucratic assignments, while a high level of discretion permits greater attentiveness to structural constraints.

3. Due to a variation in the level of interest-group pressure, in the assigned bureaucratic tasks, and in the structural constraints, state agencies differ in their perceptions and orientations. A third way in which institutional arrangements matter, therefore, is by determining the allocation of authority *among* state officials, which would be critical for resolving whose voice prevails. Given the different preferences of Congress and the administration, or of the departments of Commerce and State, *where* decisions regarding protectionism are made potentially determines the character of

[11] This suggests that state/society relations partly depend on the institutional arrangements in place, for institutions have the capacity to shape the degree of influence of nonstate actors in the process of decision making, and, therefore, that an institutional transformation may change the nature of these relations.

[12] Note that this formulation refers to autonomy of state officials from direct pressures, *not* autonomy from structural constraints, which are integral to state officials' construction of their interests.

those decisions.[13] Because of the differences in the political influence of pressure groups over various state agencies, the hierarchical distribution of authority among political agencies is also critical for determining which pressure group prevails. Whether decisions are made by Congress or the U.S. administration, for example, will directly affect the political influence of domestic pressure groups.

In short, institutions affect policy outcomes by shaping the relative position of interested actors: institutions affect the relative resources, preferences, and strategies of interested actors; they affect the balance of influence between interested actors and state officials; and they affect the relations among state officials. The history of international trade policymaking in the United States illustrates this fundamental contribution of institutions to policy outcomes.

The analytical focus on institutions should not suggest, however, that no other factors exist that improve, or weaken, the situational and structural positions of competing actors. In this book, I show that U.S.-based multinational corporations improved their political influence by putting in place institutional arrangements biased in their favor. But their greater role in the U.S. economy—itself partly a result of the opportunities allowed by the new policies—strengthened their situational status (more resources to utilize in the political game), as well as their structural position (greater dependence of U.S. economic growth on their activities), independently of the institutional transformations analyzed here. It is exactly the interplay between a group's position and the institutions governing the political game that is fundamental for the analysis here. As we will see, the political influence of internationalist-oriented business on Congress remained limited, so without the institutional changes—which shifted authority to the administration, and then to the WTO—their improved position would have had limited substantive impact. At the same time, there is no doubt that the increasing economic position of internationalists, combined with previous institutional transformations, made recent fights over institutional changes easier to win. In short, while a group's economic position surely matters, political influence cannot be measured solely by a group's resources, for the institutional context would greatly affect the ability to *convert* such resources into actual political influence.

---

[13] Related aspects will have an effect on agencies' positions and the final outcome. Take, for example, the cluster of responsibilities within a given agency. An outcome of two tasks may be quite different if they are performed by two different offices (so that in a case of conflict, an interoffice decision needs to be made), or if the same office is responsible for both tasks (so that in case of a conflict, an intraoffice compromise needs to be made).

Which Institutions Matter?

For the analysis here, I use Peter Hall's somewhat restricted definition of institutions, where institutions include "formal rules, compliance procedures, and standard operating practices. . . . As such, they have a more formal status than cultural norms but one that does not necessarily derive from legal, as opposed to conventional, standing" (Hall 1986, 19). Of the vast number of institutional arrangements that determine the rules of the political game, three in particular are correlated with the three types of relations mentioned above and have proved responsible for shaping the trajectory of protectionist practices in the United States in a way increasingly biased in favor of internationalism:

1. *Access.* State agencies differ in the degree of access they provide to non-state actors ("general access"), and the social groups they provide access to ("differentiated access").[14] The greater the general access to a state agency, the more vulnerable the agency is to social pressures, and the more important the distribution of "differentiated access" would be. Put differently, the greater the general access to a state agency, the more significant an interest group's relative situational position is, and the less important the inherent features of the state agencies, such as structural constraints and bureaucratic responsibilities, are. Congress, for example, offers differentiated access that favors domestic industries over internationalist business, whereas the administration favors internationalists. At the same time, Congress is more accessible to interest groups than the administration, so the influence of protectionists in Congress is a major factor in congressional policies, while the influence of internationalist business in the administration is not. "General access" and "differentiated access" are interrelated, and both depend on the bureaucratic role assigned to the state agency; the "compatibility" between the objectives of the agency and the demands of the interested groups; what the different social groups can offer (e.g., money, votes, or mobilization of support); personal relations and previous personal or professional affiliations; and the discretion allowed to the agency.[15]

[14] Debates over state/society relations focus on the extent to which state institutions are insulated from, and thus have autonomy with respect to, pressure groups. State-centered approaches, in particular, present political institutions as potentially autonomous entities (Evans, Rueschemeyer, and Skocpol 1985). However, for understanding state action we need to consider not only the general level of access but also who among the competing interest groups gets to enjoy that access, that is, the extent to which access is differentiated.

[15] On differentiated access as a filtering mechanism, see Bachrach and Baratz 1962. On how differentiated access is constructed and how it affects state capacity, see, for example, Skocpol and Finegold 1982.

Table 2.1 How do institutions matter?

Institutions affect relations of power	. . . and therefore the relative influence of competing interests	Correlated institutions
Between competing interest groups	The relative situational position of nonstate actors	Differentiated access
Between competing interest groups and state agencies	Autonomy of state officials; structural position of nonstate actors	General access; legalization/discretion
Between competing state agencies	The relative authority of state agencies	Hierarchical distribution of authority

2. *Discretion and degree of legalization.* State agencies differ in the degree of discretion granted to them when they make decisions. A high level of discretion or low degree of regulation provides flexibility (within the constraints of structural dependence and the bureaucratic role) and hence allows greater opportunity for external pressures. While a relatively low level of discretion may protect an agency from external pressures, it might also provide less flexibility for the agency's officials to challenge the formal bureaucratic role.[16]

3. *The hierarchical distribution of political authority.* The distribution of authority can be determined by law or can be decided informally; in both cases it is correlated with the material resources and manpower granted to the office, the relative status of the social forces having access to it, organizational hierarchies (the importance of one agency can be promoted by having the role of centralizing the positions of other offices or heading interagency or overseeing committees), the individuals heading the agencies (e.g., their status or their relations with the president), and general political priorities (e.g., foreign policy versus economic policy).

In short, various institutional arrangements—among them, general and differentiated access, discretion and degree of legalization, and distribution of authority—shape policy outcomes by affecting the situational position of interest groups, the level of autonomy of state officials, and the relative influence of competing state agencies. Table 2.1 summarizes this argument.

---

[16] The institutions that shape an agency's discretion and degree of legalization are a particular case of many other institutional arrangements that determine the "general access" of interest groups to agencies. They are worth a separate consideration since, as I show below, they have been particularly significant in weakening the extent to which social actors can influence trade policies.

Institutions at the International Level

The institutional arrangements of the U.S. state were a major terrain of, and a cause for, confrontation between advocates of trade liberalization and protectionists. Yet the institutional arrangements of the U.S. government are only one part of the institutional constellation that affected the interested actors. In addition, the international organizations governing trade relations—the GATT and then the WTO—also had an important role in the globalizing trajectory of U.S. protectionist practices. Here, again, historical institutionalism is especially useful in analyzing the interplay between interested actors and institutional arrangements, this time at the international level.

Most scholars of globalization who have engaged with the question of international politics have utilized either a neorealist or neo-Marxist view of interstate relations (Cox 1987; Gowan 1999; Shaw 2000). In spite of fundamental differences between these views, both hold that state power at the international realm is determined by the unequal distribution of economic (and military) resources, and international political outcomes are shaped by the constraints and opportunities created by the international structure and the position of nation-states within it. Both formulations maintain a concept of state power that is exogenous to the institutional environment in which this power is exercised and is not affected by it. Institutional arrangements simply reflect the existing power relations among states and have no independent effects.[17]

States do not, however, enter interactions—such as bargaining, legal disputes, or even wars—with a given amount of "power" that they then exercise on others. Instead, the institutional context in which they act would determine how effective their resources or political strategies are (Ikenberry 2001). An unequal distribution of military resources, for example, would matter more in an actual war than in diplomatic negotiations, even if these military resources do affect the outcome of the negotiations. Similarly, an unequal distribution of economic resources would matter more in diplomatic negotiations than in judicial proceedings. In other words, the extent to which the unequal distribution of resources among states influences outcomes would depend on, and can be altered by, the institutional arrangements in place.

---

[17] It is this conception that leads most scholars of globalization to dismiss the possibility that international organizations can impinge on state sovereignty, and see discussion in the concluding chapter of this book.

Among those approaches that do grant some influence to international organizations and regimes,[18] the most dominant is rational-choice institutionalism, which suggests ways in which international organizations can act as independent intervening variables in world politics by affecting the strategies and decisions adopted by states (Keohane 1984; Keohane 2002; Keohane, Nye, and Hoffman 1993; Baldwin 1993). However, this focus on the efficacy of institutional arrangements in maximizing the interests of participating nation-states has the outcome of deemphasizing power relations, conflicts, and struggles, and ignoring the orientation and pressures inscribed in the institutions themselves. I suggest that a historical institutionalist approach that integrates the constitutive role of international organizations with a consideration of disparities between the engaged member-states would be more useful for analyzing international politics. Historical institutionalists, however, have commonly confined their arguments to the domestic level and have not applied their analysis to international organizations (Pierson and Skocpol 2002).[19] In what follows I therefore outline a historical institutionalist approach to the international level.

As at the domestic level, institutional arrangements affect policy outcomes at the international level by shaping the relative influence of interested actors. Here, too, institutional arrangements affect three types of relations. First, institutional arrangements of international organizations affect the situational position of competing actors by providing differentiated access to them. "Actors" here include primarily the member-states of the organization in question, but also nongovernmental organizations, and global and domestic economic (nonstate) actors. For example, whether decisions are made by weighted voting, majority voting, or consensus would greatly affect the ability of poor countries to oppose the demands of rich countries. Institutional arrangements also affect the relative influence of the participants by shaping their strategies, alliances, and coalition possibilities.

---

[18] See the literature on international regimes (Ruggie 1982; Krasner 1983) and social constructivism (Ruggie 1998; Wendt 1999). More recently, studies have drawn on neo-Weberian analyses of the state to argue that international organizations have autonomy and purpose independent of the states that comprise them, and capacity to impose their will on those states (Barnett and Finnemore 1999, 707–10; 2004; Duina and Blithe 1999; Barnett 2002). Yet this approach makes too strong of a claim to be empirically sustainable. Autonomy and capacity are historically specific, and are always in relation to and interaction with the participating member-states.

[19] See Ikenberry (2001) for recent, and rare, application of historical institutionalism to the international realm. It is more common to see historical institutionalism applied to the case of the EU (Pierson 1996). Pierson's approach to institutions, however, tends to deemphasize political struggles, which is central to the approach I offer here.

Institutional arrangements also affect the level of autonomy (or insulation) enjoyed by an international organization's officials. When not insulated, IO officials make decisions that reflect the interests of those member-states or nongovernmental actors with greater situational position. When insulated from direct pressures, IO officials can make decisions independently of external pressures, and which reflect, instead, the agency's structural dependence or bureaucratic character.[20] An IO agency's bureaucratic character is the outcome of the formally assigned and informally inherited rules: a cluster of responsibilities, procedures, expectations, and objectives that together create the ideological and pragmatic orientations imposed on, or internalized by, the individual officials. While the neorealist description of interstate relations applies well to an institutional context of nonautonomous institutions, it fails to address the possibility, which is well captured by rational choice and historical institutionalists, of relatively autonomous institutions. Bureaucratic institutions are potentially more autonomous than member-driven organizations; and institutions with strong dispute settlement procedures are potentially more autonomous than those that have to rely on voluntary cooperation.

Finally, institutional arrangements affect the allocation of authority among the various agencies of the international organization, which in turn determines which of the competing orientations in the IO prevails. Whether decisions are made by way of diplomatic negotiations or judicial proceedings, for example, will greatly affect the relative influence of the competing member-states as well as the ability of IO officials to impose their own preferences.

Historical institutionalism hence provides a viable alternative to the common contention that international policy outcomes, even those channeled through international regimes or organizations, *necessarily* reflect the inequality of resources among states. A historical institutionalist approach, while permitting cases in which the inequality of resources among states dominates the outcomes, can also explain cases in which outcomes cannot be explained by merely pointing at the distribution of resources. Indeed, the case of GATT illustrates that the institutional arrangements of international organizations often effectively reproduce the original inequality among states by giving privileged access to those states with more economic resources, and by providing little influence to the organization itself, so that the institutional environment has no real "mediating" role between

---

[20] As with state officials, this perception suggests that the preferences of IO officials are *potentially* different from dominant non-IO actors, and that they are active participants in the struggle over favorable outcomes (Barnett and Finnemore 2004).

resources and outcomes. Yet this does not mean that these institutional arrangements are transparent, so that inequality of resources is directly reflected in the *outcomes*. Rather, they are biased, so that inequality of resources is reflected in the *institutions*, which allows states to convert nonpolitical resources into political influence. Yet there is nothing inherent in the international realm that necessitates this kind of correspondence. At least potentially, institutional arrangements of international organizations could have the effect of altering the situational or structural positions of the competing forces.

The historical institutionalist approach allows scholars not only to depict the interplay between institutions and actors at both the national and international realms of activity but also to integrate both levels of analysis.[21] The institutional arrangements of the state and of international organizations, together, affect the political positions and strategies of the interested actors— including domestic nonstate actors (e.g., industries and trade associations, workers and trade unions, NGOs), state actors (politicians and bureaucrats), nation-states (as members of the international organizations), international nonstate actors (other international organizations, multinational corporations, INGOs), and IO officials. They all struggle for favorable domestic laws *and* international agreements, as well as for favorable institutional context (an issue I address below). The fate of U.S. protectionists depended on the U.S. government's influence at the interstate level as much as on protectionists' influence at the domestic level. We therefore need to examine the political processes and institutional contexts at both levels.

At the same time, the significance of each level to the final outcome is not necessarily of equal weight. At times, domestic factors are more dominant than international ones (as was the case for U.S. trade policymaking until the 1970s); at other times, international ones dominate (as was the case for many other countries since the 1940s and for U.S. trade policymaking after the 1970s, and even more so after the mid 1990s). In contrast to other, usually static, attempts to analyze the interplay between domestic and international factors, my historical institutionalist approach suggests

---

[21] On the interplay between domestic and international factors, see Gourevitch 1978; Putnam 1988; Mastanduno, Lake, and Ikenberry 1989, 458. In the particular case of trade, see Goldstein 1996; Milner 1997; Milner and Rosendorff 1997. To capture this interplay better, it is useful to think not in terms of two distinct levels, as Putnam's two-level game (1988) does, but in terms of one field of action that incorporates both. See, for example, Ian Clark's "integrated approach to the internal and external," which takes as its unit of analysis "a unified field of political action" (Clark 1999, 65–66; see also Hobson 1997; Clark 1998; Hobden and Hobson 2002).

that the relative weight of the two political scales is historically specific. It also suggests that this relative weight would depend, among other conditions, on the institutional arrangements in place: some arrangements would provide more influence for domestic factors while others would grant influence to international ones. New institutions may divert the center of activity from one level to another. This takes the discussion to the question of institutional change.

How Do Institutional Arrangements Change?

The constitutive effect of institutions on the position of competing actors and agencies means that a change in the institutional arrangements will bring about, by creating a different balance of relative influence, new policy outcomes. Indeed, at the core of this book lies the argument that the trajectory of trade policy in the United States in the direction of greater trade liberalization was the outcome of successive institutional changes. The Reciprocal Trade Agreements of 1934, the Trade Act of 1974, and the Uruguay Round Agreements Act of 1994 were all *institutional* turning points, each resulting in a distinct logic that governed trade policy implementation for a certain period of time. But how do institutions change? It is here that a discussion of the interplay between institutions and political action becomes necessary.

The Origins of Institutions

Institutions originate in political struggles. Political actors do not fight only over substantive outcomes within a given institutional context, but also over institutional outcomes, in order to improve their relative position and therefore their future ability to make substantive changes.

One of the advantages of historical over rational choice institutionalism is that it takes "the goals, strategies, and preferences [of actors] as something to be explained," rather than assumed (Thelen and Steinmo 1992, 9). Historical institutionalists correctly insist that the identification of interests, the choice of strategies, and other features of political action are constructed within the historically specific context of the institutions in place. Historical institutionalist analyses, however, tend to put the politically motivated, strategically oriented "agent" in a straightjacket of overdetermining institutions. Strategic action and political maneuvering are structured *by* institutions, *within* a given institutional context that is itself rarely challenged, and often succumb to the institutions' own logic and endogenous dynamism.[22]

This overinstitutionalized conception of political actors not only marginalizes the strategic leverage of actors within a given set of institutional arrangements but also invites a depoliticized conception of institutions. In particular, exogenous sources of institutional creation and change, most importantly intentional political action, are often denied or dismissed. Paul Pierson (2000a), for example, finds instrumental or farsighted actions of political actors improbable. While more open to the dialectic relationship between government institutions and political power, Bo Rothstein (1992, 52) emphasizes factors, such as lack of information and the dominance of short-term interests, that stand in the way of intentional institutional design. Even when historical institutionalists confirm that institutions originate in political action, they dissociate the initial interaction from any subsequent effects. That is, they deny that the moment of institutional making has significant impact on the nature of the institutions in later periods (Mahoney 2000; Thelen 2003). Rothstein (1992) contends that in cases when the creation of institutions *is* intentional, the outcome is rarely what the creative agent expected, and Pierson explicitly asserts, "Even if institutional designers do act instrumentally, and *do* focus on long-term effects, unanticipated consequences are likely to be wide-spread" (Pierson 2000a, 483). Politics is viewed as a dynamic process that frequently produces unexpected consequences as different, ongoing processes interact (Thelen 1999, 383–84).[23]

While institutional arrangements affect the political strategies and interests of political actors in a way that often reproduces and stabilizes these arrangements, actors are also always potential contenders of the institutions within which they act (Jessop 1990, 149, 256, 260–62; Knight 1992; Clemens 1993; Clemens 2003; Sokolovsky 1998, 248).[24] Political struggles,

---

[22] For similar criticism, see Pontusson 1995; Sokolovsky 1998; Luong 2000; see also Chorev 2005a.

[23] Since the theory in its current manifestation does not allow for individuals to challenge institutions effectively, historical institutionalists look for endogenous sources of change (Thelen and Steinmo 1992, 21; Thelen 1991; Thelen 1999; Steinmo 1993; Clemens and Cook 1999; Orren and Skowronek 2002). This has led to productive areas of study, such as path dependence and other evolutionary processes (Pierson 2000b; Mahoney 2000).

[24] Historical institutionalists are correct in suggesting that actors would often choose to adapt to the institutions in place rather than challenge them. However, this may be because of slim chances of prevailing in the struggle or because of other barriers to collective action, rather than due to a process of socialization into the logic of the institutions. See footnote 4 above, for related discussion.

therefore, may target not only substantive policies within *given* institutional arrangements (themselves uncontested) but also the arrangements themselves. The motivation is clear: since state institutions have the effect of privileging some actors over others, interested actors struggle to change them to their advantage (Jessop 1990, 149; Gourevitch 1999, 137). In fact, as Rothstein (1992) acknowledges, it might be more beneficial to struggle over institutions rather than policies, for reconfiguring institutions can save one the trouble of having to fight the same battle over and over again. I will show that the three institutional transformations discussed in this book—in 1934, 1974, and 1994—were all a result of deliberate political strategies of internationally oriented businesses, in an attempt to transform the structural parameters governing trade, and in order to win long-term political advantages. Rather than particular policies, the institutional arrangements themselves were the primary object of struggle, exactly because internationalists realized that institutional arrangements would have the effect of advancing their interests on a permanent, rather than contingent, basis.

Under what conditions are institutions challenged? Thelen and Steinmo (1992, 15) rightly criticize Krasner's (1984) model of "punctuated equilibrium"—in which institutions are stable until they are "punctuated" by crises that bring about relatively abrupt institutional change—for obscuring the dynamic interaction of political strategies and institutional constraints. This should not, however, lead to the dismissal of the importance of crises in triggering institutional change. The struggles over the arrangements governing trade practices were often motivated by new economic circumstances, including both economic crises (as in the 1930s and 1970s) and economic opportunities (as in the 1990s). Economic or other sources of crises may heighten a prevailing sense of deprivation of the disadvantaged, or they may provide new opportunities for privileged actors to seize. New economic circumstances often lead to revised preferences, and hence to an incompatibility between the institutional arrangements in place, which reflect old preferences, and the newly established interests. Arguably, this should occur especially in cases where the institutions are perceived as being responsible for the crisis or as putting constraints on favorable solutions. It is not surprising that struggles over institutional arrangements often make it possible to protect or solidify existing advantages rather than to challenge them, for the likelihood for contenders to prevail in the struggle depends, among other factors, on the political influence that is *already inscribed* in the institutional arrangements in place.

In the case of U.S. trade policy, the three successful challenges to the institutions in place were initiated by advocates of free trade. Internationally competitive industries—the particular industries and sectors supporting free trade have changed over time—understood that to survive the Great Depression in the 1930s, to recover from the economic recession in the 1970s, and to take advantage of opportunities for further economic expansion in the 1990s, they had to defeat the opposition of protectionist industries.[25] Over time their situational and structural position was much improved, thanks to their greater share in the U.S. economy. However, the institutional arrangements in place—particularly the control of Congress over trade decisions—put limits on their ability to determine policy. Each time, therefore, they focused on changing the institutional arrangements themselves—moving it away from Congress, and then away from the administration as well.

Of course, not all attempts for institutional change succeed. Postwar planners failed to get the International Trade Organization (ITO) off the ground (Diebold 1952; Gardner 1980), and the attempts to strengthen interstate dispute settlement mechanisms during the Tokyo Round of multilateral trade negotiations in the early 1970s led to very disappointing substantive results (Hudec 1980). Nevertheless, the institutions that do emerge embody the politics that has brought them to life. Institutions that originate in political struggles are the solidified manifestation of the outcomes of those struggles, so the created institutions are biased in favor of those who designed them (Jessop 1990). Figure 2.1 summarizes this argument.

The fact that institutions are established with the intention, and often, the result, of serving the interests of particular social forces should not suggest that they are redundant for analyzing the final outcomes. New arrangements do not merely *reflect* the disparity of power among the competing actors at the time of the political struggle. If that were the case, an analysis of the relations of power in society rather than the institutional arrangements in place would have been required to explain trade practices at any given time. Instead, the new institutions establish a *new* balance of influence between the competing forces, for once in place institutions develop independent effects. *The successful contenders could not have achieved earlier what they could achieve once the new institutions were in place.* In the case of trade, the increased restraint in providing protectionist measures was not the outcome of a growing economic or political influence of the interna-

[25] Internationally competitive manufacturers (particularly, advanced technology businesses) and commercial and investment banks, which led the fight in the 1930s and the 1940s, were joined by U.S.-based multinational corporations, industrial users of imported inputs, and retailers in the 1970s. The service sector, investors, and companies concerned with intellectual property joined the coalition in the 1990s.

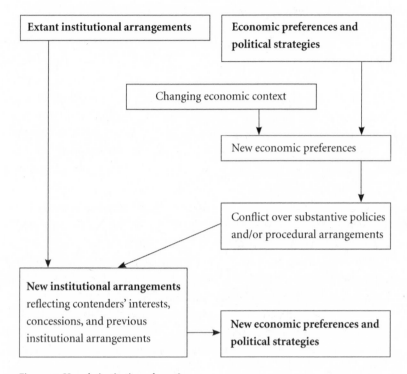

Figure 2.1. How do institutions change?

tionalist business community *prior* to the introduction of the new institutional arrangements. Each institutional transformation, on the contrary, was a reaction to the internationalists' realization that, *within the extant set of institutional arrangements,* protectionists' political strategies were disturbingly effective. Only the introduction of a new set of institutions could lead to the curbing of protectionist practices.

An even more important source of the causal effectiveness of institutions is the potential inconsistency that can exist between the balance of power inscribed into the institutions and a new balance of power, if the balance of political forces that had been solidified by the institutions changed for reasons exogenous to the institutions themselves. Institutions can also shape outcomes in cases of inconsistency between the interests protected by these institutions and a new set of interests, if the interests of the designers of the institutions have changed. This means that institutions "matter" not because they are autonomous from social forces, which they are not. It is because they do not reflect the *current* balance of social forces or the *current* interests of the designing forces that they can interfere in the "translation" of current relations of power into policy outcomes.

Institutional Dynamics

As I mentioned above, historical institutionalists commonly contend that even if strategic actors create institutions, it is improbable that they will achieve their desired results. Contingency, social complexity, and endogenous developments, they argue, prevent institutions from bringing the intended outcomes (Pierson 2000a; Schickler 2001; Pierson and Skocpol 2002, 708; Thelen 2003). While institutions do bring outcomes other than the ones intended by their designers, the reliance of historical institutionalists on developments endogenous to the institutions themselves is unsatisfactory. First, many of the intentional goals do materialize into desired outcomes. While Pierson is of course correct in insisting that we cannot *assume* a connection between current effects and original intentions (Pierson 2000b, 264; Thelen 2004, 25), in this book I offer detailed evidence of the original intentions of those who designed the institutions to evaluate whether, and the extent to which, their intentions were achieved.

Second, even those unavoidable "unanticipated" consequences should not be explained away by references to contingent developments. Rather, they are the result of *continuous* interplay between political strategies and extant institutional arrangements.[26] As Thelen (2003, 231) rightly argues, "In politics, losers do not necessarily disappear and their 'adaptation' to prevailing institutions can mean something very different from 'embracing and reproducing' those institutions." Once new institutions are in place, political actors adapt their strategies in order to maximize the benefits they can extract from the new institutional environment. These strategies can have varying results. Some strategies result in outcomes unanticipated by the original designers without transforming the institutions themselves (Hattam 1992). Others result in a "piecemeal change" of the institutions (Immergut 1992; Thelen 1999). In still other cases, adaptive politics turn into a challenge to the institutions themselves, which may result in yet another intended transformation of institutional arrangements. In other words, unanticipated outcomes are simply an outcome of counterstrategies intended to maximize benefits in the new institutional context.

[26] This part of my argument is broadly compatible with Kathleen Thelen's recent work (2004), in which she rejects a deterministic picture of institutional "lock in" and offers an important contribution to the issue of incremental change, especially through periodic political realignment and renegotiation.

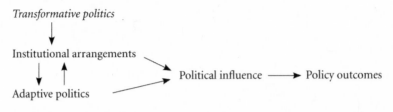

Figure 2.2. Institutional dynamics

At the same time that the intentional design of institutions explains the bias inscribed in them, the interplay between institutions and adaptive political strategies within given institutional arrangements means that this bias merely suggests a *tendency*, and that the final policy outcome would depend not only on the institutions in place but also on the strategic reaction of the interested actors, as it is shaped by the institutional arrangements in place and exogenous factors such as available resources. As Jessop formulates most carefully, policy outcomes are not inscribed in the state structure as such, but in the *relation* between the institutional arrangements and the strategies that various forces adopt toward them. There is therefore a certain openness in the state structure that is only resolved through actual political struggles, and the bias inscribed in the state institutional arrangements can only be understood as a bias *relative* to specific strategies (Jessop 1990, 10, 260). This relationship is summarized in figure 2.2.

In the next four chapters I explore the changing interplay between biased institutional arrangements and the strategic reaction to them. I show that the history of U.S. trade policy formation has been demarcated by moments of institutional change of either the U.S. state or the international organization, themselves a consequence of political struggles. Each new set of institutional arrangements altered the relative influence of competing actors, leading to new types of protectionist practices. Each successive institutional regime led further in the direction of greater trade liberalization and, as a result, in the direction of more intensified globalization.

CHAPTER THREE

SELECTIVE PROTECTIONISM, 1934–74

The United States was not always a champion of free trade principles. Rather, throughout the nineteenth and the early twentieth centuries the U.S. government faithfully adhered to the demands of its protectionist farmers and manufacturers and kept tariffs systematically high. By the mid 1940s, however, protectionism has become an exception to policies determined by liberal principles. Consequently, a steady liberalization of trade practices occurred in the post–World War II era, with tariffs on imported goods reduced from a high of 52.8 percent in 1930 to 9.9 percent in 1967.

Postwar liberalism in the United States is often explained as an outcome of new economic opportunities, which led U.S. industries to change their position in favor of free trade. For this argument to hold, however, those interested in exploring foreign markets also had to have the political influence to make this change happen—tariffs and other protectionist measures had to be renegotiated to allow U.S. business access into Europe and elsewhere. Yet, while internationally competitive manufacturing industries and banks supported trade liberalization, many other businesses remained stout protectionists. Protectionist industries, moreover, maintained their influence in Congress, which had the constitutional monopoly over trade policymaking. Consequently, Congress remained loyal to its previous protectionist stance. Thus the question arises, what permitted the policy change from protectionism to internationalism?

In this chapter I argue that the ability of internationalists to transform U.S. trade position and policies first required a shift in the site of authority away from Congress, and to the administration. Internationalist business and their supporters in the administration could not make Congress change its protectionist position, but they did manage, largely thanks to the trauma of the Great Depression, to weaken Congress's monopoly over trade issues. In the Reciprocal Trade Agreements Act (RTAA) of 1934, Congress delegated the authority to reduce tariffs to the executive branch. The administration could then engage in bilateral and, after 1947, multilateral, trade agreements, which led to a dramatic reduction in tariffs. At the same time, Congress maintained its authority over trade issues other than tariffs, and used this authority to provide protection from the administration's liberalization to "special cases." Trading partners of the United States did not particularly like this arrangement, but the international setting in which trade agreements and rules were negotiated—the General Agreement on Tariffs and Trade (GATT)—did not provide many effective opportunities to challenge U.S. policies. In short, rather than being based on a national consensus about the benefits of free trade, liberal policies resulted from an institutional shift that enabled internationalists to impose their liberal preferences.

In what follows I trace the history of U.S. trade policy formation from the nineteenth century till the end of the postwar era to identify the origins of the new institutional regime and describe its effects. The chapter begins with a brief history of U.S. trade laws from 1816 to the infamous Smoot-Hawley Tariff of 1930. I argue that protectionist industries have been consistently successful in imposing their will not only due to their superior economic and organizational resources but also because the resources available to them "fit" (Skocpol 1992, 54–57) the opportunities provided by Congress's political logic and procedures—protectionist industries could relatively easily mobilize a large number of constituencies from a great number of congressional districts. The chapter then traces the radical shift from the protectionist Smoot-Hawley Tariff of 1930 to the liberal RTAA only four years later. I show how the economic retaliation that followed the Smoot-Hawley Tariff and that allegedly contributed to the difficulties to recover from the Great Depression was used by the State Department to convince Congress to delegate tariff-setting authority to the administration. In the 1940s, Congress refused to ratify the creation of an International Trade

Organization (ITO), but the administration bypassed Congress by signing the General Agreement on Tariffs and Trade. I then describe in detail the substantive outcomes of the new institutional arrangements introduced in the RTAA and GATT. I show that the new hierarchical distribution of authority that characterized the new regime, which I call "selective protectionism," narrowed the authority of Congress and thereby weakened the political influence of protectionists, who did not have a similar influence over the executive. The act also substantively increased the influence of state agencies, particularly the Department of State, which supported the economic agenda of internationalist business. The result was a dramatic reduction of tariffs on goods imported into the U.S. market. At the same time, because alternative protectionist measures remained under the jurisdiction of Congress—the authority of the administration was limited to tariff-setting—protectionist industries could keep some of the advantages they had enjoyed before 1934. Rather than high tariffs across the board, however, Congress now provided only particularistic protection to selected industries. Finally, I argue that this simultaneous pursuit of trade liberalism and "selective" protectionism was tolerated by other countries because the institutional arrangements of the GATT favored rich countries, which allowed American domination at the international realm.

From the Tariff of 1816 to Smoot-Hawley

Article 1, Section 8, of the U.S. Constitution grants Congress the power to regulate commerce with foreign nations and to levy duties and tariffs. When the U.S. Congress first convened in 1789, one of its initial acts was to pass a bill that set tariffs on goods imported into the United States. For the next 150 years or so, tariffs were kept consistently high. Initially, Congress imposed high duties because duties were one of the sole sources of federal revenue. Between 1789 and 1800, 88 percent ($5,020,000 of $5,717,000) of the federal government's revenue was derived from Customs collections. With the Tariff of 1816, which levied a series of 25 percent duties, including almost prohibitively high duties on woolen, cotton, and iron manufactures, protection took precedence over revenue concerns and "protectionism" became a rationale and a tool of U.S. trade policy (Pastor 1980, 73–75).

Why the dominance of protectionist policies? The institutional characteristics of the U.S. Congress, most obviously the fact that Congress members are directly elected, made them relatively "vulnerable" to social pressures (Lohmann and O'Halloran 1994; Fordham and McKeown 2003).

In the struggle between protectionists and supporters of liberal trade the former prevailed because the form of representation in Congress—including the disproportionate representation of small states and the determining role of committees in shaping policies—gave advantage to relatively large, labor-intensive, but geographically concentrated industrial groups (Pincus 1975; Rogowski 2002), as many protectionist industries were (Bauer, Pool, and Dexter 1972). Concentrated benefits, moreover, provided those industries strong incentive to overcome collective action problems (Smith 1994; Bailey, Goldstein, and Weingast 1997). As a result, members of Congress often prioritized the interests of protectionist industries over internationalist business. After 1816, the Tariff of 1824 raised rates again, to an average duty charge of more than 30 percent, and included in the protected category such products as glass, lead, iron, and wool. The "Tariff of Abominations" of 1828 included tariffs on hemp, wool, fur, flax, liquor, and imported textiles. The "Adams Compromise" Act of 1832 reduced tariff rates somewhat, but retained the high 1828 rates on manufactured cloth and iron (Hiscox 2002, 47–48).

Due to the geographical concentration of U.S. industries, political struggles over trade issues have commonly been divided along regional lines. Northern industries wanted high tariffs in order to protect themselves from cheaper European products. The economies of the agricultural southern states, by contrast, were based on the export of raw materials and the importation of manufactured goods. Southern farmers, particularly cotton and tobacco growers, therefore championed cuts in tariffs. The struggle over tariff rates turned into a partisan struggle during those periods in which the parties themselves were split along regional lines, and even then members of Congress often crossed party lines following more particular regional concerns (Hiscox 2002). The Republican Party's base of support was in the Northeast and Midwest, including industries such as iron and textiles and farmers growing wool and hemp, and it therefore held a protectionist agenda. The Democratic Party's base of support was southern, and it therefore called for tariff cuts (Hiscox 1997, 82).

By the 1840s, tariff rates were raised or lowered by significant degrees as control of government changed hands. The Whig's turn to protectionism in the Tariff Act of 1842 and the subsequent liberalization in 1846 after the Democrats retook control over Congress are examples of such partisan swings (Taussig 1964, 115; Pastor 1980, 85; Hiscox 1997, 95–96). After the Civil War, internal taxes, which had been imposed with the declared intent of raising revenue, were repealed, but due to the postwar dominance of the northern Republicans, cuts in protective tariffs, which had been raised during the war with the intent of offsetting the internal taxes, were largely avoided (Taussig 1964, 173; Hiscox 1997, 132). Although specific duties had been raised in the interim, the first tariff revision after the Civil War was in 1883. Over the next five decades there were seven additional general revisions: in 1890, 1894, 1897, 1909, 1913, 1922, and 1930. The primary trend of the tariffs passed by Republican congresses was toward increasing protection. This trend was interrupted only by the tariffs of 1894 and 1913, which were supported by the Democratic Party (Pastor 1980, 75).

But no previous legislation could match the most infamous protectionist act in American history—the Smoot-Hawley Tariff Act of 1930.[1] The original intention behind the legislation was to increase the protection afforded to domestic farmers against foreign agricultural imports.[2] Once the tariff schedule revision process got started, however, it proved impossible to stop, and won the act the apt description of a "textbook case of pressure group politics run amok" (Haggard 1988, 91). As a consequence of the stock market crash of 1929 and the subsequent Great Depression, calls for increased protection flooded in from industrial interest groups, and soon the bill became a means to raise tariffs in all sectors of the economy. The act was sponsored by protectionist Republicans, joined by Democrats linked to import-competing sugar and meat producers and to protectionist urban interests in the Northeast. It was opposed by liberal Democrats and insurgents among the Republicans from the midwestern farm states: grain growers and other exporting farmers gained nothing from higher barriers to imports, and there was widespread resentment that a bill intended for farm relief had been hijacked by industrial interests (Hiscox 1997, 198–201). Still, even those who argued against the increase of some tariffs asked for it as an exception and did so without challenging the general principle of protection (Pastor 1980, 83). The act amended twenty thousand tariff schedules, mainly upward. Under the act, the average tariff rate on dutiable imports rose to 52.8 percent, one of the highest in American history.

---

[1] For a classical study of Smoot-Hawley Tariff, see Schattschneider 1935; see also Hufbauer, Berliner, and Elliott 1986; Smith 1994; Eichengreen 1989; Bailey, Goldstein, and Weingast 1997.

[2] Massive expansion in the agricultural production sector outside of Europe during World War I led, with the postwar recovery of European producers, to massive agricultural overproduction during the 1920s. This triggered declining farm prices during the second half of the decade. Already during the 1928 election campaign, therefore, Republican presidential candidate Herbert Hoover pledged to help the beleaguered farmers by, among other things, raising tariff levels on agricultural products. The Great Depression worsened the situation, with farm prices dropping 51 percent from 1929 to 1933.

The Smoot-Hawley Tariff provoked a storm of foreign retaliatory measures. Within months of the bill's passage, Canada, France, Mexico, Italy, Spain, Cuba, Australia, and New Zealand raised tariffs on American imports. By the end of 1931, twenty-six countries had enacted quantitative restrictions and exchange controls, and by 1932, even the United Kingdom abandoned its free-trade principles and established the Ottawa system of imperial tariff preferences (Pastor 1980, 79; Lake 1988, 202). These measures deepened the decline in international trade, already damaged by the world-wide depression. United States imports from Europe fell from a 1929 high of $1.334 billion to just $390 million in 1932, while U.S. exports to Europe fell from $2.341 billion in 1929 to $784 million in 1932. Overall, world trade declined by some 66 percent between 1929 and 1934 (Eichengreen 1989; Irwin 1998).

The Smoot-Hawley Tariff was, however, the last comprehensive tariff-setting law to be passed by Congress. The next trade bill that was enacted, in 1934, introduced institutional arrangements that rendered the future enactment of Smoot-Hawley-like legislation highly unlikely.

The Reciprocal Trade Agreements Act of 1934

Between 1930 and 1939, U.S. industrial output was cut in half. Unemployment averaged 18.2 percent, and per capita income fell from about $700 in 1929 to some $400 in 1933. Prices of farm products, raw materials, industrial goods, and stocks fell dramatically; U.S. trade shriveled. In 1929, the estimated value of U.S. imports and exports had reached almost $80 billion dollars. In 1934, the value had dropped to $50 billion.[3]

Past experience, including the Smoot-Hawley Tariff, proved to those who were looking for export opportunities to recover from the Great Depression, such as technologically advanced manufacturers, extractive industries, but also many agricultural segments, that Congress was too susceptible to protectionist demands. Major commercial and investment banks, particularly the "internationalized" New York financial community, which were interested in the ability of European debtors to sell in the American market, reached a similar conclusion. The influence protectionists had in Congress made it difficult to reduce tariffs and impossible to maintain reduced tariffs over time. Since internationalists could not

[3] U.S. Department of Commerce, Bureau of Economic Analysis, National Income and Product Accounts Tables, Table 1.1.6. Real Gross Domestic Product, Chained (2000) Dollars. Available at http://bea.gov/bea/dn/nipaweb/index.asp.

suppress protectionist influence in Congress, the only way to prevent further tariff increases or to "lock in" tariff reductions was to move authority away from Congress and to the executive branch of government. Such a relocation of authority was at the center of the Reciprocal Trade Agreements Act (RTAA) of 1934.

Most analyses of the RTAA explain it as a self-restraining act of Congress: legislators delegated tariff-setting authority to the president as a way to insulate themselves from unwanted protectionist pressures after the disastrous consequences of the 1930 Smoot-Hawley Tariff Act made them realize that they were incapable of passing nationally beneficial tariff legislation.[4] In the account here I emphasize instead the collaboration between the internationalist fraction of the administration that drafted the bill and internationalist business, which guaranteed the support of most Democrats and some Republicans in Congress.[5]

As early as December 1931, the American Exporters and Importers Association drew up a proposal in which it argued that moving the trade policy process from Congress to the executive branch was the "quickest and safest" way to advance trade expansion and domestic economic growth. Only in the executive branch, the association reasoned, could economic policy operate in the "national interest," as the president would be insulated from the influence of special interest groups plaguing congressional policymaking (Woods 2003, 402–3). Economic opportunities, in other words, required protectionist restraint, which, in turn, necessitated the shift of authority away from Congress. Other associations representing the internationalist segment of American business, including the National Foreign Trade Council, the National Automobile Chamber of Commerce, the American Manufacturers' Export Association, and the Foreign Commerce Club of New York, supported similar proposals (Woods 2003, 403).

These associations received the active support of the internationalist fraction of the government bureaucracy—then located in the Department of State and the Federal Reserve (Frieden 1988; Haggard 1988; Schnietz 2003, 218–19). It was therefore significant that Roosevelt asked his Secretary of State, Cordell Hull, rather than his foreign trade advisor, the protectionist

---

[4] For such interpretations of the RTAA, see Pastor 1980, 92; Baldwin 1985; Destler 1986, 11; Goldstein 1988, 188; Goldstein and Lenway 1989; Smith 1994, 139; Milner and Rosendorff 1996. For a critique, see Hiscox 1999; Schnietz 2000, 418–420.

[5] See Gardner 1980; Frieden 1988; Haggard 1988; Bailey, Goldstein, and Weingast 1997; Gilligan 1997; Schnietz 2000; Schnietz 2003; and Woods 2003. Some of these works (e.g., Bailey, Goldstein, and Weingast 1997; Schnietz 2000; Schnietz 2003) emphasize the role of Democrats in Congress, and downplay the role of economic actors.

George Peek, to prepare a draft of the trade legislation.[6] Hull believed that there was a direct relationship between an open international economy and a peaceful, cooperative world political order (Gardner 1980, 5). He also recognized that an open international economy depended on the ability to negotiate reciprocal trade agreements, and that such agreements required the transfer of tariff-making authority from Congress to the president (Haggard 1988, 110). Hull therefore asked Congress to grant authority to the president to negotiate bilateral concessions raising or lowering tariff rates up to 50 percent of the existing rates on agricultural and industrial products, providing reciprocal arrangements were made by the other party. He also asked Congress to treat the bilateral agreements reached by the president as executive agreements, requiring no ex-post congressional approval. This was a radical departure from previous practices, for while Congress had delegated authority to the president to negotiate trade treaties before, it had never been without a requirement of congressional ratification (Pastor 1980, 75–82).

Hull's liberalism was concerned primarily with international order and American power (Haggard 1988, 100), yet in his testimony before the House Ways and Means Committee, Hull advocated the bill as a tool for securing markets for American exporters and as a necessary condition for dragging the American economy out of the depths of the Depression.[7] The delegation of authority to the administration was presented by Hull as the only pragmatic arrangement available. Bilateral bargaining, he argued, required trade-offs. In exchange for concessions in the interest of internationally competitive U.S. industries, the U.S. government would have to open the domestic market to foreign products. United States negotiators would therefore need the authority to reduce tariffs, as other countries would be less inclined to engage in mutual concessions if they knew that Congress might later reject or revise the agreement. Later in the testimony Hull added,

> It is manifest that unless the Executive is given authority to deal with the existing great emergency somewhat on a parity with that exercised by the executive departments of so many other governments for purposes of negotiating and carrying into effect trade agreements, it will not be practicable or possible for the U.S. to pursue with any

[6] For a good review of the positions and struggles in the administration over the 1934 Trade Act, see Haggard 1988.

[7] U.S. Congress. Hearings before the House Committee on Ways and Means. *Trade Agreements Act.* 73rd Cong., 2nd sess., 5–6; cited in Pastor 1980, 86.

degree of success the proposed policy of restoring our lost international trade. It would seem to me that this is the one governing consideration.[8]

Supporters of the bill assured reluctant Congress members that Congress would not be cut out of the policy process, that trade policy would continue to be based on negotiation between Congress and the White House, and that channels for congressional influence would remain in place (Smith 1994, 140). The House Report stated that "the proposed bill . . . does not remove from Congress its control of policy which must underlie every tariff adjustment. Although the exigencies of present-day conditions require that more and more of the details be left to presidential determination, the Congress must and always will declare policy to which the Executive gives effect."[9]

These assurances notwithstanding, the negative impacts on import-competing American industries were not lost on those who benefited from congressional tariff setting. Among them were textile and shoe producers, scientific instrument manufacturers, toy makers, wool growers as well as the steel, rubber, mining, lace, glass, and chemical industries (Frieden 1988, 68; Schnietz 2003, 218–19).[10] They realized that by anchoring trade policy-making on reciprocal concessions negotiated by the executive branch, the reform would swing the political balance in favor of free-trade interests. Reflecting the position of these industries, the Republicans in the House Ways and Means Committee, in their minority report, criticized the bill for placing "in the hands of the President and those to whom he may delegate authority the absolute power of life and death over every industry dependent on tariff protection."[11]

In the course of the debate in the Senate Finance Committee the administration made several compromises, which ensured the passage of the bill. Most important, it agreed to limit the authority of the president to negotiate trade agreements to three years, which allowed supporters of the bill to present it as a temporary and emergency measure. Alternatively, it meant

---

[8] U.S. Congress. Hearings before the House Committee on Ways and Means. *Trade Agreements Act*. 73rd Cong., 2nd sess., 5–6; cited in Pastor 1980, 88–89.

[9] U.S. Congress. House Ways and Means Committee. *Amend Tariff Act of 1930: Reciprocal Trade Agreements*. 73rd Cong., 2nd sess., 14; cited in O'Halloran 1994, 86.

[10] Organized labor, represented by the American Federation of Labor (AFL) and the Congress of Industrial Organizations (CIO), did not take a strong position on the issue (Hiscox 1997, 205).

[11] Report of the Ways and Means Committee on Reciprocal Trade Agreements Act, cited in *New York Times*, 20 March 1934, 4, cited in Pastor 1980, 89.

that the president would have to periodically return to Congress for new authority, which promised a continuous negotiation between Congress and the executive and a setting for effective political pressures (Haggard 1988, 111–13). The act also contained an "escape clause" provision, permitting temporary protection of industries injured by liberalizing concessions. At the same time, many other amendments suggested by Republicans— including exemptions of specific protected commodities from trade agreements, limiting tariff reductions to levels equalizing "production costs" between American and foreign producers, and allowing congressional rejection of any reciprocal trade agreement after a year—were defeated (Schnietz 2000, 427), and the bill was hence free of special interest amendments (Pastor 1980, 92; Haggard 1988, 101; Smith 1994, 140).

The Reciprocal Trade Agreements Act passed both houses in a partisan vote, with the Democrats, who represented the interests of exporters, supporting the bill, and most Republicans maintaining their historical platform favoring high tariffs (Pastor 1980, 90; Hiscox 1999).[12] Once in place, however, the new institutional arrangements changed the logic of the political game. From 1934 on, Congress consistently renewed the president's authority to negotiate trade agreements.[13] Not until the Clinton presidency did Congress refuse to grant authority to the administration, *irrespective* of who controlled Congress and irrespective of the party affiliation of the president. Debates between Democrats and Republicans focused instead on the conditions under which the delegation of authority would be granted.

The RTAA had immediate implications for U.S. trade practices. In the ninety years between 1844 and 1934 various administrations altogether initiated only twenty-one trade agreements, of which eighteen failed—either because the Senate rejected them or because Senate amendments made the agreement unacceptable to the other country (Schnietz 2000, 433). In contrast, in the eleven years between 1934 and 1945, the State Department successfully concluded twenty-eight reciprocal trade agreements, which no longer needed congressional ratification. Those agreements led to a steady decline in U.S. tariffs, falling from an average of 52.8 percent in 1930 to 28.2 in 1945 and 25.5 percent in 1946 (Pastor 1980, 93–94, 332; Haggard 1988, 92; Hansen and Prusa 1997).

---

[12] The partisan nature of the voting, and the fact that among members of Congress who voted on both bills almost all those who voted for Smoot-Hawley in 1930 voted against the RTAA in 1934, are evidence against the common interpretation of the RTAA as a bipartisan congressional act of self-restraint (Hiscox 1999; Schnietz 2000, 418–20).

[13] Before the creation of GATT, in 1947, Congress extended the RTAA for three years in 1937 and 1940, for two years in 1943, and again for three years in the Trade Extension Act of 1945.

Before analyzing how the Reciprocal Trade Agreements Act of 1934 was able to transform the politics of trade at the domestic level in such a way, we need to review the establishment of the General Agreement on Tariffs and Trade, in 1947, which introduced procedures to govern trade negotiations at the international level.

ITO and GATT of 1947

The outcome of the Second World War ensured the hegemonic status of the United States and put the U.S. government in a position to shape the economic and political recovery of foreign countries. That task intensified the conflict between economic nationalists and internationalists in the U.S. administration, which was reflected in the battle of opinion over foreign economic policy between the Treasury Department and the State Department. In the Department of Treasury, under Secretary Henry Morgenthau Jr., national economic planners and New Dealers were interested in an expanded government role in managing the economy, to promote full employment, industrial capacity, and social welfare (Gardner 1980, 4). During the war, however, the primary responsibility for shaping American foreign economic policy rested with the Department of State (Gardner 1980, 16). After the death of Roosevelt in April 1945, left-wing New Dealers were further marginalized and State Department internationalists gained even greater influence (Graz 1999). Postwar planners in the Department of State, still under the direction of Cordell Hull, held that the United States, despite its comparative self-sufficiency, had a great stake in the economic well-being of the rest of the world, because it needed foreign markets for the produce of its factories and farms, and because it needed a healthy environment on which to base its efforts at world peace. They were therefore determined to break with the U.S. legacy of isolationism and to reconstruct a multilateral system of world trade (Gardner 1980, 12–13).

ITO Negotiations

In November 1947, the U.S. Department of State convened a UN conference—the Havana Conference—for the purpose of negotiating an international trade charter and for the establishment of an International Trade Organization (Reisman 1996, 83). The negotiations involved a number of countries, but were primarily between the United States and the United Kingdom, the two countries with the largest share of world trade.

The Truman administration's objective, as formulated by the Department of State, was to create a multilateral system of world trade, aimed at the reduction of trade barriers, especially quantitative restrictions, and at nondiscrimination, especially against the preferential trading practices of the United Kingdom (Diebold 1952, 12–13; Gardner 1980, 12–13). British negotiators were in favor of international collaboration, but the British emphasis was rather more on lowering trade barriers than on their nondiscriminatory application, which would have required a change in the special economic relations between the members of the British Commonwealth (Gardner 1980, 27). The British also insisted that the liberalization of trade be linked to a broad commitment to maintain full employment policies and demanded that the charter include escape clauses that would allow the use of discriminatory trade practices to protect the economy from balance-of-payments pressures and international deflationary pressures.

Initially, the Americans resisted any language or policies that would force the United States to accept a commitment to full employment, and the American negotiators sought to define very narrowly the conditions under which the use of import restrictions would be allowed (Block 1977a, 68). But in order to make substantial progress on their first priority—the removal of trade barriers—U.S. negotiators needed to show that the United States was not proposing the elimination of quotas and reduce tariffs without regard for other conditions affecting international trade (Diebold 1952). As a compromise, American drafters were willing to include in the charter detailed rules not only for tariffs, quotas, exchange controls, and state trading, but also for international commodity agreements and intergovernmental measures used to check restrictive trade practices. Also included were provisions concerning the maintenance of full employment in each country and the avoidance of policies that would create unemployment abroad, even if these were left rather general, as no one could devise detailed provisions likely to be acceptable to all the participating governments (Diebold 1952, 12). In March 1948, the Havana Charter was concluded and signed by fifty-three countries (most of the sixty-one countries that made up the United Nations at the time).

Yet the ITO Charter was stillborn, as it was opposed by *both* protectionists and internationalists in the United States, and consequently was not ratified by Congress. Domestic supporters of the ITO Charter included some of the associations representing internationalist businesses, such as the National Council of American Importers, the Committee for Economic Development, the National Planning Association, and the Committee for the International Trade Organization. Agricultural interests, such as the

American Farm Bureau Federation and the National Framers Unions, and organized labor also supported the charter (Diebold 1952, 10, 15). They were defeated, however, by the opponents of the charter. These included agricultural and manufacturing industries protected from foreign competition by tariffs and other import controls, such as the chemicals, dairy products, paper and pulp, and livestock and allied industries, as well as nut growers, makers of glassware and glass containers, woolen manufacturers, independent petroleum producers, rayon manufacturers, and makers of woven wire cloth. Associations opposed to the charter included the American Tariff League National and the Labor-Management Council on Foreign Trade Policy (Diebold 1952, 23). But businessmen who generally supported trade liberalization also opposed the charter. Representatives of the U.S. Chamber of Commerce, the National Foreign Trade Council, and the U.S. Council of the International Chamber of Commerce asserted that the charter went too far in subordinating the international commitments of signatory countries to the requirements of national economic plans and policies. They argued that the exceptions to the charter's general rules, and the escape clauses applicable to special circumstances, were so numerous that foreign countries would be able to comply with the charter without actually freeing trade from existing restrictions, and that the charter was too heavily laden with the ideological and practical paraphernalia of government regulation and control, so that it would not help, and very likely would hinder, the development of private enterprise (Diebold 1952, 14, 16–20). The Executive Committee of the United States Council of the International Chamber of Commerce summarized its objections in its "Statement of Position" on the charter:

> It is a dangerous document because it accepts practically all of the policies of economic nationalism; because it jeopardizes the free enterprise system by giving priority to centralized national governmental planning of foreign trade; because it leaves a wide scope of discrimination, accepts the principle of economic insulation and in effect commits all members of the ITO to state planning for full employment. From the point of view of the United States, it has the further very grave defect of placing this country in a position where it must accept discrimination against itself while extending the Most-Favored-Nation treatment to all members of the Organization. It places the United States in a permanent minority position owing to its one-vote-one-country voting procedure. Because of that, membership in the ITO based on this Charter would make it impossible

for the United States to engage in an independent course of policy in favor of multilateral trade.[14]

In April 1949, President Truman's request for a joint resolution permitting American participation in the ITO was sent to the House Committee on Foreign Affairs, where numerous hearings were held. But the ITO Charter died in the committee and was never put to a vote (Diebold 1952, 1). Without the participation of the United States, the International Trade Organization had no future. With the demise of the ITO, all that remained was the General Agreement on Tariffs and Trade.

The General Agreement on Tariffs and Trade

A General Agreement on Tariffs and Trade concluded the first round of multilateral trade negotiations, which took place in Geneva in 1947, and was signed by twenty-three countries. The purpose of that treaty was to begin the process of reciprocal tariff reduction and to carry part of the substance of the Havana Charter of the ITO during the year or two in which the ITO Charter was to go through the slow process of ratification (Vernon 1954, 6–7). Since the U.S. government was allowed to enter into trade agreements but could not join organizations without the approval of Congress, the GATT text was formulated to avoid any suggestion that it was an organization, including, for example, making the "Contracting Parties acting jointly" the highest GATT authority. This maneuver allowed the survival of the GATT despite the death of the ITO (Jackson 1967). The GATT then assumed the commercial policy role that had been originally assigned to the ITO and provided the organizational and legal framework for governing international trade relations.[15]

The GATT not only committed the contracting parties to the results of the tariff bargaining but to several of the obligations of the ITO Charter as well, particularly the provisions in the chapter on commercial policy. The commercial chapter introduced a commitment for the reduction in tariffs and other barriers to trade by means of reciprocal trade agreements, and a commitment for the elimination of discriminatory treatment in international commerce—the "unconditional most-favored-nation (MFN) treatment," as it is usually termed—requiring any privilege granted to one

---

[14] Cited in Diebold 1952, 20–21.

[15] For this reason, it is common to refer *both* to the actual treaty and to the organizational framework as "the GATT."

country to be accorded to all other contracting parties. The commercial chapter also introduced exceptions to these general obligations. The most important exception to the MFN rule allowed "regional" free-trade arrangements that involved discrimination in the use of trade barriers against nonmember contracting parties. Other exceptions allowed certain preferential arrangements existing prior to the GATT and granted preference schemes with less-developed countries. There was also an exception in cases of economic difficulty such as balance of payments deficit or market disruption.

But the GATT did *not* incorporate the ITO provisions on restrictive business practices, economic development, employment, or organizational structure. In that way the GATT reflected—in a way that the ITO did not—the preferences of the internationalists, for while the ITO envisioned a balance between international openness and national interests, the GATT took very little consideration of domestic concerns. At the same time, the ITO promised a strong regime whereas the GATT offered only a weak basis for an institution—the GATT covered a narrower sphere of policy, required little if any legislative action by signatories, lacked a permanent organization, and committed signatories less firmly (Finlayson and Zacher 1981, 566–69; see also Diebold 1952, 28; Gardner 1980, 379–80). As a result, the GATT had little capacity to enforce its liberal obligations on member-states, especially developed industrial countries, and most particularly the United States.

The Restrained Role of the GATT in American Politics

What role did the GATT play in the struggle between protectionists and internationalists in the United States? In chapter 2 I argued that international organizations may differ in the extent to which they permit inequality of resources among member-states to directly shape policy outcomes. The institutional arrangements of the GATT certainly reproduced the inequality among states rather than challenging it. Privileged access to those with greater economic resources and little influence to the organization itself meant that the institutional environment had no real "mediating" role between resources and outcomes (Curzon and Curzon 1973; McGillivray 2000; Wilkinson 2000; Steinberg 2002; Jawara and Kwa 2003).

Rich countries' ability to take advantage of their economic and political resources stemmed from GATT's form of decision making: decisions were to be reached by consensus.[16] Steinberg (2002) persuasively suggests that the consensus decision-making process is little more than "organized hypocrisy," where the actual practices—of "invisible weighting"—are decoupled from the rules and norms—of consensual decision making—that are maintained for external display (Steinberg 2002, 342).[17] The main source of U.S. influence is the size of its market. As Steinberg puts it, "The proportionate domestic economic and political impact of a given absolute change in trade access varies inversely with the size of a national economy" (2002, 347). This means that what from a U.S. point of view amounts to a small concession can be negotiated in return to policy changes that have a huge consequence for a smaller economy. As for "sticks," while the United States is not known to use military or financial promises in trade negotiations (Steinberg 2002, 348), it has certainly used threats of sanctions, including unilateral retaliations, or of withdrawal, to twist the arm of reluctant states. The advantageous position of the United States and other rich countries also stems from their control of the initiatives, proposals, alternative packages, draft texts, and so on. These plans and documents are first developed in the United States or Europe, discussed informally by the transatlantic powers, then in larger groups (Quad, G-7, OECD), then presented in backdoor negotiations of a few dozen countries (the so-called "Green Room"), and only then become public and open to the multilateral discussion. Initiatives from weak countries, in turn, hardly ever make it through those stages (Steinberg 2002, 354–55).

---

[16] Formally, decision making was entrusted to the collective group of Contracting Parties and decisions were to be reached through a voting procedure in which each country had an equal voice (one voice/one vote rule). From the mid 1950s, however, a practice emerged in which agreements were reached by consensus, so that diplomatic negotiations, rather than voting, were at the center of the decision-making process.

[17] The diplomatic negotiations were organized in a way hardly conducive for real consensus. Negotiations followed a "major interest" norm, which dictated that initial negotiations were between the largest principal supplier of a product and the largest principal purchaser (Jackson 1969, 243; Kock 1969, 100). The only multilateral element in this rule-making process was near the close of negotiations: a last-minute "balancing" of "offers" and "concessions" would occur in order to get countries that would benefit secondarily from the nondiscriminatory application of agreed tariff reductions to "pay" for those benefits. As a result, the same groups of developed industrial countries dominated all trade negotiations. With the advent of linear tariff reductions in the Kennedy Round (1963–67), this bilateral technique was discarded for a greater degree of multilateralism, but the ability of those few countries that were the major suppliers of most products and that possessed the largest import markets to determine the extent of linear tariff cuts and the sectors to be excluded from such cuts remained striking (Finlayson and Zacher 1981, 585–86, 591–92; McRae and Thomas 1983, 53–54).

The great influence of the unequal distribution of resources among states on the final outcome enabled developed countries, especially the United States, to control the agenda and impose their interests on others. Hence, although the GATT was formally aimed to bring trade liberalization to all member-states and to effectively restrain protectionism, in practice the GATT did not play a major constitutive role in American trade policy formation. As I illustrate below, U.S. administrations used GATT to impose liberal rules on others but at the same time, when pressed by Congress, they bypassed or violated those very rules. Instead, the GATT obligations effectively reflected the preferences of the United States (indirectly entrenching in the international realm the tension between the State Department's internationalist preferences and Congress's practices of constraint), while U.S. trade practices were shaped by *domestic* influences.

The Regime of Selective Protectionism

The dominant economic position of the United States after the Second World War led more and more business groups to support liberal trade. With Europe and Japan in ruins, U.S. manufacturers had little to fear from foreign competition at home, and the superior strength of the U.S. economy offered a great opportunity for U.S. businesses to gain a foothold in foreign markets. Large national business organizations, including the U.S. Chamber of Commerce, the U.S. Council of the International Chamber of Commerce, the Committee for Economic Development, the National Association of Manufacturers, and the National Foreign Trade Council, appeared in congressional hearings to support periodic extensions of the RTAA. The Cold War also spurred approval of a liberal trade system as a means of building an international alliance against the threat of communism (Baldwin 1984, 8–10; Pearson and Riedel 1990, 103). Yet strong opposition to trade liberalization continued in the 1940s and 1950s, with a wide range of industries—including glassware, pottery, handicraft, textiles, watch making, oil, coal, paper pulp, lead and zinc interests—testifying *against* giving the president power to cut import duties or asking for import relief (Watson 1956, 691–92; Baldwin 1984; Smith 1994; Lusztig 1998, 47–48).

The political influence of those domestic industries opposed to the reduction of tariffs, however, had been negatively affected by the RTAA, which had introduced a new institutional environment in which trade policy would be formulated and implemented. By granting the president authority to lower tariffs in return for reciprocal concessions made by other countries, the act permitted a general process of trade liberalization with only exceptional treatment to "special" cases.

Trade Liberalization in the Executive Branch

Institutionalist accounts of the RTAA maintain that the intent of the shift in authority from Congress to the executive branch was to provide an advantage to internationalist interests, for the structural characteristics of the executive rendered it less protectionist than Congress (Haggard 1988, 95; Lohmann and O'Halloran 1994; O'Halloran 1994; Bailey, Goldstein, and Weingast 1997). Indeed, U.S. presidents after 1934 have consistently maintained an internationalist position (in spite of frequent specific violations of this formal stand for expedient reasons). Michael Hiscox (1999), however, has convincingly argued that the perception of presidents as *inherently* internationalist cannot be demonstrated historically, for presidents *before* 1934 were as protectionist as their parties: several Republican presidents came out clearly for high tariffs in election campaigns, backed the most protectionist of Republican tariff bills in Congress, and even vetoed tariff reductions pushed by congressional Democrats (Hiscox 1999, 677; see also Irwin 1998; Irwin and Kroszner 1999).

Indeed, presidents are not inherently internationalist. Rather, their consistent support of internationalism after 1934 has been partly due to the institutional arrangements of the RTAA, which has not only strengthened executive authority over trade policy but has also rendered the executive more oriented toward internationalism than before. Specifically, the delegation of authority to the president intensified the administration's internationalism by providing incentive for action of business internationalists, and by strengthening the position of those agencies, such as the Department of State, supporting free trade.

First, moving the site of political struggles from Congress to the executive limited the access, and hence influence, of protectionist groups. Because of its bureaucratic structure, in which decisions are made not by elected officials but by professional civil servants who are less vulnerable to direct pressure, and because the president is elected by all citizens, the administration tends to be less vulnerable to regional or otherwise "special" social pressures than Congress (Bailey, Goldstein, and Weingast 1997) and more attentive to internationalist interests, who could more easily present their preferences as compatible with the national interest, with regard to both economy and national security. Moreover, the RTAA provided an incentive for internationalists to take advantage of the differentiated access they had to the administration. The reciprocal nature of the authority to enter bilateral trade agreements meant that the administration's ability to bring tariff reduction of other countries depended on its ability to lower its own tariffs. This provided strong reason to exporters and U.S.-based multinational corporations, which they did not have in the unilateral proceedings in Congress, to enter the political scene and to explicitly oppose tariff-related protectionist actions (Bailey, Goldstein, and Weingast 1997; Gilligan 1997). The principle of reciprocity hence "shifted the balance of trade politics by engaging the interests of export producers, since tariff reductions could now be defended as direct means of winning new markets for American products overseas" (Destler 1992, 16).

Second, the delegation of authority from Congress to the executive branch involved shifting authority from a site of decision-making generally vulnerable to social pressures to a site of decision-making that is less so. With less access provided to interest groups, bureaucratic considerations and structural pressures dominated the process of decision making. This did not *necessitate* support of a free-trade agenda. Common institutionalist accounts notwithstanding, the U.S. executive should not be seen as having a unified voice on trade. Rather, the executive has been commonly torn between liberalism and protectionism. But the RTAA put authority over trade policy implementation in the hands of government agencies in favor of internationalism. Between 1934 and 1962, the agency responsible for formulating trade laws and for negotiating international trade agreements was the Department of State, which was chief among those promoting the idea of using trade liberalization as a tool in achieving geopolitical goals and was hence a committed promoter of free trade. It was later replaced by the Office of the Special Trade Representative, which was expected to have domestic sensibilities but had the formal responsibility to support and promote trade liberalization. It was this hierarchical distribution of authority that allowed liberalism to prevail.

In short, the two interrelated developments—a new balance of influence between protectionist groups and internationalists and more weight to the State Department—ensured that the new authority of the executive would be used for further trade liberalization. As already mentioned, between 1934 and 1945 the Department of State concluded twenty-eight reciprocal trade agreements, and the average tariffs rate in the United States fell to an impressive 25.5 percent in 1946 (Pastor 1980, 93–94, 332; Haggard 1988, 92; Hansen and Prusa 1997). The process of tariff reduction intensified with the establishment of the GATT. While multilateral trade negotiations during the first decade following World War II resulted only in minor tariff reductions,[18] subsequent rounds of negotiations—the Dillon Round in 1960–62 and the Kennedy Round in 1963–67—led to quite substantial tariff reductions. In the Kennedy Round, for example, industrial countries made cuts of almost 40 percent on manufactured products (Finlayson and Zacher 1981, 571; Jackson 1997, 74). Through these GATT negotiations, the tariff level on all dutiable U.S. imports dropped to less than 12 percent in 1962 and to 9.9 percent in 1967. Global trade flow seems to have been directly affected: world trade increased from $97 trillion at the war's end to $270 trillion in 1962 (Goldstein 1993, 163; Hirst and Thompson 1999).

Selective Protectionism in Congress

The delegation of authority to the administration concerned only the reduction of tariffs. Alternative protectionist measures, such as the imposition of import quotas, remained under the jurisdiction of Congress. The result was a potentially fragile division of labor that Congress nevertheless cherished. On the one hand, therefore, members of Congress representing protectionist interests[19] did not prevent the extension of the 1934 arrangement, and Congress repeatedly extended the president's authority to negotiate the reduction of tariffs.[20] Congress also generally stopped its practice of unilaterally raising tariffs. On the other hand, Congress remained, as it was before 1934, vulnerable to protectionist pressures and hence used its remaining authority to preserve its doctrine of "no injury" (Diebold 1972), that is, to ensure that the process of trade liberalization would not hurt struggling industries. Congress often enacted measures, such as peril-point

[18] The initial limits on liberalization were partly because U.S. protectionist industries managed to convince Congress to impose general limitations on the authority granted to the president, and see below. In addition, the State Department's concern with foreign policy rather than economic considerations explains why the United States, while generally promoting liberalization, permitted an abundance of protectionist practices by its trading partners (Gilpin 1971; Krasner 1976, 337; Frieden 1988, 61).

[19] The Republican Party was increasingly split by alliances to capital-intensive export-oriented sectors and to those industries, such as textiles and steel, that began to face stiff import competition, so that by the early 1950s many Republicans had switched sides and come to support multilateral trade liberalization (Hiscox 2002, 65). Many Democrats, in turn, reversed their position when, in the late 1960s, the AFL-CIO, led by the powerful steel and textile unions, began advocating protection for these industries. The party's rural support base also grew increasingly divided along commodity lines over the trade issue (Pastor 1980, 97; Hiscox 2002, 63–65).

[20] Following the establishment of GATT, Congress extended the authority to the president in 1948, 1949, 1951, 1953, 1955, 1958, 1962, and 1968.

and escape-clause provisions, intended to curb the extent to which tariff reduction would injure particularly sensitive industries. In addition, it arranged "pockets" of special protection in which particular industries could maintain high tariffs or be protected by import quotas (Destler 1986). The institutional order established in 1934 therefore also permitted, or could not prevent, protectionist measures.

CONGRESSIONAL OVERSIGHT OF THE ADMINISTRATION

Congress used the time limits it imposed on the delegation of authority to periodically review, introduce, renew, or remove provisions that constrained the ability of the president to set tariffs that would injure import-sensitive industries.

In the Trade Extension Act of 1948, Congress extended the RTAA for only one year and introduced a "peril-point" provision, which required the Tariff Commission to set minimum rates for contemplated concessions below which domestic industries might be harmed by imports. The president could not reduce duties below the rates determined by the Tariff Commission without explaining his action to Congress. The following year, Congress repealed the peril-point provision, but it reintroduced it in the Trade Extension Act of 1951.

The 1951 act also mandated the "escape clause" into law. A version of an escape-clause provision had first appeared in the 1934 act, which guaranteed the opportunity for outside groups to present their views to the president before the completion of bilateral negotiations. If a particular industry could demonstrate that a concession would cause it "serious injury," then it was presumed that the president would not reduce the tariffs of that item. The provision was generalized in the 1942 bilateral trade agreement with Mexico: the clause in the agreement permitted the modification or withdrawal of trade-agreement concessions in order to remedy serious injury to a domestic industry from increased imports resulting from that concession (Diebold 1972, 155–56). In 1945, the administration agreed to incorporate an escape clause in all future bilateral and multilateral agreements, and the clause was also incorporated in the multilateral agreements of the GATT. In 1947, an executive order established a formal governmental mechanism to act on applications of domestic industry for escape-clause relief. The provision of the 1951 law allowed the president to withdraw trade concessions and impose duties on imports of any article that caused or threatened to cause serious injury to a domestic industry. The Tariff Commission was given the authority to determine injury. The president then had discretion to act on the commission's recommendation or to reject it.

If he chose the latter, he would have to inform the Congress of his reasons (Pastor 1980, 98–101). Four years later, the Trade Act of 1955 modified these requirements, making it easier for industries to receive import relief (Zeiler 1992, 36; O'Halloran 1994, 91). The Trade Act of 1958 granted Congress the right by a two-thirds concurrent vote to override the president's refusal to invoke the escape clause and thereby force the president to implement a recommendation of the Tariff Commission.

The Trade Extension Act of 1955 also included a national security clause that allowed industries "vital to national security" to apply for exemption from tariff reductions. In the 1958 act, Congress rewrote the national security escape clause "so that virtually any domestic industry could obtain protection from foreign competition if it were determined that such competition were weakening the internal economy and thereby impairing national security" (Pastor 1980, 103–4).

Congress also limited the negotiation flexibility of the president by blocking the inclusion of "sensitive" sectors, such as textiles, into the multilateral trade negotiations (Aggarwal 1985). It also set limits on the rate of tariff reduction the executive could negotiate—Congress gave permission to lower tariffs by only 15 percent in the acts of 1953 and 1955, and by only 20 percent in the act of 1958. Another obstacle for trade liberalization was procedural: the RTAA established an item-by-item negotiations method, which necessitated the daunting task of separate negotiations for each item.

In the early 1960s, however, the Kennedy administration confronted a pressing issue that necessitated, state officials believed, a substantive multilateral lowering of trade barriers. The establishment of the Common Market in Europe required a reaction, they argued, that would offset the effects of the trade diversion created by the formation of a European block (and that would form a harmonious trade partnership between the two centers of noncommunist industrial power). The internationalist business associations such as the Committee for Economic Development, the Committee for a National Trade Policy (CNTP), and the Chamber of Commerce agreed. The American Farm Bureau Federation and the AFL-CIO, in turn, accepted the need to change trade policy in reaction to intra-European cooperation.

Consequently, the Trade Expansion Act (TEA) of 1962 delegated a particularly broad authority to the president: the authority to reduce tariffs by 50 percent, over five years. It also gave the president the authority to abolish the item-by-item negotiations method and to utilize the European linear method of across-the-board negotiations (Bauer, Pool, and Dexter 1972, 77; Zeiler 1992). The TEA was liberal also with regard to other issues. The act repealed the peril-point provision, putting in its place a much weaker prior notification and advice requirement. Instead of establishing a peril point for each commodity, the Tariff Commission would advise the president as to the probable economic effects of tariff reductions. The escape clause and national security clause were revised in such a way as to make proof of injury more difficult (Goldstein 1993, 188). At the same time, legislative veto of escape-clause determinations was made easier: it required only a majority of both houses by concurrent resolution instead of the previous two-thirds. As a concession to organized labor, the act also added a trade adjustment assistance program to provide loans to help firms shift into new lines of production, as well as unemployment and retraining payments to workers affected by trade concessions.

Another concession was institutional. Concerned that the State Department had been unduly influenced by the foreign policy aspects of trade (and that the Commerce Department was incompetent and insufficiently responsive to agricultural interests), Congress delegated the trade negotiating authority to a newly established Office of Special Trade Representative (STR) in the Executive Office of the president. The Special Trade Representative was expected to play the "executive broker" role between domestic interests and foreign governments, between the executive branch and Congress, and among the concerned government agencies (Destler 1995, 107; Dryden 1995, 50–59).

Protectionist elements opposing the 1962 bill included the Trade Relations Council, the Nation-Wide Committee on Import-Export Policy, and the Liberty Lobby. Individual industries opposing the bill included textiles, carpets, glass, chemical, lumber, and oil. The administration thwarted protectionist amendments to the bill by satisfying in advance the demands of enough injured industries to neutralize them or even give them a stake in the bill's passage. By arranging Voluntary Restraint Agreements (VRAs) for the textile and apparel industries, providing assistance for softwood lumber producers, ordering tariff increases to the carpet and glass industries recommended by the Tariff Commission, and exempting from negotiations products on which the Tariff Commission had made a finding of injury (including lead, zinc, and oil), "the union of various protectionist elements . . . which, voting together, could have crippled the bill, failed to materialize."[21] This "special" treatment, provided to some industries in the context of the 1962 act, exemplifies a more general phenomenon of "selective" protection.

[21] Congressional Quarterly, *Almanac,* 1962, 283, cited in Pastor 1980, 116.

CONGRESSIONAL SELECTIVE TREATMENT OF SPECIAL CASES

The progressively liberal steps taken by Congress, especially in 1962, such as allowing the administration to cut tariffs across the board rather than item-by-item, increased the possibility of injury to import-competing industries (Diebold 1972; O'Halloran 1994, 93). In the administration, the various commissions and agencies to which the domestic interests hurt by imports could appeal for relief were not very effective and therefore only sparsely used (Goldstein and Lenway 1989). With no effective support from the administration, import-impacted industries repeatedly turned to Congress for relief. Congress, in turn, coped with these industry-specific pressures by providing, as if external to the general process of trade liberalization, protectionist measures to a limited number of "special" cases (Destler 1986, 22). Congress arranged such "pockets" of special protection by passing laws that provided higher tariffs or import quotas to particular industries (see also Hufbauer, Berliner, and Elliott 1986; Destler 1986, 22–25). In response to the sugar industry lobbying, for example, Congress created a quota framework for regulating domestic production and imports in 1934, allocated percentage-of-market quotas to domestic producers and foreign countries in the Sugar Act of 1937, and assigned fixed tonnage quotas to domestic producing areas in the Sugar Act of 1948. Only at the end of 1974 did President Ford allow the fixed tonnage quotas to expire. In response to the meat industry lobbying, Congress passed the protectionist Meat Import Act of 1964. In response to the fish industry demands, Congress enacted the Nicholson Act, which prohibited the unloading of fish caught by foreign vessels in U.S. waters. In reaction to similar pressures, Congress increased tariffs on canned tuna in oil in 1951, enacted the Federal Aviation Act of 1958 in support of the air transport industry, and passed the Copyright Act of 1970 in support of the book manufacturing industry. The oil industry used the national security clause attached by oil-state legislators to the RTA of 1955 to obtain, in 1957, "voluntary" controls on U.S. importers of oil which were replaced, in 1959, with a Mandatory Quota Program.

Since it was the executive that could reach agreements with importers, the president was often contacted by special groups for relief. Protectionist industries soon realized, however, that a congressional threat of import quotas was the most efficient way to attract the president's attention to their plight. Congress then became instrumental in making the administration negotiate bilateral agreements that would restrain exports to the United States. The textile industry was one of the most persistent and influential of those lobbying Congress for the sake of the administration's intervention. The industry was negatively affected by international competition relatively early. From 1958 to 1960, imports of cotton goods increased nearly 150 percent. As a result, the cotton textile trade surplus, which had been $125 million in 1958, shrank to $19 million in 1960. Two years later, the industry took advantage of the administration's interest in the trade bill of 1962 to promote their concern. As Representative Carl Vinson, the leader of the textile group in the House, said: "Unless quotas are imposed that will provide the necessary protection to the textile industry in the United States, I think I can safely predict that at least some of the members who voted to extend the Trade Agreements Act of 1958 will have second thoughts if a bill to extend the Act is presented on the floor in 1962."[22] To ensure the support of the cotton textile industry, Kennedy presented a seven-point agenda.[23] The program called for federal aid to assist with modernization, including revised depreciation allowances, loans, and research and development programs, and for studies of the two-price global cotton system and a possible imposition of an eight-and-one-half cent "equalization fee" on cotton textile imports. The plan also allowed for easier resort to the escape and national security clauses. Most important, Kennedy promised to arrange a GATT meeting in order to negotiate a protective trade agreement (Zeiler 1992, 79). The result was a GATT Short Term Agreement (STA), in which it was agreed that a sector that suffered "market disruption" from imports could ask importers to reduce textile shipments to lower levels. If its request was denied, the sector could apply for a GATT waiver to limit imports. A five-year Long-Term Arrangement Regarding International Trade in Cotton Textiles (LTA) followed. The LTA froze imports for two years and controlled the rise in quota levels over the next three years. As a complementary act, Congress also passed a bill limiting cotton textile imports from nonsigners of the LTA (Zeiler 1992, 85–87). The LTA was renewed twice, in 1967 and in 1970, and was then replaced, in 1974, by a Multi-Fiber Agreement (MFA).[24]

The steel industry also grew protectionist. Until the late 1950s, the U.S. steel industry was the world's preeminent producer of the major raw material commodity and enjoyed complete control over its domestic market. But in 1959 imports surged to 4.4 million tons from merely 1.7 million tons the year before (an increase of 260 percent), and steel imports exceeded exports for the first time. By 1968, only ten years later, imports of steel

[22] Congressional Quarterly, *Almanac*, 1962, 287, cited in Pastor 1980, 109.

[23] Already as a presidential candidate, in an attempt to win the South and New England, Kennedy pledged that a solution to the cotton textile problem would be a "top priority objective" of his administration (cited in Zeiler 1992, 75).

[24] On the political struggles preceding the MFA, see chapter 4.

consisted of 18 million tons, which amounted to 16.7 percent of the market (Hall 1997). In response, the industry put extensive effort in recruiting the U.S. government to help it fight the import penetration threat. In 1966, the American Iron and Steel Institute (AISI) began to lobby for temporary tariffs, and by the end of 1967, a political coalition including the textile, oil, and steel industries obtained enough support in Congress to introduce a steel import quota bill that would have imposed unilateral quotas to limit steel imports for five years (Hall 1997, 51,115). The Johnson administration, though, objected to the imposition of quotas: "I think those protectionist bills just must not become law and they're not going to become law as long as I am President," Johnson announced. "Those proposed quotas would invite massive retaliation from our trading partners throughout the world . . . prices would rise. Our world market would shrink. So would the range of goods which American consumers choose when they buy" (cited in Hagy 1993, 196–97). But a widening trade gap and budget deficit were putting increasing pressure on an overvalued dollar, so the administration had an incentive to restrict imports as means of shoring up the dollar (Hall 1997, 116). The solution came from Japanese and German steelmakers, who offered to voluntarily restrict their exports. In December 1968, the Johnson administration entered into Voluntary Restraint Agreements for basic steel with Japan and the six members of the European Coal and Steel Community (ECSC). The agreement limited total steel imports into the United States to 14 million tons for 1969 (compared to the 18 million tons of imports in 1968). It located 41 percent of the allowed volume for Japan and the ECSC each, and 18 percent for the rest of the world. The voluntary limits were to be in effect for three years, with a 5 percent increase allowed each year. These VRAs launched a new era for the steel industry, during which it achieved protectionist measures by threatening the administration and foreign producers with congressional action. In 1972, the VRAs were extended for three more years by the Nixon administration, which needed the steel industry's support for Trade Act of 1974 (Hagy 1993, 199; Hall 1997, 119).[25]

---

[25] The 1972–74 VRAs, however, were not tested in the marketplace. Demand for steel in the global economy temporarily increased, and imports declined to 12.4 percent of the market share in 1973. It was therefore difficult to make a political case for protectionism, and in 1974 American steel companies allowed the VRAs to expire without putting up a fight. There was also a legal reason not to extend the VRAs. The Consumers' Union of the United States filed a lawsuit against the State Department and the firms that participated in the 1972 VRAs, in which it argued that the VRAs were a violation of the Sherman Anti-trust Act and a violation of the 1962 Trade Expansion Act. Some of the charges were later dropped and others were dismissed by the court. Yet dissenting opinions in the case demonstrated that the new VRAs were bound to be controversial.

Discussion

United States international trade policies in the postwar era were formed within an institutional regime of *selective protectionism* in which liberal principles prevailed, but which still allowed for protectionist exceptions. The notion of "selective protectionism" only partially parallels Ruggie's (1982) well-known description of the postwar era, which is often used in the literature as a starting point to analyze the contemporary era of (neoliberal) globalization (Evans 1997; McMichael 2003). Ruggie's notion of "embedded liberalism" captures a particular arrangement, in which liberal trade practices, which provided relatively unrestricted freedom for global capital, were "embedded" in a social compact that committed advanced industrial states to insulating their citizens from the costs of such an international economic system. Under this formulation, protectionist measures were not an exception to, but an integral part of, the logic of the postwar order, and were intended to assure—within the general framework of multilateralism, nondiscrimination, and a general obligation for free trade—domestic economic growth, full employment, balance of payments, and other domestic concerns (Ruggie 1982, 393; see also Zeiler 1998; Graz 1999). While the notion of "embedded liberalism" captures well the tension in the United States between trade liberalization and protectionist practices—a tension which is surprisingly overlooked by most scholars of trade, who emphasize instead the liberal elements of the postwar period—this chapter suggests that Ruggie's reference to the international regime as the *source* of this emerging balance between multilateralism and domestic issues is inadequate.[26] Ruggie's description of the principles and norms of the international trade regime relies on those provisions of the ITO relating to full employment and other domestic issues. But the ITO was not ratified, and since the GATT took only the commercial chapter from the ITO, it emphasized multilateralism largely at the expense of domestic responsibilities.[27] The postwar international regime, in other words, did not incorporate the domestic concerns to which Ruggie refers. In any event, the GATT offered too weak of a basis for an international regime. In contrast to Ruggie's perception of the GATT as a regime consisting of *shared* principles and norms

---

[26] But see Haggard (1988, 93–94), who rightly suggests that the RTAA of 1934 left ample room for effective protectionist strategies. Haggard, however, focuses on the fact that Congress retained powers of oversight and does not pay sufficient attention to actual protectionist measures.

[27] As mentioned earlier, even the ITO Charter was fairly vague regarding the domestic responsibilities of member-states.

that limited the discretion of its member-states, the weak institutional features of the GATT instead allowed member-states great and unequal influence over both the organization and its decisions. The implications for the United States were that the sources of trade policies—including protectionist ones—were at the domestic level, rather than the international one.

At the domestic level, I argue in this chapter, the contestation focused on institutional arrangements, particularly the location of authority. A century and a half of defeats in Congress and, most particularly, the Smoot-Hawley Tariff, led supporters of free trade to the conclusion that Congress was too susceptible to protectionist demands and that, since they could not offset the influence protectionists had in Congress, the only way to ensure tariff reductions was to move authority away from it, and to the administration. The punitive effects the Smoot-Hawley Tariff had on American exporters, and the desire to reverse them in the context of the economic devastation of the Great Depression, softened congressional resistance. A collaboration between business internationalists and state officials at the Department of State led to the enactment of the RTAA of 1934, which for the first time in American history granted the president the authority to lower tariff rates in international trade agreements without the need for ratification from Congress. The RTAA formed a delicate balance between liberalism and protectionism, which allowed a first, if still modest, step in the institutional project of globalization.

The delegation of tariff-setting authority to the administration permitted a substantial reduction in tariffs, because the administration, in particular the Department of State, supported free-trade principles, and because it provided incentives for internationalists to use their political influence to lobby for tariff reduction and against protectionist practices. At the same time, the authority that was left to Congress meant that domestic industries opposed to trade liberalization maintained some influence over trade policy. At the international level, the procedures of negotiations preserved the political advantage of rich countries and permitted American dominance. Consequently, the GATT reproduced the American trade agenda and could not impose effective restrictions on the U.S. Congress. The outcome was a regime of *selective protectionism*, in which protectionism became, for the first time, a doctrine of restraints and exceptions to a liberalizing process that was not in itself challenged.

The postwar balance between trade liberalization and protectionist exceptions satisfied the demands of protectionist industries but was also accepted by internationalists. The "special" legislation kept industry-specific protection out of trade-liberalizing statutes, and hence stopped protectionist groups from upsetting the overall liberal direction of trade policy (Destler 1986, 25; Smith 1994, 141–42). Special deals were also seen as a way to split the opposition and prevent the emergence of cross-sectoral coalitions (Bauer, Pool, and Dexter 1972). However, once selective protection came to be viewed by internationalists, in the early 1970s, as potentially damaging to the general process of trade liberalization, a new struggle over institutional arrangements emerged. This is the topic of the next chapter.

CHAPTER FOUR

THE ORIGINS OF CONDITIONAL PROTECTIONISM

Selective protectionism survived for forty years, but the economic recession of the late 1960s led to its demise. Because of the new economic conditions, many manufacturing industries faced stiff international competition and turned protectionist. In their turn, manufacturers who were potentially competitive in the international market pressed for greatly improved access to foreign markets, demanding "fair" trade from U.S. trading partners. The clash between protectionists and internationalists was therefore inevitable, and protectionists, at least initially, had the upper hand. Most spectacularly, when the administration failed to negotiate voluntary restraint agreements on behalf of the textile and apparel industries, Congress initiated a protectionist bill that would have unilaterally imposed import quotas not only on textiles and apparel but on a variety of other goods as well. The reversal of postwar liberal victories seemed almost certain. But it was not. In a counterattack, internationalists managed to block the textile bill that the protectionists had promoted. More fundamentally, internationalists established a second institutional transformation: the Trade Act of 1974 delegated further authority from the unreliable Congress to the executive branch, thereby weakening protectionists' political influence and curbing future protectionist threats.

The chapter begins with a detailed description of the economic recession in the late 1960s and how it altered the interests and demands of U.S. manufacturers, with some reverting to protectionism while others searching for ways to increase their operations abroad. I show that, initially, the administration sought to respond to the new demands following the logic of selective protectionism, pressing for trade liberalization while permitting special treatment for few declining industries. However, I argue that the ability of the textile and apparel industries to insist on their protectionist goals and to lead, if inadvertently, to the mobilization of other protectionist industries as well, made it painfully clear to internationalists that the institutional regime of selective protectionism no longer served their interests. Once internationalists recognized that the institutions governing selective protectionism allowed for protectionist successes in a way that directly undermined their (newly defined) interest in "free but fair" trade, they fought to change them.

The chapter then proceeds with an analysis of the site internationalists chose to fight protectionist successes: negotiations over the Trade Act of 1974. I provide detailed evidence that shows that one of the main purposes of internationalists in fighting for the Trade Act was shifting authority also over nontariff trade measures from Congress to the executive. The transformation of authority to the administration was achieved by revising the U.S. trade remedy laws. These laws provide statutory remedies for industries and workers to counterbalance import surges or unfair trade practices of importers. The Trade Act of 1974 made the conditions under which relief was granted easier to meet. I show that officials in the Council of International Economic Policy, Office of Special Trade Representative, as well as the National Security Council, who were responsible for the formulation of the bill in the administration, advocated the amendments exactly to limit the congressional role in trade policy formulation. Associations representing the largest U.S. international companies, most prominently the Emergency Committee on American Trade (ECAT), as well as the Committee for a National Trade Policy (CNTP) and the U.S. Council of the International Chamber of Commerce, aided the administration in formulating the relevant provisions and testified in Congress in favor of the changes.

I provide a detailed account of the struggles over each one of the four trade remedy laws that were reversed: trade adjustment assistance, escape clause, antidumping law, and countervailing duty law. I describe the original reasoning behind the specific amendments proposed, and the bitter debates that ensued regarding each suggested revision. I show that the suggestion to make the provisions more lenient was strongly advocated by internationalists while greeted by protectionists with great suspicion. I also show that, while asking for more lenient conditions, internationalists also insisted that the process of decision making at the administration should be as bureaucratized and legalized as possible, to reduce the effectiveness of protectionist political pressures. At the same time, they supported presidential discretionary powers to reject positive (though not negative) determinations. Combined, these measures were meant to block the most blatantly protectionist measures, while allowing for measures that posed only minimal threat to the general process of trade liberalization.

The ability of protectionist industries to mobilize Congress on their behalf in selective cases was of little use in opposing comprehensive institutional challenges. I suggest that this was due to the logic of selective protectionism, which effectively disorganized the protectionist forces, and due to political manipulations of the Nixon administration, which managed to buy off the most influential industries. Protectionist industries, labor, and their supporters in Congress did fight back in regard to particular provisions and gained important concessions, but they failed to block the institutional change itself.

Managing Protectionism in the Early 1970s

Under the regime of selective protectionism, various U.S. administrations advanced free trade by negotiating the reciprocal reduction of import duties in bilateral and multilateral trade agreements. Congress, in turn, discontinued its practice of unilaterally raising tariffs. Instead, Congress arranged "pockets" of protection for selected industrial sectors and pressured the administration into negotiating voluntary restraint agreements with trading partners regarding specific commodities. These protectionist exceptions to politically influential industries were welcomed by the internationalists, for they kept industry-specific protection out of trade-liberalizing statutes, in particular, those statutes that enabled the president to lower tariffs, and hence stopped protectionist groups from upsetting the overall liberal direction of trade policy.

This tacit agreement between internationalists and protectionists was upset by the economic recession of the late 1960s. Whereas from 1962 to 1968 the economy had grown at 4.6 percent a year, it grew only 2.4 percent in 1969, and then fell 0.3 percent in 1970 (Judis 2000, 110; Harrison and Bluestone 1988). The recession was largely a result of the economic recovery of Western Europe and Japan and the consequent rise of international competition in the U.S. market (Brenner 1998), and was therefore accompanied by a radical increase in the rate of manufactured imports relative to domestic production, which skyrocketed from less than 14 percent in 1969, to nearly triple that, 38 percent, only ten years later. The first absolute trade deficit in recent U.S. history occurred in 1971 (Ferguson and Rogers 1981, 10; Block 1977a).

In response to the increased import penetration into the U.S. market, a great number of American companies—manufacturers of products ranging from textiles and steel to pianos, minks, and silverware—asked for protectionist measures.[1] They were joined by organized labor, which saw jobs threatened by competition from low-wage workers abroad, some of them employed by U.S. multinationals that had "exported the jobs" of American workers in order to take advantage of lower wage costs (Destler 1980, 135). While the AFL-CIO had supported the liberal Trade Expansion Act of 1962, by 1970 it was calling for an *"orderly* expansion of world trade" (*New York Times,* 2/22/1970, italics added).

Internationally competitive industries also altered their economic strategies and political preferences. In reaction to the saturation of the American market, they intensified their exports to foreign markets[2] and stepped up their direct foreign investment abroad.[3] Consequently, U.S.-based multinational corporations and American exporters now had much greater interest in furthering the process of trade liberalization than during the postwar boom. Reliance on foreign markets made these companies more sensitive to barriers to trade and to direct investment imposed by U.S. trading partners. Internationally competitive businesses therefore urged the U.S. government to act against various other states' use of border taxes, nontariff barriers, and other discriminatory treatments.[4] This meant, in essence, that many American corporations replaced their traditional support of "free trade" with demands for "fair trade." Two associations representing the largest international U.S. companies, which had in the past led the free-trade campaign, became particularly active in lobbying against the unfair trade practices of other countries that impeded access to their markets. The

[1] Businesses responded to the recession also, of course, by developing new *economic* strategies, including the reorganization of work and labor-management relations. On flexible specialization and post-Fordism, see Harrison 1994; Amin 1994; Sabel 1994; Esser and Hirsch 1994.

[2] Sectors that maintained a positive trade balance included capital goods (including jet planes, computers, and other advanced electronic equipment), coal and lumber, agriculture, and exported services (including banking, shipping, and insurance)(Block 1977a, 157).

[3] Direct investment outflow steadily increased from $1.654 trillion in 1960 to $3.530 trillion in 1972, and $4.968 trillion in 1973 (Block 1977a, 157).

[4] Memo, Undersecretary of Commerce to President Nixon, February 2, 1969, box 19, FG 21 Commerce, WHSF, WHCF, Subject Files, 1969–74, NPMP.

Committee for a National Trade Policy (CNTP) circulated a report, entitled "The Imperatives of a Trade Policy in the National Interest," which urged the administration "to declare publicly and unequivocally its commitment to negotiated 'free trade' (including codes of *fair international competition* where necessary)" and "to impress upon the governments of economically advanced countries . . . the need to reduce as quickly as possible those import barriers which have emerged as serious, discriminatory restrictions against U.S. exports."[5] The Emergency Committee on American Trade (ECAT), which was founded in 1967 by David Rockefeller, president of Chase Manhattan Bank, and Arthur Watson, president of IBM, with the objective "to publicize our opposition to any increase or expansion of import quotas" (quoted in Martin 1994, 60), also shifted its views somewhat. ECAT called for "rules that would make access to markets similar throughout the world," and asked, in particular, "for the removal of barriers to American exports" (*New York Times*, 1/3/1969, 35, 3). Although ECAT called for international cooperation by way of "vigorous and tough multilateral trade negotiations to assure fair access for American trade and investment abroad,"[6] it also drafted and submitted for the administration's consideration bills aimed at increasing the president's authority to *unilaterally* retaliate against discriminatory foreign treatment of U.S. exports.[7]

The political response to the economic conditions of the 1970s put the U.S. government in the uneasy position of facing both intensified demands for protection and similarly vehement demands for fairness. C. Fred Bergsten, the chief economic aide of Nixon's National Security Adviser, Henry Kissinger, was one of the first state officials to acknowledge these changing economic sentiments:

> U.S. trade policy clearly needs new direction and focus. Most of the constituencies which have supported the essentially free trade

[5] "The Imperatives of a Trade Policy in the National Interest," CNTP Report, February 1969, box 1, WHCF, Subject Categories, FG 6–10 STR, NPMP.

[6] ECAT to Peter Flanigan, Director of CIEP, May 18, 1970, box 14, NPMP, WHCF, SF, FG.

[7] One suggestion was to extend an existing authority to retaliate against discriminatory treatment of agricultural exports to also cover nonagricultural exports. Another was to give the president authority to retaliate, through trade restrictions, against foreign direct investment controls if those controls negated the value of tariff concessions made by the foreign country. The first recommendation was supported by the Trade Executive Committee, which recommended that such a provision be included in the 1969 trade legislation, and was the source of Section 301 of the Trade Act of 1974 (see below). The second was judged to be too open to abuse, and was thus rejected. Memo, Paul W. McCracken, chairman of CEA, to President, June 20, 1969, box 401, SF, NPMP, NSCF.

approach of the last 35 years have either reversed their positions or become relatively ineffective, and no new forces have developed to take over from them. Therefore, the traditional approach must either be jettisoned or at least modified substantively, or be resumed on the basis of a new coalition of supporting political forces.[8]

Initially both protectionists and fair-traders followed strategies, and the administration and Congress responded to them, under the assumption that it was possible to pursue trade liberalization while at the same time attending protectionist demands as special cases. Protectionist industries thus pursued the legislative route, asking Congress for import quotas and other forms of aid. Congress, as in the past, was willing to address the requests of selective industrial sectors. In spite of the supposed division between the Republican and Democratic parties—the former by then had formally embraced free-trade ideology, the latter had turned increasingly protectionist—support for declining industries crossed party lines. The chairman of the House Committee on Ways and Means, Wilbur Mills, a Democrat, stated that he would sponsor legislation to redress the balance of trade in favor of specific American industries. John W. Byrnes, a ranking Republican member of the same committee, announced that things had to be done to counter foreign economic invasions in certain industry markets in the United States (Pastor 1980, 124–25). Almost three hundred members of the House sponsored quota legislation in the ninety-first Congress (1969–70). By March 1970, the House Ways and Means Committee calendar included twenty-three bills limiting footwear imports, twenty-two bills setting import quotas on meat, forty-three on milk and dairy products, forty on mink, fifty-eight on steel products and pig iron, forty-five bills directing the president to negotiate limits on textile imports, and forty-seven bills empowering the president to set ceilings on imports competing with troubled industries on the basis of percent of domestic market (*National Journal*, 3/7/1970, 501). Some of these initiatives explicitly violated the logic of "selective protectionism for special cases." Instead, Congress showed willingness to block the process of trade liberalization for the benefit of declining American companies.

The Nixon administration resisted this protectionist trend. It was divided, instead, between those maintaining the traditional adherence to liberal trade policy and those swayed by calls for fair trade. Top officials at the Department of State, the National Security Council, and the Council of

---

[8] Memo, C. Fred Bergsten, December 9, 1970, Box 2, FG, NPMP, WHCF, SF.

Economic Advisers maintained their support for free trade. Leading the fair trade camp were Treasury Secretary John B. Connally, and the head of the Council of International Economic Policy (CIEP), Peter G. Peterson.[9] Both embraced the argument that the deteriorating economic conditions in the United States were due to lack of reciprocity. In past trade negotiations, they argued, the United States had given away much more than it had gotten, and it had failed to insist that other countries live up to their international trade obligations. In a leadership meeting in November 1971, Connally presented his views in strong language: "The world has been riding the U.S., a good horse, to death in the post-war years, and this has got to stop." He went on to complain about the Japanese, stating that "the Japs [*sic*] could sell a Toyota here for about the same $2,000 price as a Pinto, while in Japan, the Pinto would cost some $5,200," and about the Europeans for blocking their markets to Japanese products. He concluded by arguing that "we are fighting for a fair share for our own people" and that "we want a New Deal, a Fair Deal for Americans in the world."[10] On his part, Peterson argued that the emergence of discriminatory trading agreements abroad had contributed to the decline in the U.S. trade position (*New York Times*, 1/23/1972, IV, 13, 1), and "alerted the President . . . [that] we were getting the short end of the stick; couldn't afford it much longer; and action was required."[11] In July 1971, the Commission on International Trade and Investment Policy (the Williams Commission) reiterated "a growing concern in this country that the United States has not received full value for the tariff concessions made over the years because foreign countries have found other ways, besides tariffs, of impeding our access to their markets."[12]

---

[9] Nixon established CIEP in 1971, to function as the economic analogue to the National Security Council.

[10] Memo for the president's file, Patrick J. Buchanan, November 16, 1971, box 86, WHSF / Staff Members & Office Files, President's Office Files, President's meeting file, 1969–74, NPMP. At the same time, Connally passionately insisted that the pursuit of fairness was not protectionism in disguise: "We do not intend to become provincial. We shall not resort to protectionism. We shall carry our burdens on the international scene. But to do so it is essential to attain an equilibrium in our overall financial balance with the rest of the world. We seek no advantage of others. We propose to suffer no disadvantage. We seek a balance which will be to the benefit of all the nations. . . . To fail in our effort would be to fail not only as an Administration, nor even as a Nation. At stake is nothing less than the foundation for the freedom and security of this generation, and those that follow." John Connally addressing the Economic Club in the fall of 1971. Cited by Eugene T. Rossides before the American Footwear Industries Association, March 2, 1972, box 64, WHCF, SF, TA, NPMP.

[11] Memo, George Crawford to Peter Flanigan, Director of CIEP, January 27, 1972, Box 3, WHCF, SF, TA, NPMP.

[12] *Williams Commission Report*, ix.

In spite of official opposition to protectionism, and under the pressure of commitments Nixon had granted during his presidential campaign and the threat of pending legislation, the Nixon administration had to address the predicament of at least some of the declining sectors. A month after entering the White House Nixon declared, in a press conference, that the best interests of the United States would be served by "moving toward freer trade rather than toward protectionism" and took "a dim view of this tendency to move toward quotas and other methods that may become permanent, whether they are applied here or by nations abroad."[13] At the same time, he affirmed the possibility of giving protection to some industries, such as textile and steel (*New York Times*, 2/7/1969, 1, 7). The division of responsibility in the administration contributed to the erroneous perception of trade liberalization and protectionism as two separate issues. General policy was formulated by the internationally oriented National Security Council (NSC) under Henry Kissinger, and trade negotiations were conducted by the Office of the Special Trade Representative (STR) in conjunction with the Department of State. Responsibility for bilateral negotiations concerning the restriction of specific commodities, however, was granted to the Department of Commerce. The fallacy of this perception was made painfully clear in the case of the textile industry.

Protecting Textiles

During the postwar period the textile and apparel industries were some of the most persistent and influential sectors lobbying for special protection, with evident success. An early achievement of the textile industry was the Long-Term Arrangement (LTA) of 1962, which provided a framework that allowed bilateral agreements for import quotas on cotton textiles (see chapter 3). But the LTA diverted the efforts of exporting countries away from cotton and toward man-made fibers, resulting in rapidly increasing imports of such products. Imports of man-made fibers grew from 328.4 million square yards in 1964 to 4.3 billion in 1971. (Because of the rapidly expanding U.S. market, however, the increase in the proportion of U.S. consumption of man-mades filled by imports was far less striking—from 1.3 percent in 1962 to 3.6 percent in 1968.) A considerable portion of these imports (28 percent) came from Japan, the largest single seller in the U.S.

[13] Here Nixon reiterated the conclusions of the Task Force on Foreign Trade Policy, headed by Alan Greenspan, that concluded that it would be better to maintain the previous free-trade orientation of the preceding administration. "Report of the Task Force on Foreign Trade Policy," box 401, NSCF, SF, NPMP.

market (Destler, Fukui, and Sato 1979, 35). Responding to this import surge, the American textile industry called in 1968 for comprehensive restraints on man-made fiber textile imports. The industry directed its lobbying efforts both at Congress,[14] and the presidential election campaign. The textile industry was concentrated in the South, and therefore played an important role in Nixon's attempts to win the presidential elections. In addition, some textile magnates had contributed heavily to Nixon's campaign. Roger Milliken of Deering Milliken, for example, had raised $1 million in 1968 for the special Southern operation.[15] To secure the industry's support of his candidacy, Nixon endorsed the textile industry's cause, pledging both to improve the administration of the LTA and to extend the limitation on the annual increase of cotton textile imports to all other textile articles involving wool, man-made fibers, and blends.[16]

Once in office, the Nixon administration resolved to handle the issue of the textile industry "within the framework of a liberal trade policy."[17] The administration therefore decided "to handle this on a voluntary basis rather than having to go to a legislation which would impose quotas."[18] The American Textile Manufacturers Institute (ATMI) initially accepted voluntary restraint agreements as an adequate solution. Accordingly, the administration launched an effort, led by the Commerce Department, to get comprehensive bilateral agreements with the key exporters—Japan, Korea, Taiwan, and Hong Kong—in an effort to convince them to voluntarily limit their textile exports to the United States.[19]

---

[14] In March 1968, the Senate passed a general textile quota proposal as an amendment to a major tax bill. The provision, however, was deleted in the Senate-House conference.

[15] Memo, Harry Dent to Haldeman and Chapin, August 15, 1971, box 38, WHCF, SF, BE, NPMP.

[16] Nixon made a verbal commitment to textile industry leaders in August 1968, and few days later he sent a telegram to that effect to more than a hundred congressional sponsors of textile import quota legislation during the 90th Congress. Memo, Richard Nixon, August 21, 1968, Box 63, WHSF, WHSF, SF: CF; NPMP, Memo, Robert Ellsworth, special assistant to the President, to H. R. Haldeman, Chief of Staff, February 21, 1969, Box 63, WHSF, WHSF, SF: CF, NPMP; Letter, Roger Milliken, Chairman of Deering Milliken, to Nixon, September 12, 1969, Box 399, NSC, SF, NPMP.

[17] NSC Review Group, Memo, April 5, 1969, Box 2, WHCF, Subject Categories, FG 6–10 STR, NPMP.

[18] Memo, Robert E. Ellsworth, Special Assistant to the President, to H.R. Haldeman, Chief of Staff, February 21, 1969, Box 63, WHSF, WHSF, SF: CF, NPMP.

[19] ATMI argued that the State Department, to which the responsibility for the international negotiations had initially been assigned, could not be relied on fully to press the industry's case with foreign nations, and insisted that this responsibility be transferred to the Department of Commerce. Memo, Robert E. Ellsworth, Special Assistant to the President, to H.R. Haldeman, Chief of Staff, February 21, 1969, Box 63, WHSF, WHSF, SF: CF, NPMP.

Strong opposition to the negotiations was initially expressed by the Textile and Apparel Group of the American Importers Association.[20] As soon as the negotiations lingered with no foreseen resolution, however, they were joined by supporters of fair trade.[21] ECAT opposed the textile initiative because of the negative effects that stalled negotiations would have on foreign countries' adherence to fair trade rules and their pace of liberalization.[22] In a letter to Robert E. Ellsworth, special assistant to the president, the chairman of ECAT and Pepsi's chief executive, Donald Kendall, noted his "concern about the costs to the United States economy that could result" from the effort to negotiate voluntary limits on textiles. "There are a number of sensitive and important discussions and negotiations going on with foreign governments that could suffer from the textile negotiations," he wrote. Among the issues at stake were the European border tax adjustment system and, more pressing, Japanese limitations on investment and trade. "Pressure to negotiate this 'voluntary' textile quota," Kendall warned, "might make foreign nations much less willing to give us what we want."[23]

This conflict of interests between the protectionist and fair-trade camps reached a high point when, after almost a year and a half of futile negotiations, the textile industry abandoned its previous support of voluntary trade agreements and demanded, instead, unilateral measures of protection. On March 19, 1970, the Board of Directors of ATMI adopted an official resolution stating, "The situation demands an immediate legislative solution. Accordingly, we respectfully urge the President to . . . propose promptly . . . legislation to impose effective, comprehensive, quantitative limitations on imports into the United States of all textile articles."[24]

[20] Letter, Textile & Apparel Group of American Importers Associations to Nixon, February 3, 1969, Box 59, WHCF, SF, TA, NPMP.

[21] The unexpected refusal of the foreign governments to comply with U.S. demands was, in Japan, due to domestic political pressures (Destler, Fukui, and Sato 1979), and in Korea, Taiwan, and Hong Kong, due to economic concerns resulting from the end of the war in Vietnam. U.S. expenditures for the war had provided these countries with an added economic stimulus, and they were seeking opportunities to increase their exports in order to compensate for the expected decreases in U.S. expenditures. Textiles were a key component of such increases. Letter, Donald Kendall of ECAT to Robert E. Ellsworth, Special Assistant to the President, February 24, 1969, Box 59, WHCF, SF, TA, NPMP.

[22] Memo, C. Fred Bergsten, chief economic aide of National Security Adviser, to Henry Kissinger, National Security Adviser, November 12, 1969, box 399, NSC Files, SF, NPMP.

[23] Letter, Donald Kendall, Chairman of ECAT, to Robert E. Ellsworth, Special Assistant to the President, February 24, 1969, Box 59, WHCF, SF, TA, NPMP.

[24] A Resolution Adopted by the Board of Directors of the American Textile Manufacturers Institute, Inc., at San Francisco, March 19, 1970, box 399, NSC Files, SF, NPMP.

Subsequently, the textile industry established a coalition with shoe manufacturers for the purpose of initiating a joint effort in Congress for legislative quotas. ATMI also moved against any legislative approval of the reversion of Okinawa to Japanese sovereignty, in order "to teach the Japanese a lesson."[25] Less than a month later, Wilbur Mills, the chairman of the House Ways and Means Committee, submitted to the committee a bill (H.R. 16920) providing for statutory textile and footwear quotas. The "Mills bill" proposed to limit textile imports for 1970 to the 1967–68 average, with future year increases proportionate to the growth of U.S. domestic consumption. Quotas would be allocated by country and by category. It exempted from these limits any country with which the United States had negotiated an agreement limiting textile and leather footwear imports.

When Mills, shortly after Nixon's election, had raised the possibility of initiating a trade bill imposing import quotas as a way to "motivate" the Japanese to reach a voluntary agreement with the U.S. government,[26] the administration had opposed it on the grounds that the use of unilateral measures "would place us in violation of our international obligations and make us liable for retaliation from other countries."[27] The free trade camp in the administration continued to oppose any congressional initiation. Bergsten saw quota legislation as "smashing of our thirty-five year policy of freer trade," and warned that "enactment into law of the Trade Bill would be a disaster for U.S. foreign policy."[28] Paul W. McCracken, chairman of the Council of Economic Advisers, asserted, "It is not overly alarmist to say that . . . we may be on the verge of a trade war with Europe and Japan."[29]

But the failure of the negotiations with Japan made it impossible for the administration to continue to argue that voluntary agreements were a viable alternative to legislated quotas. Therefore, and in spite of internal opposition, Nixon agreed to support the bill. Following the logic of selective protectionism, however, the administration refused to support "protectionist trade legislation well beyond textile quotas,"[30] specifically in regard to import quotas on shoes.[31]

[25] Memo, Harry Dent to president, March 24, 1970, box 399, NSC Files, SF, NPMP.

[26] Memo of conversation, Stans with Mills and Byrnes, May 2, 1969, box 11, WHFS / Staff Member & Office Files, Peter Flanigan, 1969–74, Subject Files, 1969–74, NPMP.

[27] Letter, Carl Gilbert to Senator Schweiker, March 10, 1970, box 52, RG 364, USTR, General Counsel, 1962–75, NPMP.

[28] Memo, Bergsten to Kissinger, March 12, 1970, box 399, NSC Files, SF, NPMP; Memo, Bergsten to Kissinger, November 24, 1970, box 399, NSC Files, SF, NPMP.

[29] Memo, McCracken to the president, July 2, 1970, Box 58, WHCF, SF, FG, NPMP.

[30] Memo, Kissinger to President, July 13, 1970, Box 401, NSC Files, SF, NPMP.

[31] The shoe quota threatened to jeopardize relations with Italy and Spain. Kissinger went as far as claiming that protectionist steps would lead to "new gains for the Communists in

Yet, as the administration soon realized, it was impossible to provide import quotas only for textiles. Lobbyists for approximately seventy product categories for which import quota bills had been introduced pressed strongly for equal treatment of their claims (Destler, Fukui, and Sato 1979, 208). Worse, John W. Byrnes, a ranking Republican member of the committee, added a "basket" clause to the bill requiring the president to take action to restrain imports whenever the import/consumption ratio exceeded a certain percentage (Destler, Fukui and Sato 1979, 209).[32] Nixon reacted by announcing that he would veto the trade bill if it imposed quotas on any item other than textiles.[33]

Internationalist business also fought vigorously against the bill. As Kendall noted in the congressional hearings, "In the case of Japan, we believe that the current fixation with textiles that has required so much attention over the past year while the problem of open markets has been neglected is like playing ball in a sand lot rather than in the big ball park."[34] Ellison Hazard Steinberg, also speaking in the name of ECAT, warned that quotas would worsen the international climate for widespread American investments in operations overseas: "Our plants overseas are dependent to a large extent on cooperative relations among the countries concerned. We would not wish them to be caught in the middle of a trade war."[35] Kendall also tried to mediate a textile agreement with Japan, but was blocked by ATMI (Destler, Fukui, and Sato 1979).

Italy." Memo, Kissinger to president, July 8, 1970, Box 401, NSC Files, SF, NPMP. The administration offered an alternative domestic program to meet the shoe industry's problems. In addition, the president requested a Tariff Commission investigation to see whether there was a case for import restraints. Memo, Kissinger to president, July 13, 1970, Box 401, NSC Files, SF, NPMP.

[32] The administration was not vehemently opposed to a basket provision as such. There were, in fact, serious considerations of suggesting such a provision, but only as *a replacement* for the import quotas on shoes and textiles, and one less strict than Byrnes's formulation. This should be seen as an early manifestation of the willingness of the administration to support measures that would shift authority and discretion away from Congress. See, Memo, Bergsten to Kissinger, August 4, 1970, box 401, NSC Files, SF, NPMP.

[33] Memo, C. Fred Bergsten, chief economic aide of National Security Adviser, to Henry Kissinger, National Security Adviser, July 23, 1970, Box 1, WHCF, SF, TA, NPMP.

[34] Letter, ECAT to Peter Flanigan, Director of CIEP, May 18, 1970, box 14, WHCF, SF, FG, NPMP.

[35] Letter, ECAT to Peter Flanigan, Director of CIEP, May 18, 1970, box 14, WHCF, SF, FG, NPMP.

Nevertheless, on November 10, 1970, the bill passed in the House by a 215–165 margin.[36] In the Senate, however, "some very effective behind-the-scene lobbying . . . carried on by members of ECAT," brought a different outcome.[37] Through filibuster threats and various parliamentary maneuvers, the consideration of the bill was blocked, and the bill never became law (Destler, Fukui, and Sato 1979, 242).

Although the bill failed to pass, the textile industry ultimately got what it had originally demanded. In 1974, the administration concluded a multilateral "voluntary" Multi-Fiber Agreement (MFA) on textiles and apparel, which implemented new restraints on imports by way of bilateral agreements (Cline 1990, 11). But the Mills bill had more far-reaching consequences. The textile experience made U.S.-based multinational corporations and American exporters realize that the intensified demands for protection directly contradicted their interest in imposing fair trade practices on other countries. The attempt to reach an agreement on textile import quotas with Japan slowed down the administration's efforts to reduce Japan's own nontariff barriers to trade. Even more disturbingly, the Mills bill breached the logic of selective protectionism by turning a bill aimed at textiles into a general protectionist bill that included, in addition to benefits to several industries, a general formula for limiting imports. The textiles case also showed that the existing institutional arrangements exacerbated the conflict instead of mollifying it. The demands clashed not only because of an inherent incompatibility, that is, the inconsistency of U.S. demands for others to reduce their barriers to trade while at the same time maintaining and imposing similar barriers at home. The demands clashed also because the division of responsibility between Congress, which had control over unilateral protectionist measures, and the administration, which was responsible for bilateral negotiations and agreements, made it difficult to reach a compromise between protectionist and internationalist interests. Internationalists realized that this division of authority, *given the new preferences,* advantaged protectionists over internationalists. It was this realization that motivated the internationalists to challenge the institutional arrangements that had governed protectionism since 1934.

---

[36] Eighty-five Republicans and 143 Democrats voted for the bill; 88 Republicans and 90 Democrats voted against, suggesting the cross-partisan nature of the debate.

[37] Memo, Jonathan Rose, CIEP, to Peter Peterson, Director of CIEP, March 18, 1971, box 2, TA, NPMP, WHCF, SF.

Making New Institutional Arrangements

A trade bill, which the U.S. administration needed so it could launch a new round of multilateral trade negotiations,[38] was the arena that advocates of free or fair trade in the administration—supported by U.S.-based multinational corporations, as well as exporters, industrial users of imported inputs, and retailers (Destler and Odell 1987)—chose to challenge the institutional arrangements in place.

The draft bill reflected quite faithfully the hierarchy of opinions in the administration. The Departments of Commerce and Labor, which were relatively attentive to domestic industries and supportive of protectionist claims, had little influence on the wording of the bill. The "free trade" camp was well represented by the Department of State, the National Security Council, the Office of the Special Trade Representative, and the Council of Economic Advisers. The by-then similarly influential fair trade camp was represented by Peterson of CIEP and Connally, who in addition to being the secretary of treasury was also appointed as the administration's chief economic spokesman. Consequently, the bill was a patchwork of "free" and "fair" trade concerns.[39]

To address the problem of unfair trade practices by other countries, insofar as they affected the access of American companies and products to

[38] John Connally's influence on Nixon initially led to an attempt to solve the monetary crisis of 1971 unilaterally. Nixon's New Economic Policy (NEP) of August 15, 1971, included a ninety-day freeze on prices, rent, and wages; the closing of the gold window; and a 10 percent import surcharge for a temporary, but undefined, period. Adherents of multilateralism and liberal trade eventually succeeded in moderating the effects of Nixon's restrictive policies. With regard to the trade aspects of the NEP, Kissinger convinced Nixon to abandon the initial plan according to which an improvement of $13 billion—that would be achieved through the unilateral removal of tariff and nontariff trade barriers by U.S. trading partners—would be needed in its balance of payments before the surcharge could be lifted (Hersh 1983, 462n). Foreign countries instead only had to commit to a new round of multinational trade negotiations, hence the need of trade legislation. On the monetary economic crisis of the 1970s, see Silk 1972, chaps. 10–13; Block 1977a, chap. 7. On Nixon's NEP and the resulting international negotiations, see Safire 1975, 491–528; Solomon 1977; Odell 1982; Gowa 1983.

[39] The bill also contained one title involving explicit foreign policy concerns. The administration wanted Congress to implement a trade agreement between the United States and the Soviet Union in which the United States agreed to provide the Soviet Union, which was not a GATT member, Most-Favored-Nation (MFN) status. But even before the administration bill was submitted, Senator Henry Jackson and Congressman Charles A. Vanik sponsored resolutions denying MFN status to countries that barred emigration. The intention was to use the trade agreement to force the Soviet Union to permit the emigration of Jews out of the country. Kissinger, however, was willing to give up on the bill completely if such conditions were introduced. Only after Kissinger achieved a compromise between the Soviet authorities and the congressmen at home could the bill pass. For an exhaustive study on the struggle over MFN status to the Soviet Union, see Stern 1979; on Kissinger's role see also Kochavi 2005.

foreign markets, the administration formulated a unilateral solution and a multilateral one.[40] The unilateral measure, which faithfully followed ECAT's suggestion, asked Congress for presidential authority to retaliate against any country that maintained "unjustifiable or unreasonable tariff or other import restrictions" against the United States, or pursued other discriminatory or subsidy policies that damaged the U.S. trade position.[41] That was the basis of Section 301 of the Trade Act.

In addition, the administration asked Congress for an authority to negotiate and implement the reciprocal reduction not only of tariffs, which was granted by Congress more or less continuously since the RTAA of 1934,[42] but also of nontariff barriers. The problem was that the president had no constitutional authority to implement international agreements that required changes to domestic laws. Hence, congressional ratification was required for any international agreements with implications to domestic legislation. Congress, however, often refused to ratify changes that had negative implications for domestic constituencies. Following the Kennedy Round of multilateral trade negotiations, it refused to ratify the International Antidumping Code and an agreement to eliminate the American Selling Price (ASP) method of calculating import duties that U.S. negotiators had signed. Hence, before U.S. negotiators could expect other nations to make new concessions regarding nontariff barriers, a reliable method for assuring congressional support for U.S. concessions was required. The solution preferred by the administration, and included in the draft legislation

---

[40] The adherence to fair trade was also reflected in the bill's stated objective "to provide the tools to protect our position and restore equity if our trading partners fail to negotiate an equitable trade liberalization package." The focus on "equity" reflected the victory of the Treasury Department over the National Security Council, which held that "the major point of foreign policy is that we should not box ourselves into a commitment to 'restore equity' if our trading partners fail to negotiate an equitable liberalization package. This implies that we would significantly increase trade barriers with the result that others would surely retaliate. . . . The risk here is that for questionable tactical reasons it commits the President to do something which later on he may not wish to do, and which would have disastrous economic and foreign policy implications." The Concept of 1973 Trade Legislation, CIEP, January 11, 1973, box 5, WHCF, SF, TA, NPMP; Memo, Hormats to Kissinger, January 16, 1973, box 402, SF, NPMP, NSCF.

[41] Under then-current law, the president could strike back at discrimination against U.S. manufactured goods abroad only by withdrawing tariff concessions. Only if the discrimination were against U.S. agricultural products could he otherwise raise tariffs or impose quotas in retaliation.

[42] The Trade Act of 1974 granted the administration a five-year mandate to enter into trade agreements to eliminate all tariffs below 5 percent, and to reduce all tariffs above 5 percent ad valorem by as much as 60 percent.

sent to Congress, was a legislative veto mechanism. The president would send proposed changes to Congress, which would become law *unless* a majority in either the House or the Senate voted to reject them within ninety days. Members of the Committee on Finance in the Senate, however, insisted that the procedure was unconstitutional. By that time, the Nixon White House was preoccupied with the Watergate scandal and was completely absent from the discussions. Still, committee members and the Office of the STR managed to agree on an alternative: Congress would vote on bills implementing international trade agreements within a limited period and without any amendments (Destler 1997, 7–8). This "fast track" procedure, which did not allow Congress to modify U.S. international trade concessions—only to accept or reject the international trade agreement as a whole—was as revolutionary as the delegation of authority over tariffs in 1934, for it strengthened the credibility of the U.S. administration at the international realm, at the expense of Congress's ability to unilaterally defy compromises made during international trade negotiations.

The administration's draft bill also proposed to strengthen four existing trade laws providing statutory remedies for industries and workers who demonstrated that they had suffered injury due to import surges, or against importers who used unfair trade practices. The four provisions were trade adjustment assistance, the escape clause, antidumping law, and countervailing duty law. While at times conceived as protectionist, these provisions—particularly the antidumping (AD) and countervailing duty (CVD) laws—had the unique feature of following a similar logic to that used by fair traders in their quest for access to foreign markets. The duties imposed were aimed at deterring importers from employing unfair-trade practices in their competition with American manufacturers in the U.S. market.

The administration's decision to strengthen trade remedy laws as part of an otherwise liberal trade bill has been commonly interpreted as a concession to protectionist industries and labor, a compromise necessary to gain their support for the bill (Pastor 1980, 142–43; Destler 1986, 114–17). Indeed, the administration was concerned that it did not have the necessary congressional and public support for passing the bill.[43] Deputy STR, William Pearce, warned:

A great deal needs to be done to develop public support for the bill. For a variety of reasons, many groups that supported enactment of

[43] By the 1970s position over trade was only loosely partisan (Hiscox 2002) and concerns about passing the bill in Congress were not expressed in terms of party politics, in spite of the fact that throughout the Nixon administration the Democratic Party controlled both houses.

the last major trade bill are no longer reliable. Most groups affiliated with organized labor will oppose the Administration's bill. Others (for example, the Committee for a National Trade Policy) have lost leadership, financial support and effectiveness. Despite good intentions, they cannot be counted on without extensive reorganization. Even groups that have remained strong and effective (for example, the Emergency Committee for American Trade) must be convinced that an Administration bill has a reasonable chance to pass without damaging amendments. All business-oriented groups are likely to reserve judgment until plans on such issues as taxes and investment are clear. Extensive consultations will be required to develop a dependable core of private backing around which major support can be mobilized.[44]

Consequently, the administration launched—with the active help of supporting business associations, particularly ECAT—a serious lobbying effort. The effort was aimed less at the public at large and more at "interest group organizations in the international economic field which have 'clout' in Congress."[45] The administration identified the U.S. Chamber of Commerce, the National Association of Manufacturers (NAM), the American Retail Federation, the American Iron and Steel Institute (AISI), and the American Importers Association (AIA) as key organizations.[46] Organized labor was a special concern, since it was sponsoring a competing bill, the Burke-Hartke bill (formally, the Foreign Investment Act), which provided thoroughgoing quantitative restrictions on imports and was aimed to discourage foreign direct investment by U.S. corporations.

Several government officials who supported the changes suggested that making the trade laws more lenient could pacify opposition of the bill. Deane Hinton, deputy director of CIEP, for example, argued that "the bill we will draft will have enough safeguards built into it to persuade the moderates (and maybe even some individual workers) that responsible confidence is better than irresponsible defeatism."[47] The fact that Congress

[44] Memo, Pearce, December 13, 1972, box 5, WHCF, SF, TA, NPMP.
[45] Memo, Pearce, December 13, 1972, box 5, WHCF, SF, TA, NPMP.
[46] Memo, February 12, 1974, WHCF, SF, TA, NPMP.
[47] Deane Hinton, Deputy Director of CIEP, to Peter Peterson, Director of CIEP, December 17, 1971, box 3, WHCF, SF, TA, NPMP. See also Comprehensive Trade Legislation: Issues and Options, STR, January 8, 1973, box 5, WHCF, SF, TA, NPMP; STR Paper, "Summary of Agency Positions on Import Relief and Adjustment Assistance," December 12, 1972, box 5, WHCF, SF, TA, NPMP.

further strengthened the provisions could also suggest that amending the trade laws was used as means to balance the liberal character of the bill.

Yet the changes to the trade laws could not have been motivated solely as a concession, for two reasons. First, the administration neutralized the objections of protectionist industries with more effective means, by buying them off with special arrangements and policy exceptions outside the contours of the bill. The primary targets were the most influential industries: "Steel and textiles, once you keep them out of a trade bill, you can resist the efforts of the other interests."[48] The textile and apparel industries were shielded from the planned multinational negotiations by the MFA; imports of steel were governed by "voluntary" bilateral agreements since 1972; and certain categories of import-sensitive products, including textiles and apparel, footwear, watches, and steel products, were excluded from the Generalized System of Preferences (GSP).[49] The administration also negotiated policy exceptions with manufacturers of ceramic dinnerware, ball bearings, nonrubber footwear, color TV sets, industrial fasteners, CB radios, and petroleum (Verdier 1994, 276). In other words, the administration guaranteed the passage of the bill by buying off industries, rather than compromising the bill's liberal orientation. The strengthening of trade laws, in this context, would have been redundant.

Second, the trade laws were not sufficiently "protectionist" to satisfy struggling industries' demands, and to use them as concessions was therefore futile. As the chairman of ECAT, Donald Kendall, wrote to the director of CIEP, "The recommended program will fall short of making converts or supporters of a liberal trade policy from among those industries and unions now in the import restrictionist camp."[50] And Secretary of Labor James D. Hodgson noted: "Any endeavor to make inroads into the labor movement protectionist position would find us swimming upstream against a very strong current."[51]

Indeed, the provisions were only rarely perceived or justified as being a concession to gain protectionists' support for the trade bill, a concession that would allow protectionists to advance their interests and that could undermine the internationalist agenda. Instead, the provisions were endorsed

---

[48] Harry Lamar, Ways and Means Committee staff member, quoted in Pastor 1980, 158.

[49] Letter, William D. Eberle, STR, to Russell Long, Chairman of Committee on Finance, November 7, 1974, box 53, RG364, US TR, General Counsel, 1962–1975, NPMP.

[50] Letter, Donald Kendall, Chairman of ECAT, to Peter Peterson, Director of CIEP, January 10, 1972, box 22, WHCF, SF, TA, NPMP.

[51] Memo, James D. Hodgson, Secretary of Labor, to Peter Flanigan, Director of CIEP, June 29, 1972, box 4, WHCF, SF, TA, NPMP.

by advocates of trade liberalization in the administration, in particular STR and CIEP, in close cooperation with internationalist business, in an effort to *restructure* protectionist measures in a way that would limit their negative effect on free and fair trade. While the safeguard and unfair-trade law provisions of the bill were not aimed at eliminating protectionist action as such, they did intend "to facilitate the adjustment process with *minimum disruptive effects.*"[52]

The negotiations with Japan and the textile bill made free- and fair-trade advocates realize that the institutional arrangements in place did not allow them to pursue their agenda but rather gave protectionist industries political leverage that they had used quite effectively. The new institutional arrangements, inscribed into the modified trade remedy laws, sought to shift authority over protectionist measures from Congress to the administration and, in the administration, to legalize the process of decision making, so as to reduce the effectiveness of political pressures, while leaving to the president discretionary powers to reject positive determinations. By providing the administration means, independent of Congress, to deal with protectionist demands, these arrangements were meant to minimize potential interruptions to the process of trade liberalization.

Shifting authority to the executive would restrict Congress from passing protectionist legislation, such as the Mills bill, which, by that time, was perceived as being the most harmful kind of protectionist measure. As a CIEP document reasoned, these measures were to "blunt protectionist pressure from industries and businessmen," thus avoiding "pressure from them for a highly restrictive approach to safeguards (including pressure for arithmetic trigger formulas)"[53] C. Fred Bergsten, Kissinger's chief economic aide, similarly wrote, "Any administration will have to defend U.S. commercial interests vigorously around the world. . . . Credible policies in this direction are necessary, at a minimum, *to avoid having Congress take trade matters increasingly into its own hands*" (Bergsten 1971, 633, italics added). The measures under the jurisdiction of the administration were considered less bluntly protectionist than congressional quota legislation. Trade adjustment assistance was celebrated as "the most valid alternative to import restrictions yet conceived" (Bergsten 1971, 630), since the remedies offered did not include restraints on imports and did not impose any direct burden

---

[52] The Concept of 1973 Trade Legislation, CIEP, January 11, 1973, box 5, WHCF, SF, TA, NPMP. Italics added.

[53] The Concept of 1973 Trade Legislation, CIEP, January 11, 1973, box 5, WHCF, SF, TA, NPMP.

on trading partners. Escape clause, AD, and CVD laws were also viewed as credible alternatives for legislation. In contrast to adjustment assistance, these measures did directly affect the flow of trade. However, AD and CVD measures did not trigger retaliation and did not require compensation. In contrast to legislated import quotas, safeguards and unfair-trade laws were consistent with international trade agreements.[54]

Importantly, the *legalization* of the decision-making process would render the political influence of protectionists less determinant of the final outcome. Rules, not political considerations as such, were to govern the decision of whether a specific industry was eligible for protection. Under selective protectionism, domestic industries backed their claim to protection by referring to economic difficulties. The question, for example, whether the steel industry's troubles derived from technological "backwardness" or from international competition did not seem to matter much, as long as the industry had the political leverage to get congressional support. Under the new arrangements, in contrast, a request for relief would have to be supported by evidence of injury and a causal link to imports. In the case of AD and CVD laws, industries would have to demonstrate unfair practices in order to gain protection.

In order to ensure that protectionist claims would be referred to the administration and not to Congress, protectionists had to find it in their interest to use the administrative channels. Making the requirements of the trade laws more lenient provided incentives for protectionists to refer their demands to the administration. As I describe below, the discussion preceding the formulation of the Trade Act reveals that this was indeed the main reasoning provided for making the provisions more lenient.

Disregarding the promise embedded in making unfair-trade laws more lenient, protectionist industries and labor opposed the administration's liberal trade bill. The "fast track" procedure threatened to radically weaken the ability of Congress to oppose anti-protectionist concessions offered by the administration to U.S. trading partners; and protectionist industries complained that the amended unfair trade laws would not bring substantive enough changes. The protectionists' political position at the time was quite promising: the protectionist legislation in the late 1960s and early 1970s demonstrated Congress's support, and the Watergate scandal made the administration too preoccupied to effectively lobby on behalf of its bill. Watergate should have also strongly discouraged Congress from putting

[54] Bergsten 1971, 630; see also Comprehensive Trade Legislation: Issues and Options, STR, January 8, 1973, box 5, WHCF, SF, TA, NPMP.

any more authority in the hands of an untrustworthy president. Yet, an accumulation of several factors worked against the interests of the protectionists, who eventually lost the struggle over the trade bill.

First, the initial bill was not drafted in Congress, where one could expect greater attentiveness to protectionist needs, but in the administration—and long before Watergate turned into a public scandal. In the administration, the task was granted to agencies supporting free and fair trade (STR and CIEP) or concerned with foreign issues (NSC). The Department of Commerce was also relatively active, but its most protectionist proposals were flatly rejected by the other agencies. ECAT had access to the Special Trade Representative and to the president himself—Donald Kendall, the chairman of ECAT, was a personal friend of Nixon. As a result, ECAT actively participated in the drafting deliberations, and its recommendations received equal attention as those provided by state agencies. Protectionist industries, in contrast, did not have much access to or support in the administration.

Even in Congress, protectionist industries failed to utilize their potential resources. During negotiations over general trade bills in Congress, protectionists exerted weak influence because they lacked an umbrella association to represent them. Instead, protectionists were divided along industrial lines, each promoting its own distinct objectives. The absence of a unified voice was itself an outcome of institutional conditions and opportunities—the logic of selective protectionism did not encourage industries to cooperate with each other, since the chances for congressional support increased if protectionist bills were narrowly constructed. In addition, protectionist industries did not cooperate with organized labor. The Burke-Hartke bill, supported by AFL-CIO, was rejected by internationalist and protectionist businesses alike, and diverted organized labor's attention away from the administration's bill. Given these limited political opportunities, the most that domestic industries could ask for were provisions in the trade bill that dealt with their own particular interests. As we saw, the administration largely prevented such demands by offering some industries concessions outside the contours of the bill.

Finally, the Watergate scandal, which should have discouraged Congress from providing additional discretionary powers to the president, proved of little consequence to foreign economic policy issues. As I mentioned, negotiations in the administration over the bill occurred before the scandal erupted and were therefore not disturbed by it. By the time of the congressional hearings, in 1974, however, the administration was completely absent (Destler 1997, 8). The Special Trade Representative, William D. Eberle, however, was an active presence and a constructive influence. Congressional hearings suggest that Watergate was *not* a concern in the discussions. While Watergate had moved Congress to impose itself more forcefully in foreign policy issues (Gelb and Lake 1973; Franck and Weisband 1979; Cronin 1980), this has not been the case with economic issues.

As I describe in detail below, the final formulations of the trade adjustment assistance, safeguards, and unfair-trade law provisions were a skewed compromise between the two camps, with the internationalists having the upper hand—while Congress made the provisions more lenient than what the internationalists had originally desired, the internationalists largely succeeded in putting in place the institutional arrangements within which these lenient provisions would be implemented.

Trade Adjustment Assistance

Under the Trade Adjustment Assistance Program (TAA), which originated in the Trade Expansion Act of 1962, workers could obtain jobless benefits, retraining, and relocation aid, and firms could obtain loans, tax breaks, and technical aid, if the Tariff Commission, a quasi-judicial federal agency, determined that they suffered injuries as a result of increased imports. However, the test of injury that was required to trigger adjustment assistance was so tightly drawn and so stringently interpreted that the law proved inoperable. Of the fifteen petitions filed between 1962 and 1968 not a single case of adjustment assistance was authorized. A study of the Tariff Commission on adjustment assistance declared that "an analysis . . . leads to an inescapable conclusion—the criteria established in the Trade Expansion Act as a requisite for a decision favorable to the petitioning industry, firm, or workers have been difficult to satisfy."[55]

Despite initial declarations that improving adjustment assistance could contribute to the "neutralization" of labor on trade issues,[56] and that "abandoning adjustment assistance . . . would pose serious problems for the enactment of liberal trade legislation on the Senate side," administration officials soon admitted that it would be impossible to pacify labor.[57] As the deputy director of CIEP, Deane Hinton, argued, "There isn't much he [the President] could do to wean organized labor away from 'its' bill in

[55] Memo, U.S. Tariff Commission to president, May 15, 1973, box 6, WHCF, SF, TA, NPMP.

[56] Memo, Guenther to Stans, October 1972, box 5, WHCF, SF, TA, NPMP.

[57] Memo, Brady, CIEP, to Flanigan, Director of CIEP, January 24, 1973, box 5, WHCF, SF, TA, NPMP.

any scenario."[58] Throughout the negotiations in Congress the AFL-CIO maintained the position that "the entire thrust of the bill is to negotiate away—with little likelihood of any gain for the U.S.—the remaining industrial sector and its millions of jobs that Americans depend on."[59]

Yet support for adjustment assistance continued, as it was considered the "best alternative to import restrictions which could both zero in on specific problems and avoid disrupting international trade relationships" (Bergsten 1971, 634). Since the remedy of adjustment assistance was not restraints on imports, but financial (or other) remedies to workers or firms, adjustment assistance had no distorting effect on trade and did not invite any burden on the trading partners. Moreover, administration officials and business genuinely believed that an effective system of assistance would curtail the demands for congressional intervention. According to Bergsten (1971, 634), "Adjustment assistance must be resuscitated politically to forestall new restrictions to meet import problems," and STR William D. Eberle anticipated that the new trade adjustment assistance program "would reduce the pressure for quotas or other import restrictions."[60]

Exporters and multinational corporations—including ECAT, CNTP, and NAM—shared the view of adjustment assistance as a better alternative to congressional import restrictions.[61] CNTP, for example, urged the use of trade-adjustment programs as "the primary instrument of industry assistance," and added that "the criteria for imposing such trade restrictions should be tightly drawn so as to make trade controls, if needed at all, only a marginal part of a balanced policy of constructive help."[62]

Organized labor and protectionist industries, however, were less enthusiastic. The Amalgamated Clothing Workers of America claimed that the suggested adjustment assistance program "is not only a case of too little too late but it is not a practical answer to the problems that face us now and will continue to face us in the future."[63] Representatives of the protectionist

---

[58] The reference here is to the Burke-Harke bill. Deane Hinton, Deputy Director of CIEP, to Peter Peterson, Director of CIEP, December 17, 1971, box 3, WHCF, SF, TA, NPMP.

[59] AFL-CIO Charge – Jobs and Trade, October 10, 1973, box 2, WHCF, SF, FG 6-10 STR, NPMP.

[60] Memo, William Eberle, STR, to Haig, March 4, 1974, box 403, NSCF, SF, NPMP.

[61] Memo, Peter Peterson, Director of CIEP, to Laurence H. Silberman, Undersecretary of Labor, January 17, 1972, box 22, WHCF, SF, TA, NPMP; Letter, Executive Vice President of Caterpillar Tractor Co. to Peterson, January 17, 1972, box 22, WHCF, SF, TA, NPMP; Letter, Donald Kendall to Peterson, January 10, 1972, box 22, WHCF, SF, TA, NPMP.

[62] CNTP testimony, U.S. Congress, May 14, 1973, House Committee on Ways and Means, *Trade Reform*, 93rd Congress, 789, italics added.

[63] Amalgamated Clothing Workers of America testimony, June 6, 1973, House Committee on Ways and Means, *Trade Reform*, 93rd Congress, 3870.

industries expressed similar sentiments. Frederick Dent of Mayfair Mills, a textile corporation, argued against adjustment assistance and in favor of a sound international trade policy.[64] Similarly, Roger Ahlbrandt of Allegheny Ludlum Industries, speaking on behalf of the steel industry, argued that "adjustment assistance is not the answer to this problem."[65] Concerned that the administration would adopt adjustment assistance as the only remedy, he "urge[d] our friends in government to remedy the source of the illness rather than to seek palliative care."[66] AISI thus informed Congress that it "share[d] the view of labor that financial and other forms of Adjustment Assistance only after injury has occurred do not constitute responsible trade policy."[67]

Underlying the revitalization of the adjustment assistance program was the willingness of the American government to take on itself the cost of trade liberalization rather than imposing it on its trading partners. But this was also its main weakness, and the reason it was eventually constructed in a way less generous than had been originally perceived. George Shultz, who replaced Connally as secretary of treasury in May 1972, strongly opposed "adding additional trade adjustment assistance benefits without providing additional revenue" (cited in Destler 1980, 146). In an attempt to strike a balance between a more effective program and budgetary concerns, the administration bill liberalized the eligibility criteria for workers' adjustment assistance, dropping the requirement that injuries had to be caused by prior tariff concessions and requiring that imports needed only to have *contributed substantially* to job losses, rather than being the major cause, but the amount and duration of benefits were reduced below those authorized in 1962. In addition, the administration proposed a revised unemployment insurance program for all workers as well as a liberalized pension-vesting scheme, thereby dropping the link to trade (Destler 1980, 152).

The business community, concerned with the additional costs the insurance plan would impose on industry, opposed it. Minimum federal standards for unemployment compensation "seem to be a red flag for business," the director of CIEP was informed, "in that they fear Congress would set the level so high as to discourage people from working."[68] Pro-trade businesses—

---

[64] Letter, Frederick Dent, President, Mayfair Mills, to Peter Peterson, Director of CIEP, January 7, 1972, box 22, WHCF, SF, TA, NPMP.

[65] Letter, Roger Ahlbrandt, President of Allegheny Ludlum Industries, to Peter Flanigan, Director of CIEP, March 1, 1972, box 64, WHCF, SF, TA, NPMP.

[66] Letter, Roger Ahlbrandt, President of Allegheny Ludlum Industries, to Peter Peterson, Director of CIEP, January 7, 1972, box 22, WHCF, SF, TA, NPMP.

[67] AISI testimony, June 7, 1973, House Committee on Ways and Means. *Trade Reform.* 93rd Congress, 3966.

[68] Memo, Robert Morris to Flanigan, February 22, 1973, box 6, WHCF, SF, TA, NPMP.

including ECAT, NAM, the U.S. Council of the International Chamber of Commerce, the U.S. Chamber of Commerce, CNTP, and the American Importers Association—all argued that the government should "pay money earlier trying to get at the root cause of the problem rather than pay burial expenses after the dislocations have occurred."[69] NAM contended that "the Administration's apparent abandonment of trade adjustment assistance in favor of federal standards for unemployment insurance and expanded private pension regulation is *not* the answer" for effective industry and worker adjustment.[70] Associations representing U.S.-based multinational corporations, somewhat tactlessly, explained the moral and economic reasoning behind granting special attention to trade-dislocated workers compared to those workers hurt by shifts within the domestic economy.[71] The AFL-CIO, in turn, also rejected the administration's solution, stating that while the present program had been ineffective and too few workers had received aid, it was better than the unemployment compensation program proposed.[72] Congress agreed and, dismissing the administration's budgetary considerations,[73] further liberalized the eligibility criteria in the bill. Imports would have to contribute only *importantly*, and not substantially, to job loss for workers, and the injury test was to be based on an absolute, rather than a relative, increase in imports. Congress also increased the duration and value of benefits offered to workers.

In short, administration officials supported easing the eligibility requirements of the adjustment assistance program not only because this was seen necessary in order to get the bill through Congress, but also because it was regarded as the most effective alternative to import restrictions. If the first reason can be seen as mere submission to labor's protectionist sentiments, the second showed that this submission was acceptable only because it was expected to have limited effects on the general process of liberalization. Budgetary constraints, however, made the adjustment assistance program less attractive to the administration. The compromise achieved thus contained an easing of the requirements, while limiting the potential budgetary burden on the administration.

---

[69] NAM testimony. May 22, 1973, House Committee on Ways and Means, *Trade Reform*, 93rd Congress, 2001.

[70] Letter, NAM to Peter Flanigan, Director of CIEP, March 19, 1973, box 6, WHCF, SF, TA, NPMP. Underlying in original.

[71] U.S. Council of the International Chamber of Commerce testimony, May 15, 1973, House Committee on Ways and Means, *Trade Reform*, 93rd Congress, 980.

[72] AFL-CIO testimony, May 17, 1973, House Committee on Ways and Means, *Trade Reform*, 93rd Congress, 1219.

[73] Memo, Deane Hinton, Deputy Director of CIEP, May 16, 1973, box 53, RG364, USTR, General Counsel, 1962–75, NPMP.

Escape Clause

Under the escape clause, as amended in the Trade Expansion Act of 1962, an industry could obtain relief from imports if the Tariff Commission found that it had suffered *serious* injury, the *major cause* of which was the increase in imports resulting from earlier U.S. tariff concessions. The president had the discretion to reject the commission's recommendation for escape-clause relief if he found it to be against the national economic interest. Congressional legislative veto required a majority of both houses by concurrent resolution (Goldstein 1993, 188). Obtaining presidential approval posed the greatest hurdle for petitioners, for presidents often rejected affirmative recommendations. Between 1962 and 1974, all but two escape-clause applications failed.

Several considerations played a role in support of strengthening the escape clause. First, as in the case of adjustment assistance, the administration conceded that "the present law has proved too stringent."[74] Second, the STR suggested that improved statutory remedies to the problem of injury caused by import competition would help to retain public and congressional support for a policy of freer and fairer trade.[75] Third, the escape clause was considered a credible alternative to legislation (Bergsten 1971, 630), which was also consistent with U.S. international obligations.[76]

Indeed, internationally oriented associations encouraged the administration to improve the escape clause. Already in 1969 Kendall wrote to Nixon, "I would hope that your legislative proposals would include a liberalization of the 'escape clause' . . . so that administrative relief from injurious imports would be possible. Availability of such relief would considerably *diminish, if not obviate, the pressures on Congress, and on yourself, for either legislative quotas or voluntarily negotiated quotas*."[77] Similarly, David

[74] STR Paper, "Summary of Agency Positions on Import Relief and Adjustment Assistance," December 12, 1972, box 5, WHCF, SF, TA, NPMP.

[75] Comprehensive Trade Legislation: Issues and Options, STR, January 8, 1973, box 5, WHCF, SF, TA, NPMP; STR Paper, "Summary of Agency Positions on Import Relief and Adjustment Assistance," December 12, 1972, box 5, WHCF, SF, TA, NPMP.

[76] Comprehensive Trade Legislation: Issues and Options, STR, January 8, 1973, box 5, WHCF, SF, TA, NPMP.

[77] Letter, Donald Kendall, Chairman of ECAT, to president, July 14, 1969, box 399, NSC Files, SF, NPMP, italics added. For similar sentiments, see CNTP testimony, May 14, 1973, House Committee on Ways and Means, *Trade Reform*, 93rd Congress, 789; Memo, Peter Peterson, Director of CIEP, to Laurence H. Silberman, Undersecretary of Labor, January 17, 1972, box 22, WHCF, SF, TA, NPMP; Letter, Executive Vice President of Caterpillar Tractor Co. to Peter Peterson, Director of CIEP, January 17, 1972, box 22, WHCF, SF, TA, NPMP; Letter, Donald Kendall, Chairman of ECAT, to Peter Peterson, Director of CIEP, January 10, 1972, box 22, WHCF, SF, TA, NPMP.

J. Steinberg, CNTP executive director, asserted in a press release: "Failure of both the executive and legislative branches of government to deal credibly, coherently and constructively with the nation's adjustment problems . . . has fed the fires of protectionism, with dire implications for vital U.S. objectives at home and abroad."[78] The Atlantic Council urged the president to ask for "more flexible authority to provide temporary, transitional relief from excessive imports" so as to prevent "excessive economic effects . . . to a few sensitive industries or groups of workers, which would create new protectionist pressures."[79]

While advocating leniency as a means of channeling complaints, international business wanted to make sure that it was not *too* lenient. CNTP, for example, saw "no justification for additional restrictions on textiles or any other product except, if needed at all, as a temporary, marginal part of a balanced policy of government assistance to an ailing industry."[80] Here they were joined by importers and retailers—represented by the American Importers Association, the National Retail Merchants Association (NRMA), the American Retail Federation, the American Institute for Imported Steel, and others—who argued that every effort should be made to utilize the provision for adjustment assistance rather than those which provided for increased barriers to imports.[81]

In the administration, there was "a general consensus among the agencies that the statutory criteria for relief from import competition should be liberalized. The question is how much."[82] In the bill, the administration suggested a substantive loosening of the conditions for getting relief. The requirement that import relief should be granted if import competition was the *major* cause (i.e., larger than all other causes combined) of serious injury or threat thereof, was replaced with the requirement that imports be the *primary* cause (i.e., the largest single cause) of the injury. The requirement that the injury had to result from a previous tariff concession was dropped (Destler 1980, 145, 158). In order to offset the anticipated effects, the bill suggested that relief should be granted for a finite period of five

[78] CNTP, Press release, March 22, 1971, box 2, WHSF, Staff Member and Office Files, Peter G. Peterson, 1971, SF, NPMP.

[79] Letter, The Atlantic Council to the president, January 5, 1973, box 5, WHCF, SF, TA, NPMP.

[80] CNTP, Press release, March 22, 1971, box 2, WHSF, Staff Member and Office Files, Peter Peterson, 1971, SF, NPMP.

[81] NRMA testimony, May 29, 1973, House Committee on Ways and Means, *Trade Reform*, 93rd Congress, 3012.

[82] Memo, John R. Garson, Acting General Counsel, to William Pearce, Deputy STR, May 18, 1972, box 63, RG364, USTR, General Counsel, 1962–1975, NPMP.

years, with the possibility of extension, and that authority would be given to the president to compensate trading partners to minimize the risk of retaliation against U.S. exports. Congress accepted most of the administration's changes, but loosened the escape-clause requirements further. For example, the final act required that import competition be merely *substantial*, rather than *primary*, cause of injury.

An important debate in Congress regarding the escape clause revolved around the question of presidential discretion. As mentioned above, one advantage of the safeguards and unfair-trade measures was that they were legalized. Providing formal requirements and semi-judicial procedures ensured that political pressure would play a lesser role in the determination of cases. Internationalists, however, saw no reason not to play it both ways, and advocated selective discretion, which would grant the president the authority to reject affirmative (but not negative) determinations. Such discretion could protect the administration from adhering to unwanted decisions, without allowing political pressure in cases of negative determinations.[83] The administration hence asked to preserve the president's "complete flexibility" in deciding on and fashioning relief.[84]

Protectionist industries strongly opposed presidential discretion, for past experience showed that obtaining presidential approval posed the greatest hurdle for escape-clause petitioners.[85] Senator Ribicoff, reflecting labor's sentiments, asserted: "What is the use of seeking liberalization of this [escape] clause if you have been so reluctant to apply even a stricter clause?"[86]

The final act allowed the president to reject an affirmative recommendation if he found that it was not in the national interest. The president also retained discretion concerning the kind of remedy to offer. He was required, however, to act within sixty days, and Congress could override the

[83] Some businesses were ambivalent about the discretion, realizing that discretion, even if only concerning affirmative decisions, would invite interest group pressure and could therefore politicize a process that had the benefit of being strictly termed by law. CNTP asserted that discretion "opens the door to extensive pressures for import controls. . . . The President would be exposed to formidable pressures to do what these petitions are aimed at securing— restriction of the imports in one way or another." CNTP testimony, May 14, 1973, House Committee on Ways and Means, *Trade Reform*, 93rd Congress, 787.

[84] STR Paper, "Summary of Agency Positions on Import Relief and Adjustment Assistance," December 12, 1972, box 5, WHCF, SF, TA, NPMP; Comprehensive Trade Legislation: Issues and Options, STR, January 8, 1973, box 5, WHCF, SF, TA, NPMP; The Concept of 1973 Trade Legislation, CIEP, January 11, 1973, box 5, WHCF, SF, TA, NPMP.

[85] AISI testimony, June 7, 1973, House Committee on Ways and Means, *Trade Reform*, 93rd Congress, 3957.

[86] U.S. Congress, 1973, House Committee on Ways and Means, *Trade Reform Act of 1973*, 93rd Congress, 233, cited in Destler 1980, 180.

president's decision by concurrent resolution, forcing the implementation of the original recommendation (Destler 1992, 143).

Antidumping and Countervailing Duty Laws

United States law provided remedies for domestic industries against two unfair-trade practices of foreign exporters to the United States: dumping and export subsidies. Under the Antidumping Act of 1921, if the Treasury Department determined that imports to the United States had been sold at less than fair value (that is, less than the selling price in the home market), and the Tariff Commission (as of 1954) determined that the practices of dumping caused or threatened to cause injury to the U.S. industry, an antidumping duty was imposed, equal to the "margin" of dumping, that is, to the difference between the "fair value" and the actual sales price. There was no limit on the time Treasury could take to conduct its investigation. Under the countervailing duty law, which was first enacted in 1897, if the Treasury Department found that a foreign exporter had received a government subsidy in the form of a direct grant or a tax rebate, it imposed a special duty equivalent to the subsidy on the imported product. No injury had to be demonstrated.

Until the 1970s, the antidumping and countervailing duty laws had been little enforced. The Department of Treasury regularly imposed low bonds, dropped cases when continued prosecution was seen as politically unwise, accepted foreign producers' promises to raise prices, and foot-dragged when it was time to collect assessed duties (Goldstein 1993). In addition, and in order to avoid "serious international trade and political problems" in applying the mandatory countervailing duty law, Treasury had kept complaints "under consideration" for years, "where it was against the U.S. national interest to act affirmatively."[87] Under the leadership of John Connally, this attitude changed, and the Treasury Department applied the antidumping law with increased frequency and formulated regulations that effectively worked to the benefit of domestic petitioners.[88] Consequently, there was a substantial increase in affirmative outcomes. In remarks before the American Footwear Industries Association, Eugene T. Rossides, assistant secretary of the treasury, boasted that for the thirteen-year period 1955–67, the administration made twelve affirmative findings of dumping,

[87] Memo, Morgan, Treasury, to William P. Simon, Treasury Secretary, February 8, 1973, Fiche 12, Simon Papers, Gerald R. Ford Library.

[88] News, Department of Treasury, September 13, 1972, box 1109, RG59, Subject-Numeric Files, 1970–73 Economic, FT, NPMP.

whereas in the short three-year period 1969–71, thirty-six cases of dumping were found.[89] Similarly, businesses received no relief at all from the countervailing duty law from 1959 through 1966. From 1967 to 1971, in contrast, the department found on eleven occasions that imports to the United States were being subsidized and that countervailing duties should be imposed (*National Journal*, 7/24/1971, 1544).

While the State Department was concerned with the possible adverse effects these changes would have on relations with other countries,[90] others administration officials saw the benefit of diverting protectionist demands into administrative channels,[91] and industries—such as steel and textile—were in fact approached and encouraged to take advantage of the procedures.[92] These opposite reactions were reflected in the deliberations on whether to amend the unfair-trade laws. Some CIEP members were concerned that unfair-trade provisions punished other countries for practices that the U.S. government itself engaged in. One member rhetorically asked, "Can we impose countervailing duties if our skirts are dirty? Can we impose duties when a subsidy by a foreign country is similar to steps we have taken?"[93] But the director of CIEP, Peter Flanigan, viewed amending the antidumping and countervailing duty laws as providing "new kinds of authority . . . which would permit us to rely much more heavily on tariffs as a temporary relief measure than on quotas or the kinds of restraints involved in . . . Voluntary Restraint Agreements."[94] Administration officials, in other words, counted on more vigorous and effective enforcement of antidumping and countervailing duty laws to help stem protectionism in Congress. Nixon said as much in a letter addressed to the National Retail Merchants Association: "We are also strictly enforcing our laws concerning unfair competitive practices like dumping. We have taken these steps precisely because we want to *avoid the dangers of legislated restriction*."[95] As a *National Journal*

[89] Remarks of Eugene T. Rossides before the American Footwear Industries Association, March 2, 1972, box 64, WHCF, SF, TA, NPMP.

[90] Memo, Armstrong to Acting Secretary of State, July 14, 1972, box 1109, RG59, Subject-Numeric Files, 1970–73 Economic, FT, NPMP.

[91] Memo, Peter Flanigan, Director of CIEP, to Eugene T. Rossides, Assistant Secretary of the Treasury, March 29, 1972, box 22, WHCF, SF, TA, NPMP.

[92] Letter, Ahlbrandt to Peter Peterson, Director of CIEP, August 18, 1971, NPMP.

[93] Memo, Candy Staempfly to Lawrence Brady, Special Advisor for Congressional Relations in CIEP, February 2, 1973, box 6, WHCF, SF, TA, NPMP.

[94] Letter, Peter Flanigan, Director of CIEP, to Handrick Houthakker, CEA, January 30, 1973, box 44, WHCF, SF, TA, NPMP.

[95] Letter, President Nixon to Williams, president of NRMA, November 3, 1972, box 5, WHCF, SF, TA, NPMP; italics added.

analyst concluded, "Taken together, the two laws [antidumping and countervailing duty] are part of a broader Administration strategy to beat back the protectionist pressures that threaten to reverse four decades of liberal trade policy for the United States" (*National Journal*, 9/23/1972, 1496).

Administration officials in favor of strengthening the unfair-trade laws were joined by internationalist-oriented businesses that "support[ed] the need for a tough . . . trade policy conducted within the guideposts of international treaty obligations."[96] In a letter to the president, the U.S. Chamber of Commerce asserted that "our national trade policy can be strengthened with the vigorous application of countervailing duties, dumping and escape-clause provisions *without restoring to intractable quotas.*"[97] Similarly, Kendall urged the administration "to put teeth into and simplify" unfair-trade laws.[98]

The amendments introduced into the administration trade bill focused on the issues of time limits and discretion. On the one hand, the administration offered to impose time limits on the determination process. In the past, Treasury had used the absence of time limits not to decide on CVD cases. As an official in the Department of Treasury admitted, "Through this device we have in effect inserted a discretionary element into the law despite its mandatory language."[99] The imposition of time limits was thus an indirect way of limiting the informal discretionary practices of the Treasury and ensuring that the Treasury would follow up on petitions: "There seems to be widespread agreement that complaints about long delays in handling cases are valid and such a speedup is urgently needed."[100] On the other hand, the administration asked for permanent discretion to allow the secretary of the treasury to refrain from countervailing where the result would cause "significant detriment to the economic interests of the United States." The administration also asked for authority to waive countervailing duties throughout the multilateral trade negotiations, for up to five years, to facilitate negotiations limiting export subsidies. "Recognizing that time limits and a right of

---

[96] NAM testimony, U.S. Congress, May 22, 1973, House Committee on Ways and Means, *Trade Reform*, 93rd Congress, 1925.

[97] Letter, Chamber of Commerce of the U.S.A to President, November 25, 1970, box 9, WHCF, SF, TA, NPMP, italics added.

[98] Letter, Donald Kendall, Chairman of ECAT, to president, September 17, 1971, box 13, WHSF / Staff Members & Office Files, President's Office Files, President's Handwriting, 1969–74, NPMP.

[99] Memo, Morgan, Treasury, to William P. Simon, Secretary of Treasury, February 8, 1973, Fiche 12, Simon Papers, Gerald R. Ford Library.

[100] Memo, Handrick Houthakker, CEA, to Paul W. McCracken, Chairman of CEA, August 26, 1970, box 1, WHCF, SF, TA, NPMP.

judicial review of negative decisions will undoubtedly be imposed by Congress for action on countervailing duty complaints," Treasury Department officials argued, "some sort of compromise must be worked for granting rather broad discretionary authority to the Secretary."[101]

NAM, along with ECAT and the U.S. Chamber of Commerce, supported the administration's suggestions, stating, "We believe the proposed changes for strengthening the antidumping and countervailing duty instruments of trade policy to be desirable."[102] Calls to prevent a loosening of the requirements came from importers and retailers. AIA and NRMA opposed the imposition of time limits,[103] and asked that an injury test be added to all countervailing duty actions.[104] In addition, they wanted to add presidential discretion in the antidumping cases and argued, regarding countervailing duty actions, that discretion should be given not to the Treasury Secretary but to the president. Protectionist industries and labor, in contrast, wanted to expedite the process further and to eliminate discretion altogether. AISI noted, "Extraneous pressures would be brought to bear upon the decision-making process which is basically a quasi-judicial process. We referred to the need to depoliticize the administration of these laws."[105]

Congress accepted most of the amendments proposed by the administration regarding the antidumping and countervailing duty laws, and added other lenient provisions. Some changes were technical but clearly biased in nature, such as redefining the cost of production so as to inflate the calculated sum. Other changes were procedural. Congress added a provision granting U.S. producers judicial appeal of negative determinations on their countervailing duty and antidumping petitions, and imposed specific time limits, both to the antidumping and countervailing duty laws, within which the secretary of treasury would have to act. Congress also rejected the request for permanent discretion of the secretary of the treasury to refrain

[101] Memo, Morgan, Treasury, to William P. Simon, Secretary of Treasury, February 8, 1973, Fiche 12, Simon Papers, Gerald R. Ford Library.

[102] NAM testimony, U.S. Congress, May 22, 1973, Hearings before the House Committee on Ways and Means, *Trade Reform*, 93rd Congress, 1925.

[103] AIA testimony, U.S. Congress, May 14, 1973, Hearings before the House Committee on Ways and Means, *Trade Reform*, 93rd Congress, 778.

[104] AIA testimony, U.S. Congress, May 14, 1973, Hearings before the House Committee on Ways and Means, *Trade Reform*, 93rd Congress, 765; NRMA testimony, U.S. Congress, May 29, 1973, Hearings before the House Committee on Ways and Means, *Trade Reform*, 93rd Congress, 3012.

[105] AISI testimony. U.S. Congress, June 7, 1973, Hearings before the House Committee on Ways and Means, *Trade Reform*, 93rd Congress, 3957.

from countervailing. Instead, it provided the administration discretionary authority to waive a countervailing duty application for four years, which either house of Congress could override (Destler 1980, 160, 182).

The House of Representatives passed the Trade Reform Act of 1973, on November 12, 1973, in a vote of 278 for and 143 against (163 Republicans and 115 Democrats for; 19 Republicans and 124 Democrats against). The Senate voted and passed the bill on December 13, 1974, in a vote of 85 for and 4 against (38 Republicans and 47 Democrats for; 1 Republican and 3 Democrats against).

Discussion

The institutional arrangements of the RTAA of 1934 addressed the interests of internationalist business only under conditions of steady economic growth and little international competition. The regime of *selective protectionism* was undermined when, following the end of postwar prosperity, industries changed their preferences and political strategies. United States–based multinational corporations and American importers soon realized that the intensified demands of domestic industries for protection directly contradicted their quest for trade liberalization in other countries.[106] The textile negotiations with Japan and the Mills bill, in particular, revealed that a general process of trade liberalization with protectionist exceptions was no longer attainable, and that the existing institutional arrangements exacerbated the conflict rather than mollifying it. It is possible that internationalists would have preferred to simply block protectionist initiatives in Congress, but this they could do only with great difficulty and expensive compromises. As in 1934, therefore, internationalists reacted to their disadvantaged position in Congress by advocating new institutional arrangements, designed to shift the location of authority over protectionist practices away from Congress. The revised trade adjustment assistance, escape clause, and unfair-trade laws meant to curb protectionism so that demands, even if met, would not threaten the general process of trade liberalization. This

---

[106] The crisis preceding the Trade Act of 1974 aptly illustrates the causal effectiveness of institutions. The institutional framework of selective protectionism reflected the relations of power during the 1930s. The inconsistency between the balance of forces and interests embodied in the RTAA of 1934 on the one hand, and the interests following the economic recession of the 1970s on the other, meant that institutions favored policies that did not reflect the current conditions, which led to undesirable outcomes.

was accomplished by providing effective channels of relief, but under institutional arrangements that would limit the negative impacts of those very actions. I call this new kind of state intervention "conditional protectionism," because of one novel element in the new regime: the conditioning of protectionist state action on eligibility requirements.[107]

The detailed account offered in this chapter of the making of the Trade Act of 1974 shows that the institutional transition from the regime of *selective protectionism* to the new regime of *conditional protectionism* was intentional. The institutional shift of 1974, just like the one in 1934, was the deliberate creation of internationalists and their supporters in the administration, precisely in order to curb protectionist demands. This finding has important implications to our understanding of globalization and the role of political action in bringing it about. It suggests that globalization is not merely a political *process*, that is, an outcome of political transformations, but a political *project*, that is, an outcome of political transformations that were *intentionally designed* precisely to bring about the economic outcomes that followed. It also allows us to identify the actors who were behind the globalization project: in the United States, this was a tight coalition of top administration officials and the leading associations representing the largest internationally oriented corporations, ranging from banks and computer manufacturers to soft drinks. Finally, as I explore in more detail in chapter 5, it shows us the nature of the globalization project: the goal was not to completely eliminate nonliberal practices, but rather to establish a careful balance that would allow those protectionist measures that do not disturb the project as a whole.

The making of the regime of *conditional protectionism* questions historical institutionalists' argument that state institutions are rarely challenged. Once in place, the theory contends, actors develop interests and strategies that "lock" them into the extant institutional structure. While political action may be a source of institutional change, this is, almost necessarily, an unintentional outcome (Rothstein 1992, 52; Pierson 2000a). While I agree that actors often design strategies that are compatible with the institutional environment rather than trying to challenge the institutions in place—in chapter 5 I show how protectionists successfully adapted to the new institutional regime—I also contend that institutional arrangements can be an outcome of an intentional act of strategic political actors attempting to assure future benefits. By channeling authority from Congress

---

[107] Others call it "process protectionism" (Nivola 1993, 97) or "administered protection" (Bhagwati 1988, 43).

to the administration, first in 1934 and then in 1974, internationalists consciously designed an institutional context more favorable to their globalization project. It remains to be seen whether the new institutional regime met the expectations of the internationalists that had supported the change. This is the topic of the next chapter.

CHAPTER FIVE

CONDITIONAL PROTECTIONISM, 1974–94

In the previous chapter I showed that the Trade Act of 1974 intended to weaken protectionism. But was the plan successful? Could the modified trade remedy laws curb protectionism? Many trade scholars characterize the 1980s in the United States as a period of "new" protectionism, but others convincingly showed that the heightened protectionist sentiments elicited only a relatively restrained response by the government and that the most vehement protectionist claims were successfully filtered out. Still, was the curbing of protectionism due to the new institutional regime created in the Trade Act of 1974? Some trade scholars argue that the decline in protectionist practices in the 1980s reflected a decline in protectionist demands, or an improved mobilization of those opposing them.[1] However, major lobbying efforts, followed by congressional attempts to pass strict protectionist legislation, show that protectionist demands did not diminish. They

[1] Milner (1988) suggests that the transformation in the U.S. government's response correlated with a shift in the preferences of domestic actors, who due to their position in the global economic market no longer demanded higher duties or import quotas. Destler and Odell (1987) suggest that protectionist practices were prevented due to the better mobilization of international business, who have mounted, since the 1970s, vigorous and increasingly overt political efforts to oppose new import restrictions. Elsewhere, Destler (1992) also refers to the economic decline of protectionist industries as an explanation for their weakened political influence.

also show that protectionist interests preserved their influence in Congress. Had authority over trade practices remained in the hands of Congress, we probably would have witnessed a substantial rise in duties and import quotas. Instead, in this chapter I provide a detailed account of how the delegation of authority to the administration, enabled by the amended trade remedy laws, curbed protectionist demands.[2]

The chapter offers a detailed account of the administration's intervention on behalf of protectionist industries from 1974 to 1994. (1994 saw another institutional shift, which I analyze in chapter 6.) It describes the negotiations, strategies, and counter-strategies that allowed the administration to monopolize protectionist demands and to bring about a shift from Congress's offer of "selective" high tariffs or import quotas to administrative practices aimed at reducing injury to industries (based on the escape clause), and penalizing unfair trade practices of foreign competitors (based on the antidumping and countervailing duty provisions and on Section 301 of the Trade Act of 1974).[3]

The chapter proceeds chronologically, starting with the Ford administration and concluding with President Clinton. The chronological account reveals not only the general shift from congressional laws to administrative practices, but also that the administrative practices have changed over time. Initially, during the Ford and the Carter administrations, protectionist industries relied mostly on the escape-clause provision. However, I show that the industries abandoned this strategy as soon as they realized that presidents used the discretion given to them by law to consistently block positive determinations. I then describe how the Carter administration persuaded

---

[2] Another possible source of change in U.S. governmental action is the international balance of power. The economic recovery of Europe and Japan has possibly made it more difficult for the U.S. Congress to act unilaterally or illegally without negative economic or political implications, hence, its restrained activity. While international considerations were indeed more prominent after the 1970s, I show below that this had less to do with the shifting international position of the United States, and more with the relocation of authority from Congress to the administration at the domestic level.

[3] Trade remedy laws belong to the category of *non*tariff barriers to trade (NTBs), which were increasingly popular in the 1970s and the 1980s. Other measures included selective procurement, product standards, "buy American" requirements, administrative authorizations to import, price monitoring procedures, customs clearance procedures, discriminatory use of state contracts, and manufacturing and export subsidies (Krauss 1978; Tumlir 1985; Sassoon 1990, 10). It should be noted that the concern over nontariff barriers reflected not only an actual increase in such practices but also the adoption of a new, broader, definition of protectionist practices. During the immediate postwar era, protectionism had referred exclusively to trade-restricting and trade-expanding devices, such as tariffs or export subsidies; during the 1970s, protectionism came to refer more broadly to the totality of effects of government intervention on international trade.

first the steel industry and then others to use AD and CVD laws instead of demanding protectionist bills from Congress. In the 1980s, again in order to block unwelcome congressional initiatives, Reagan also initiated Section 301 cases. Bush and Clinton continued this trend. Throughout this period, Congress did not remain completely passive. While usually refusing to pass "selective" laws, Congress protected protectionists' interests by fighting for greater leniency of unfair-trade laws and demanding organizational restructuring in the administration—both intending to improve the rate of positive determinations.

The account of the different trade remedy laws also reveals that protectionists' rate of success in the escape clause, antidumping and countervailing duties, and Section 301 varied depending on the level of discretion permitted in each remedy setting. A high level of discretion, as in the escape-clause cases and the early CVD cases, led to low rates of state protectionist intervention, owing to the ability of state officials supporting free-trade principles to influence the final outcome. A high level of legalization, in contrast, led to higher rates of state intervention, because of the ability of Congress to prevail in struggles with GATT members over the wording of the laws in question.

The historical evidence offered in this chapter shows that the internationalists' plan succeeded: the use of trade laws rather than legislation proved effective. Although often criticized as protectionism in disguise, unfair trade laws, unlike protectionist measures, were not aimed at protecting uncompetitive U.S. producers or at keeping the American market closed. Rather, their objective was to combat unfair trading practices of other countries. This objective and the means used to pursue it had less disruptive effects on trade liberalization than the objective and the means characterizing selective protectionism. Moreover, the shift from escape-clause to AD and CVD laws and later to Section 301 suggests a systematic trajectory where an emphasis on the protection of the American industries at home was replaced with an emphasis on the liberalization of foreign markets.

Finally, this chapter reveals that protectionists reacted strongly against the demise of their political opportunities and influence. While Congress was no longer easily convinced to pass protectionist bills, protectionist industries could still press Congress to fight on their behalf, particularly making the unfair trade laws as favorable as was legally possible. Consequently, at least some protectionist industries managed to get satisfying remedies from the administration.

The Escape Clause under the Ford and Carter Administrations

Recently we have witnessed an increase in the filings of international trade complaints with the International Trade Commission, the Treasury Department and with our office [of Special Trade Representative]. As you know, grievances have involved cheese, canned hams, automobiles, specialty steel, shoes and other sensitive issues. The volume of these complaints is increasing the concern of foreign governments that the U.S. may be shifting to a protectionist direction. . . . As you know, however, the increased filings are due to the Trade Reform Act of 1974 which made government more responsive in resolving international trade grievances combined with current economic circumstances.[4]

Under the amended escape clause, Section 201 of the Trade Act of 1974, an industry could obtain import relief if the U.S. International Trade Commission (ITC) found that it had suffered serious injury, the substantial cause of which was an increase in imports. When the ITC made an affirmative determination, it made a recommendation to the president that relief be provided and suggested the type of remedy to provide. The president had the discretion to deny an ITC positive recommendation or to alter the suggested remedy. If the president rejected an ITC recommendation, his decision was subject to congressional override by a concurrent resolution that put into effect the ITC's recommendation.

In response to the leniency introduced to the escape-clause provision in the Trade Act of 1974, protectionist industries dramatically increased the number of escape-clause petitions they filed. Between 1963 and 1974, the average number of escape-clause investigations was approximately two per year. By contrast, the average number of petitions between 1975 and 1979 was more than eight per year. (After 1979, for reasons I discuss below, the average number declined again, to less than two per year.) There was also an increase in the rate of affirmative decisions made by the ITC. While the ITC acceptance rate was 38 percent between 1963 and 1974, it was 61 percent between 1975 and 1979 (and then decreased again, to 33 percent).[5] Yet the president could deny positive ITC determinations, and although the presidential

---

[4] Memo, Frederick Dent, STR, to L. William Seidman, Executive Director of the Economic Policy Board, August 21, 1975, Seidman papers, box 91, STR (3), Gerald R. Ford Library.

[5] However, the legal requirements might not be the primary explanation for the change in the ITC rate of success, since the rate of success after 1962 did not decline, in spite of what scholars agree has been a tightening of the conditions in the Trade Act of 1962, and since the

Table 5.1 Petition activity and acceptance rate of escape-clause cases, 1948–94

Years[a]	Average number petition/year (total)	ITC acceptance rate[b]	Presidential acceptance rate[c]	Total acceptance rate
1948–62	7 (102)	0.38	0.38	0.14
1963–74	2 (26)	0.38	0.20	0.08
1975–79	8.5 (42)	0.61	0.27	0.16
1980–94	1.5 (21)	0.33	0.57	0.19

Sources: U.S. president: *Trade Policy Agenda and . . . Annual Report of the President of the United States on the Trade Agreements Program* (Washington, DC: GPO, 1957–91); U.S. Tariff Commission: *Operation of the Trade Agreements Program*, 1948–90; U.S. International Trade Commission: *The Year in Trade: Operation of the Trade Agreements Program*, 1991–2002.

[a] Organized by legislative periods. From 1948 to 1951, the escape clause existed by executive order. The escape clause appeared in legislation as Section 7 of the Trade Agreements Act of 1951, as Section 301(b) of the Trade Expansion Act of 1962, and as Section 201 of the Trade Act of 1974.

[b] Including tie votes.

[c] Not including an award of adjustment assistance alone. Including awards different than the ones recommended by ITC.

acceptance rate gradually increased, it remained extremely low. The rate of presidential acceptance of ITC determinations—accepting the commission's findings in whole or in part and taking protective action, not including the award of adjustment assistance alone—was 20 percent between 1963 and 1974, and 27 percent between 1975 and 1979. (It was 57 percent between 1980 and 1994). The total rate of success after 1975 was therefore never higher than 20 percent (see summary in table 5.1). Moreover, presidents also repeatedly deviated from the suggested remedy, awarding less than the ITC had suggested. The presidential acceptance rate of approval with the recommended ITC relief was 3 percent (Goldstein 1993, 209).

There is little doubt that the discrepancy between ITC and the president's determinations was due to the president's political considerations (Finger, Hall, and Nelson 1982). In his remarks at a 1977 Export Development Day luncheon, the chairman of the ITC, Daniel Minchew, emphasized the distinction between a legally constrained ITC and a politicized president:

> We don't make policy at all. . . . We are simply independent administrators of a statute that dictates what cases we must take, how long we can spend on them, what very few forms of relief we must

---

decline in the ITC acceptance rate after 1979 was not preceded by radical legal changes. For statistical analyses of ITC decisions in safeguards that attempt to differentiate between legal, economic, and political considerations see Takacs 1981; Baldwin 1985; Hansen 1990; Anderson 1992; Baldwin and Steagall 1993.

recommend, and what criteria we can or cannot take into account. . . .
We can only consider whether or not imports of the commodity have
increased and to what extent they have or have not damaged the domestic industry. On the other hand, we cannot consider the effect that
our proposed tariffs or quotas may have on consumers, or on foreign
policy, or on defense capabilities. The statute reserves these considerations for the President, after he has received our recommendation.
He is free to reject our advice—we don't take it personally.[6]

The paltry number of positive determinations approved by various presidents suggests that presidential considerations worked against the protectionist industries. A careful analysis of the deliberations of the interagency
Trade Policy Committee (TPC), which was resurrected under President
Ford and had the statutory responsibility for making recommendations to
the president on escape-clause cases, reveals why political considerations
against positive determinations prevailed over considerations in favor of
ITC determinations.

The Trade Policy Committee worked in the following way: after a discussion among the members of the committee, a list of optional recommendations for the consideration of the president was prepared. Each
option included a list of reasons in support of the recommendation and the
agencies or officials supporting it. These memos to the president expose the
position of each TPC member and reveal that these positions closely followed the considerations that the member's agency was bureaucratically assigned to take into account. Hence, agencies concerned with foreign policy,
such as the Department of State and the National Security Council (NSC),
and agencies concerned with macroeconomic matters, such as the Department of Treasury and the Council of Economic Advisers (CEA), systematically opposed granting relief. The Justice Department, mostly concerned
with the creation of cartels, also commonly opposed relief. In contrast,
those agencies concerned with the welfare of domestic industries and workers, specifically the departments of Commerce and Labor, usually supported
relief. Following his mandate "to provide a balanced approach to trade policy,"[7] the Special Trade Representative (STR) had to mediate between his responsibility to support and promote trade liberalization (and to adhere to
international obligations and laws) and the expectation that he would have

[6] Remarks of the Honorable Daniel Minchew, Chairman of the U.S. International Trade
Commission, before the Export Development Day Luncheon, 26 May 1977, Staff offices, Domestic Policy Staff (DPS), Eizenstat, box 227, Jimmy Carter Library.

[7] Letter, Secretary of Labor to STR, February 14, 1975, Gerald R. Ford Library.

"domestic political sensitivity" and that he would view alternative options also in "domestic political terms."[8] As a result, the STR often supported no relief or a relief that was less substantial than that suggested by ITC, but at the same time was also quite attentive to congressional complaints. The presidents, in turn, gave most weight to the opinions of the STR and the secretary of state.[9] Arguments based on foreign relations and the international economy won out over those based on domestic political considerations. The latter were effective only in the presence of a reliable threat of congressional override.

The Treasury and CEA, in arguing against supporting ITC positive determinations for providing relief, emphasized the negative economic consequences of such actions. Of most concern was the effect that affirmative determinations would have on U.S. exporters due to the threat of retaliation,[10] and on industrial users of the imports in question.[11] In addition, TPC members expressed a concern that positive decisions would lead to the mimicry of U.S. practices and thus to increased protectionism abroad,[12] and a concern that "granting protection . . . could encourage domestic protectionist forces to bring more escape clause cases."[13] During the Tokyo Round of multilateral trade negotiations, TPC members warned that positive decisions would have an adverse effect on the multinational trade negotiations.[14] They also warned that higher prices would adversely affect consumers.[15] Under the Carter administration, agencies cautioned that

[8] Letter, Frederick Dent, STR, to William Seidman, Executive Director of the Economic Policy Board, Seidman files, box 101, STR-Specialty (1), Gerald R. Ford Library.

[9] This was the case in regard to trade issues in general, not only escape-clause debates. For example, Ford initially required the STR to consult only with the Department of State on trade negotiations. Only following the negative reaction of the departments of the Treasury, Commerce, and Labor did Ford ask the STR to consult with the entire TPC. Letter, William M. Nichols, Acting General Counsel of OMB, to Edward H. Levi, Attorney General, March 10, 1975, WHCFSF, box 29, TA 5 3/19/75–3/31/75, Gerald R. Ford Library.

[10] Memo, Robert Strauss, STR, to President Carter, 24 January 1978, WHCFSF TA-19, Jimmy Carter Library.

[11] Memo, Seidman to president, April 12, 1976, Gergen files, box 5, Footwear imports, Gerald R. Ford Library.

[12] Memo, Dent to president, April 21, 1976, Buchen files, box 11, Economy-trade: stainless steel flatware, Gerald R. Ford Library.

[13] Memo, Stu Eizenstat, Executive Director of the Domestic Policy staff at the White House, to president, 9 February 1978, Staff offices, DPS, Eizenstat, box 225, Jimmy Carter Library.

[14] Undated (circa February 1976), Seidman papers, box 100, STR-Specialty (3), Gerald R. Ford Library.

[15] Undated (circa February 1976), Seidman papers, box 100, STR-Specialty (3), Gerald R. Ford Library.

granting import relief was inconsistent with the administration's anti-inflation program.[16]

TPC members also used the specifics of particular cases to reject positive recommendations. Although considerations regarding the economic situation of petitioning industries were under the jurisdiction of the ITC, TPC members often offered economic arguments opposed to ITC findings to support their position. In a case concerning the honey industry, TPC members argued against a positive recommendation on the basis that the case for finding that the industry was threatened with injury had been exceptionally weak.[17] They also considered the potential usefulness of the relief, again in order to oppose affirmative recommendations. In a case concerning the high-carbon ferrochromium industry, for example, agencies argued that the imposition of import relief would not be an effective means to promote adjustment.[18] In two other cases, one concerning the stainless steel table flatware industry and another concerning the nonrubber footwear industry, members argued that the measures recommended by the ITC would provide unneeded protection to a significant portion of the industry.[19] Rarely were the deteriorating economic conditions of the industry mentioned to *support* an affirmative decision made by the ITC.[20]

The Department of State and NSC officials, in turn, often referred to the negative foreign relations implications of affirmative escape-clause determinations. They argued that positive recommendations were a threat to the goal of "maintaining constructive relationships with our trading partners"[21] and warned that restrictive actions would cause "great apprehension abroad over the direction of our trade policy" and "serious adverse foreign reactions."[22] Objections to the recommendation to grant relief to

[16] Memo, Stu Eizenstat to President, 9 February 1978, Staff offices, DPS, Eizenstat, box 225, Jimmy Carter Library; Memo, Esther Peterson to Strauss and Eizenstat, 6 June 1978, Staff offices, DPS, Eizenstat, box 226, Jimmy Carter Library.

[17] Memo, Dent to president, August 16, 1976, Seidman papers, box 98, STR-Honey (4), Gerald R. Ford Library.

[18] Memo, Strauss to president, 24 January 1978, WHCFSF TA-19, Jimmy Carter Library.

[19] Memo, Dent to president, April 21, 1976, Buchen files, box 11, Economy-trade: stainless steel flatware, Gerald R. Ford Library; Memo, Alan Greenspan (CEA) to president, April 7, 1976, Gergen files, box 5, Footwear imports, Gerald R. Ford Library.

[20] Domestic economic conditions—the fact that more than six hundred plants employing 163,000 workers in thirty-seven states were affected—were considered in support of the nonrubber footwear industry, but the decision was eventually rejected. Memo, Dent to president, April 5, 1976, Gergen files, box 5, Footwear imports, Gerald R. Ford Library.

[21] Memo, Dent to president, March 1, 1976, WHCFSF, box 26, TA 4/34 1/21/76–3/9/76.

[22] Memo, Dent to president, March 1, 1976, WHCFSF, box 26, TA 4/34 1/21/76–3/9/76; Undated (circa February 1976), Seidman papers, box 100, STR-Specialty (3), Gerald R. Ford Library.

the high-carbon ferrochromium industry, for example, were raised not only because South Africa, which was to suffer most heavily from import restrictions, could effectively retaliate by raising the prices of exports of chrome bearing ore to the United States, but also because of the way it might affect the very delicate U.S.–South Africa relations.[23]

Economic and foreign policy considerations were a major factor in President Ford's unexpected decision to deny relief to the nonrubber footwear industry following an ITC positive determination, in February 1976. This was the largest escape-clause case brought to date, involving $1.1 billion in imports, and there were many reasons to expect that the administration would embrace the recommendation. First, the Ford administration made a commitment to the nonrubber footwear sector just prior to the passage of the Trade Act of 1974;[24] and the Trade Act, reflecting this commitment, contained a requirement that the president negotiate an international arrangement as soon as practicable. Second, it was the administration itself that originally urged the industry to file an escape-clause petition, after TPC members had agreed that an escape-clause investigation would be the best way to bring about an international agreement.[25] Finally, the industry, the unions, and several congressmen turned the case into "a major test of

---

[23] Memo, Strauss to president, 24 January 1978, WHCFSF TA-19, Jimmy Carter Library.

[24] Herald Malmgren, deputy STR, wrote to Senator Hathaway: "As for other provisions of the Trade Act of 1974 concerning nonrubber footwear, I can assure you that this Administration will . . . give immediate attention to devising some suitable form of arrangement with the governments of other nations whose exports to us are the significant cause of disruption to the footwear industry. The purpose of such arrangements would, of course, be to reduce or eliminate the disruptive effect of imports." Untitled, Seidman papers, box 95, STR-Footwear (1), Gerald R. Ford Library.

[25] TPC members agreed that "the Administration would approach the nonrubber industry and ascertain that the industry intends to file an escape clause petition with the ITC; if the industry decided not to file an escape clause petition, the Administration would so file; after the petition is filed . . . the Administration would open consultations with the five key exporting nations, namely, Spain, Argentina, Brazil, Taiwan and South Korea. The purpose of these consultations would be to explain this action and the consequences of same, including the negotiation of bilateral restraint agreements, which these trading partners may wish to consider. Following these initial consultations, it then would be appropriate to decide on what additional steps should be taken, if any, prior to the finding of the ITC." The CEA was opposed to the government arguing the position of the U.S. nonrubber footwear industry. The Department of State, in turn, objected to having negotiations with the foreign countries while the ITC investigation was taking place and argued that "relations with Spain could well be adversely affected at a time when we are undertaking difficult and sensitive renegotiation of military base agreements." Memo, Dent to president, June 11, 1975, Lazarus files, box 11, FG 65–3 ITC, Gerald R. Ford Library; Memo, Greenspan (CEA) to Connor, June 20, 1976, Seidman papers, box 95, STR-Footwear (1), Gerald R. Ford Library; Memo, Dent to president, June 11, 1975, Lazarus files, box 11, FG 65–3 ITC, Gerald R. Ford Library.

whether the Administration will uphold the commitments made to the Congress in obtaining the Trade Act of 1974"[26] and urged the administration to establish import quotas and to negotiate quota agreements with key supplying countries.[27]

Commerce, Labor, CIEP, and STR thus recommended that moderate relief be granted in the form of a tariff-rate quota.[28] State, Treasury, Agriculture, and CEA, however, strongly opposed relief and suggested that the remedy best suited to the needs of the shoe industry was an increased effort to deliver adjustment assistance.[29] National security adviser Brent Scowcroft, who also objected to the provision of relief, wrote President Ford a note, in April 1976, summarizing the potential negative international implications of this course of action,

> A decision to grant import relief in this case . . . would be used by Europeans, Brazilians and others as evidence that the Administration too had "gone protectionist." The perception of a U.S. move towards protectionism is likely to have two results: retaliation (perhaps against U.S. agricultural exports) and emulation. . . . The risk, therefore, is that a decision to impose import restrictions on shoes could trigger a rush to new import barriers by other countries. This in turn would harm U.S. exports, provoke political acrimony, jeopardize the multilateral trade negotiations, and set back the collective recovery efforts of the industrialized world.[30]

Ford decided to reject the ITC recommendation of import relief, and instead instructed the secretaries of Labor and Commerce to expedite petitions for adjustment assistance.[31] Secretary of State Henry Kissinger and

[26] Memo, dent to President, April 5, 1976, Gergen files, box 5, Footwear imports, Gerald R. Ford Library.

[27] Senate Finance Committee's Trade Oversight Hearings, undated, Gorog files, box 1, Footwear industry, Gerald R. Ford Library; Memo, Seidman to president, April 12, 1976, Gergen files, box 5, Footwear imports, Gerald R. Ford Library.

[28] Memo, Dent to president, April 5, 1976, Gergen files, box 5, Footwear imports, Gerald R. Ford Library.

[29] Memo, Henry Kissinger, Secretary of State, and William Simon, Secretary of Treasury, to president, April 7, 1976, Gergen files, box 5, Footwear imports, Gerald R. Ford Library; Memo, Greenspan, CEA, to President, April 7, 1976, Gergen files, box 5, Footwear imports, Gerald R. Ford Library; Memo, Seidman to president, April 12, 1976, Gergen files, box 5, Footwear imports, Gerald R. Ford Library.

[30] Memo, Brent Scowcroft, NSC, to president, April 12, 1976, Gergen files, box 5, Footwear imports, Gerald R. Ford Library.

[31] Press release #222, April 16, 1976, Loen and Leppert files, box 25, STR, Gerald R. Ford Library.

Secretary of the Treasury William Simon congratulated Ford on his decision:

> Juxtaposed to nearly universal criticism of the steel decision is the overwhelmingly positive reception that greeted your decision in the shoe case—a decision reinforced by your decisions on stainless steel flatware and ceramic tableware. The shoe decision was correctly greeted as sound and courageous. These decisions, in combination with the decision on autos, reversed a swelling fear that the U.S. was about to turn protectionist in a pre-election atmosphere of intense political pressure.[32]

The president's bias against relief was restrained, at times, by domestic pressure, conveyed as a threat of congressional override. Although Congress has never actually voted to override the president (Destler 1995, 146), a reliable possibility of override was nevertheless quite effective. President Ford's decision to grant relief to the specialty steel industry was based on STR's conviction that a decision not to provide relief would be quite likely overridden by Congress,[33] and the fact that Congress had no authority to override the president's decision in the footwear case was an important factor in the decision to reject the ITC's recommendation in that case.[34] Congress employed other forms of pressure on the administration. On several occasions, including the case of the nonrubber footwear industry in 1977, and the bolts, nuts, and large screws of the iron and steel industry in 1978, Congress responded to the president's rejection of ITC recommendations by requesting a *new* ITC investigation. In both cases, the ITC recommended relief for a second time and President Carter went along with the recommendation. Another way for Congress to obtain a positive determination was to threaten the executive with protectionist legislation, as was the approach chosen in the case of the carbon and alloy steel industry in 1984 (see below). On other occasions, as in the case of the mushroom

[32] Memo, Henry Kissinger, Secretary of State, and William Simon, Secretary of Treasury, to president, June 5, 1976, WHCFSF, box 26, TA 4/34 6/8/76–10/31/76, Gerald R. Ford Library.

[33] Memo, Dent to president, March 1, 1976, WHCFSF, box 26, TA 4/34 1/21/76–3/9/76; February 24, 1976, Cannon files, box 56, Economic and energy meeting, 2/25/76, Gerald R. Ford Library.

[34] The ITC injury finding in the footwear case was unanimous. But because the commissioners were divided with regard to the *form* of relief to be granted (high tariffs, tariff quotas, or adjustment assistance), there was arguably no commission recommendation, and therefore a congressional override could not be taken. February 24, 1976, Cannon files, box 56, Economic and Energy Meeting, 2/25/76, Gerald R. Ford Library.

industry in 1976, the Trade Subcommittee of the House Ways and Means Committee passed a concurrent resolution calling on the president to negotiate with representatives of foreign governments in an effort to obtain agreements limiting exports. It called for a referral of the case to the ITC if these negotiations were unsuccessful.

Over the years, Congress became increasingly impatient with the administration's bias. While some members at the interagency committee under Carter warned about it, their warnings fell on deaf ears. In the 1978 case of the bolts, nuts, and large screws industry, for example, Special Trade Representative Robert Strauss argued that a compromise position was in the long-run interest of the administration. He argued that a demonstrated willingness to be somewhat forthcoming would help build the cooperative and supportive framework that the administration needed to avoid more severe protectionist actions, and for the administration to ask for, and receive, cooperation on more important trade and economic issues.[35] Carter, adopting the opposite recommendation of State, Treasury, CEA, and OMB, denied any relief.[36] Strauss expressed the same concern in the 1978 case of the refined copper industry. Relief, he argued, would reassure Congress of the administration's willingness to protect seriously depressed industries, thereby discouraging attempts to revise the trade laws to limit presidential discretion.[37] Those arguing against relief, responded quite harshly:

> Relief would be interpreted . . . as evidence that we are unable to resist special interest pressure for government action to raise prices. Our record of responsiveness in trade issues involving steel, stainless steel, shoes, televisions, and CB radios should be enough for an indication of our willingness to grant protection where warranted to forestall Congressional attempts to rewrite the trade laws. Even if we ultimately need to extend relief in some questionable cases to convince Congress of our open mindedness, we should select cases involving industries that are smaller, less central in the industrial structure, and where it is clearer that imports are the main cause of injury. Finally, the MTN agreements will not be considered by Congress until April at the earliest. . . . It is too early to be trading unwarranted

[35] Memo, Eizenstat to president, 9 February 1978, Staff offices, DPS, Eizenstat, box 225, Jimmy Carter Library.

[36] Memo, Eizenstat to president, 9 February 1978, Staff offices, DPS, Eizenstat, box 225, Jimmy Carter Library.

[37] Memo, Eizenstat and Howard Gruenspecht to president, 18 October 1978, WHCFSF TA-20, Jimmy Carter Library.

protection for prospective MTN votes, especially in the view of the low level of Congressional interest in this case.[38]

The NSC Special Representative for Economic Summits, Henry Owen, added that import relief would damage relations with Canada, Peru, Chile, Zambia, and other copper exporters.[39] Carter decided to reject the ITC's recommendation.

The decision regarding copper was made in August 1978. By October of that year, some members of the administration were expressing an even greater concern. Regarding the case of the bicycle tire and tube industry, the executive director of the Domestic Policy Staff at the White House, Stu Eizenstat, was in favor of import relief,

> for to do otherwise would make a mockery of the Trade Act of 1974. We have frankly gotten to the position where it is utterly impossible for a majority of the agencies to agree on import relief regardless of how egregious the situation. I am frankly quite concerned that we are completely perverting the purpose of Section 201 of the Trade Act of 1974 by failing to grant relief in this case. It appears to me that it is only a question of time until Congress rears up against our implementation of this act. This particular case seems to be a prime example of the reason this is likely to occur. Here we have an industry down to its last domestic manufacturer. . . . Imports have grown steadily to well over 80%.[40]

Carter decided not to grant relief.

Ultimately, those in the Ford and Carter administrations who were averse to the use of the escape clause rendered the provision obsolete. Their assessment that the "granting of no relief would set a precedent for not using escape clause provisions to assist industries suffering from domestic recession"[41] proved correct, and the initially high rate of petitions experienced a dramatic decline. President Ford granted relief in two out of nineteen cases; Carter granted relief in six out of twenty-five cases. The tendency to

[38] Memo, Eizenstat and Howard Gruenspecht to president, 18 October 1978, WHCFSF TA-20, Jimmy Carter Library.

[39] Memo, Owen to president, 18 October 1978, WHCFSF TA-20, Jimmy Carter Library.

[40] Memo, Eizenstat to president, 30 October 1978, Staff offices, DPS, Eizenstat, box 226, Jimmy Carter Library.

[41] TPC report, undated (circa February 1976), Seidman papers, box 100, STR-Specialty (3), Gerald R. Ford Library.

reject affirmative ITC recommendations continued during the Reagan administration, which granted relief to three out of seventeen sectors that filed a petition. By the time George H. W. Bush entered office in 1989, presidential rejection effectively ceased to be an issue, as there were hardly any escape-clause cases to consider. Only two escape-clause investigations were conducted throughout his presidency. President Bush did not grant relief to either of them.

Unfair-trade Laws under the Carter and Reagan Administrations

The rejection of escape-clause cases was softened by an explicit encouragement to use the antidumping (AD) and countervailing duty (CVD) laws. TPC members of the Ford administration complained that "foreign production and employment levels have been cut back much less than in the U.S., partly due to greater foreign government involvement in their industries through measures such as financing of inventory build-up, reimbursing labor costs, and negotiation of international arrangements."[42] They therefore recommended that "the U.S. industry . . . seek adjustment assistance and bring countervailing duty complaints against such foreign subsidies."[43]

During the postwar years, the Department of Treasury, which was the agency responsible for administrating unfair-trade laws, was known for its reluctance to provide relief (see chapter 4). The Trade Act of 1974 included provisions aimed at altering the attitude of the department. It imposed, for example, time limits that meant to prevent the indefinite delay of AD and CVD investigations. Initially, however, the Department of Treasury seemed to continue with its delaying tactics.[44] The department did not hesitate before suspending investigations or waiving the imposition of duties. A complaint requesting the assessment of countervailing duties against Common Market dairy products illustrates this tendency. The complaint was filed in 1968, but was not reviewed by the Treasury until 1974 (and only after the department faced a writ of mandamus that had been filed in the district court in Washington for the purpose of requiring it to render a decision on

---

[42] TPC report, undated (circa February 1976), Seidman papers, box 100, STR-Specialty (3), Gerald R. Ford Library.

[43] TPC report, undated (circa February 1976), Seidman papers, box 100, STR-Specialty (3), Gerald R. Ford Library.

[44] The delaying tactics continued simultaneously with a radical increase of positive determinations, after 1969, of those petitions that were investigated.

the complaint).[45] Soon after, the Treasury suspended the investigation when the Commission of the European Communities (EC) discontinued its subsidies on certain cheese exports destined for the U.S. market. When the EC announced the resumption of restitution payments on some cheese exports to the United States in February 1975, the Treasury published a preliminary CVD determination concluding that the restitution payments were subsidies.[46] But it again waived the imposition of a countervailing duty after the Europeans agreed to drop export subsidies on the cheeses that competed most directly with U.S. cheeses.[47]

Treasury officials showed a similar reluctance in AD cases. In August 1975, the United Automobile Workers submitted several petitions alleging dumping margins on cars exported to the United States, mainly from European countries. The investigation revealed that twenty-four foreign car producers had been selling cars in the United States at prices below those charged in their home markets, and yet the Treasury decided to discontinue the investigation on the condition that eight of the twenty-four foreign firms promised to eliminate their dumping margins by raising prices in the U.S. market or cutting them at home. The sixteen other companies, the Treasury said, while technically selling more cheaply in the United States, had found themselves in this situation because of fluctuating currency exchange rates and because of their confusion concerning the proper value to place on pollution control equipment that was required in the United States but not at home.[48]

[45] Draft of a letter, Henry Kissinger, Secretary of State, and William Simon, Secretary of Treasury, June 21, 1974, (FICHE 10), Gerald R. Ford Library.

[46] Treasury's decisions prompted a tense debate in the administration. The Department of State argued that the Treasury should waive the countervailing duties, citing the adverse implications for U.S.-EC relations. The Department of Agriculture suggested not to impose duties if the EC agreed to include agricultural subsidies in the multilateral trade negotiations. In contrast, the Office of the STR argued that such a position would be "viewed as a sellout by the domestic dairy industry with serious political repercussions for the Administration." STR also mentioned Ford's personal pledge to the industry, in a campaign speech, in which he had promised that "if the Europeans re-institute their export subsidies on dairy products directed at this market, I will impose countervailing duties on their products." Undated, Kosters files, box 4, Office of STR, correspondence, 2/1/75–2/23/75, Gerald R. Ford Library; Memo, Guenther through Kosters to Seidman, March 3, 1975, Kosters files, box 4, Office of STR, correspondence, 3/1/75–4/30/75, Gerald R. Ford Library; *National Journal Review*, 3/1/1975, 335.

[47] May 1975, WHCFSF, box 1, TA 4/1/75–6/30/75, Gerald R. Ford Library; *National Journal Review*, 5/3/1975, 671; *National Journal Review*, 5/24/1975, 782.

[48] Memo, Macdonald, Assistant Secretary of the Treasury, to Cannon, Assistant to the President for Domestic Affairs, May 18, 1976, Cannon files, box 35, trade policy, March-August 1976, Gerald R. Ford Library; *National Journal*, 5/8/1976, 644.

Finally, the Secretary of Treasury liberally used his discretion, granted to him in the Trade Act of 1974, to waive or suspend countervailing duties if it was likely that such duties would "seriously jeopardize the satisfactory completion" of the then impending Tokyo Round of multilateral trade negotiations. During the period in which discretion was available (it lasted until September 1979), the Department of Treasury waived duties in 92 percent of the cases (Jackson 1984, 157).

In short, in the first few years after 1974 the Department of the Treasury continued to use its authority to prevent the imposition of duties. Only in 1977 were unfair-trade laws put at the center of trade-policy implementation. The short-term goal for the Carter administration was to divert the steel industry's lobbying efforts away from congressional legislation. From then on, unfair-trade laws were utilized not simply to block protectionist demands but as a viable alternative in effectively responding to those very demands.

Protecting Steel

In 1977, a depressed domestic steel market, battered by a new surge of imports, caused a flood of steel plant closings and job losses (Hodin 1987, 270–71). The steel industry's initial lobbying efforts focused on Congress. In response, members of the Congressional Steel Caucus introduced more than twenty protectionist bills designed to help the industry through various means, including placing quotas on steel imports, increasing tariffs on certain iron and steel products, establishing separate steel sector negotiations at the multinational trade negotiations, and imposing "buy American" regulations on government procurement (Hodin 1987, 305–6; Prechel 1990, 658). The Carter administration, however, strongly opposed any action that would have led to retaliatory protective measures or disrupted the Tokyo Round negotiations. Carter also wanted to avoid a rise in steel prices, which would have exacerbated the inflation that was plaguing the country (Borrus 1983, 89). The administration thus refused to support the congressional initiation of import quotas. At the same time, it could not just ignore the growing unemployment in the Northeast and Midwest caused by steel plant closings. Furthermore, there were national security issues to consider: a substantial dependence on imported steel, it was argued, would leave the United States without assured access to an essential component in the production of armaments for conventional warfare (Block 1980b, 526).

The solution that Carter embraced, in an effort to avoid a more radical protective congressional action and to address broader economic issues, was to support a more aggressive enforcement of unfair-trade laws.[49] Hence, in discussions regarding the steel industry, representatives of the administration repeatedly told members of Congress that if the domestic industry felt there was dumping or unfair and subsidized competition, the industry should file appropriate countervailing or antidumping complaints under existing law.[50] For example, in a testimony before the House Ways and Means Trade Subcommittee, on September 20, 1977, Special Trade Representative Robert Strauss "pointed out that industry has not yet made full use of the import relief remedies in the Trade Act, particularly the anti-dumping section which appears to be a significant part of the steel trade's current problem."[51] Finally, in October 1977, a formal meeting was organized between President Carter and executives from the steel industry, labor leaders, members of Congress from steel districts, and consumer representatives. In the meeting Carter ruled out any kind of quantitative restrictions, declaring them to be an unacceptable policy option, but he also condemned foreign unfair-trade practices and declared that he would, in the future, ensure the more vigorous enforcement of American antidumping laws (Marks 1978). By the end of the meeting the industry and the administration agreed to a quid pro quo: the steelmakers said they would drop their push for import quotas, and the Carter administration promised to begin prosecuting antidumping cases more aggressively (Hodin 1987, 285–86).

This active marketing of the unfair-trade provisions confirms my claim that the executive perceived unfair-trade laws as a viable alternative to legislated import quotas. A more aggressive enforcement of fair trade policy seemed like a good solution, for reasons already elaborated in chapter 4: unfair-trade laws were considered to be less bluntly protectionist than congressional quota legislation; they did not trigger retaliation and did not require compensation; and were consistent with international trade agreements. At the same time, they could provide an adequate response to domestic economic conditions.

---

[49] Even before the crisis of 1977, officials in the Treasury and the STR office encouraged the steel lobby to look for relief under the antidumping law. According to a high-level policy official at the office of the STR, "the issue . . . from that time [1974] on . . . was dumping. . . . It was the turning point . . . we encouraged [steel executives] to use the antidumping statute, and to bring filing petitions with Treasury," cited in Hodin 1987, 93.

[50] Letter, Charles A. Vanik, Chairman of the Committee on Ways and Means, to President Carter, October 11, 1977, WHCFSF Trade TA-17, Jimmy Carter Library.

[51] Memo, John C. L. Donaldson, STR, to Frank Moore, Congressional Liaison, September 21, 1977, Office of Congressional Liaison, Moore files, box 49, Jimmy Carter Library.

In this particular case, however, the administration's response turned into a bureaucratic disaster. Within a three-month period, the industry filed twenty-three petitions against Britain, France, Italy, the Netherlands, Belgium, West Germany, Japan, India, and South Korea, in a host of product sectors. The dumping petitions were so numerous that they effectively overwhelmed the Treasury Department's ability to cope with the time-consuming and complex investigation process (Cline 1983). It soon became apparent, moreover, that under the existing regulations only European producers could be charged with selling products at less than fair value. But if dumping duties were imposed only on European producers, the Japanese, who were operating under capacity, would simply supplant them. The result would not be a reduction in steel imports, but a windfall for Japanese producers and further divisiveness in European–U.S. trade relations. Foreign policy considerations made this possibility unacceptable to the administration (Hodin 1987, 94–95; Goldstein 1993, 224).

Instead, the administration adopted the Trigger Price Mechanism (TPM).[52] The innovative element in this mechanism was its emphasis not on quotas, but on prices. Under the TPM, a base price for foreign steel was set, and any steel sold below this price was assumed to be dumped and would automatically trigger antidumping penalties (Hall 1997, 126). The TPM thus ensured fair trade without strictly enforcing the antidumping laws and was considered less disruptive to the U.S. relationship with its trading partners than a quantitative restraint solution.[53] The industry's endorsement of the TPM led to a prompt withdrawal of antidumping petitions, and to the virtual end to congressional pursuit of legislative remedies.[54]

The reformulation of unfair-trade provisions in the Trade Act of 1974, together with the explicit promise made by Carter to be more aggressive in enforcing them, led to a "strategic shift within the steel industry from

[52] This was one of the recommendations of the Solomon Task Force, which was created in October 1977 to develop a steel plan (Hodin 1987, 329–30).

[53] Because the prices were set at the Japanese cost of production (allowing an 8 percent for profit) and the Japanese cost of production was higher than the European, Europeans were in effect allowed to dump steel that otherwise would be subject to a tariff (Hodin 1987, 351–555).

[54] The TPM proved to be short-lived, however. In the beginning of 1980, reacting to a new growth in market share to imports, the American steel industry filed a massive number of antidumping suits. The Carter administration consequently suspended the TPM in March 1980. The TPM was restored in September, with a higher product trigger prices, and the American steel companies withdrew their suits for the time being (Hall 1997). In January 1982, seven steel companies filed thirty-eight antidumping and ninety-four countervailing duty cases against seven EC countries and Spain, Brazil, Romania, and South Africa. The TPM was again suspended, this time for good.

exerting political or economic pressure on the state to using the state's legal structure to achieve its economic goals" (Prechel 1990, 658). Other industries, too, recognized that the substantive and procedural changes introduced in the Trade Act of 1974 to the antidumping and countervailing duty laws made it easier to obtain a positive outcome compared to the escape clause. (In particular, it was easier to demonstrate injury under the antidumping law than under the escape clause, and the countervailing duty law had no injury requirement at all). Further, by using unfair-trade laws they avoided the barrier of presidential discretion.

Once discovered, "AD/CVD laws have become the usual first choice for industries seeking protection from imports into the United States" (Horlick and Oliver 1989, 5). The result was a skewed trade-remedy system, with a declining use of the escape clause and an upsurge in new petitions alleging unfair foreign trade practices. The average number of antidumping investigations between 1931 and 1974 was nineteen per year. The average number of investigations between 1975 and 1994, in contrast, was forty-four per year. (An average of twenty-five between 1975 and 1979, and, following the Trade Agreements Act of 1979, an average of fifty between 1980 and 1994). Similarly, the average number of countervailing duty investigations between 1931 and 1974 was five per year, while the average number of these investigations between 1975 and 1994 was twenty-five per year (see summary in table 5.2).

In line with industries' expectations, the rate of success after 1974 was quite high, compared to both the rate of success before 1969, and the rate of success in escape-clause cases. Between 1935 and 1968, the rate of success of antidumping cases was 18 percent. With the change in attitude in the Nixon administration, described in chapter 4, the rate of affirmative outcomes substantively increased to 40 percent. Between 1975 and 1994, the acceptance rate of AD cases reached 50 percent (see table 5.3). In the countervailing duty cases, the rate of success between 1975 and 1994 was 30 percent (Goldstein 1993, 217; see also CBO 1994, 41).

Table 5.2 Antidumping and countervailing duty, 1931–94

Years	AD (average number of petitions/year)	CVD (average number of petitions/year)
1931–74	19	5
1975–94	44	25

Sources: AD and CVD cases initiated before January 1, 1980, are reported in http://ia.ita.doc.gov/stats/pre80ad.txt; AD and CVD cases initiated from January 1, 1980, until December 31, 1999, are reported in http://ia.ita.doc.gov/stats/caselist.txt; USTR annual reports, various years.

Table 5.3 Rate of positive determinations in antidumping cases, 1935–94

Years	Average number petition/year (total)	Acceptance rate
1935–68	20 (677)	0.18
1969–74	23 (116)	0.4
1975–79	25 (60)	0.5
1980–94	50 (911)	0.5

Source: AD and CVD cases initiated before January 1, 1980, are reported in http://ia.ita .doc.gov/stats/pre80ad.txt; AD and CVD cases initiated from January 1, 1980, until December 31, 1999, are reported in http://ia.ita.doc.gov/stats/caselist.txt; USTR annual reports, various years.

Adaptive Politics: Redefining Unfair-trade Laws

As soon as domestic industries altered their strategies and began filing AD and CVD petitions, they also looked for ways to increase the rate of positive determinations. Trading partners, on their part, wanted to avoid a bias against their industries. Without presidential discretion to reverse positive determinations, and because of the somewhat technical nature of the AD and CVD laws, much depended on the wording of the laws. As a result, a struggle, often mediated by the administration, emerged between Congress and GATT members over the content of the trade remedy laws. During the regime of conditional protectionism, Congress often had the upper hand.

Following the Trade Act of 1974, members of the Ninety-fourth Congress (1975–76) referred to unfair-trade laws only once, in a resolution disapproving a waiver granted by the secretary of the treasury of an imposition of countervailing duties on imports of leather handbags from Brazil. In the Ninety-fifth Congress (1977–78), supporters of domestic industries in Congress began the efforts to increase the leniency of the provisions and to change the institutional arrangements governing them. These included two resolutions in support of the vigorous enforcement of unfair-trade laws and four different bills, in 1978, to amend unfair-trade laws to improve procedures relating to the determination of certain unfair foreign trade practices. In the end, however, GATT members had the first opportunity to alter U.S. unfair-trade laws.

The Tokyo Round, which was launched in 1973 and concluded in 1979, marks an important turning point in the development of the GATT. Thanks to the "fast track" procedures introduced in the Trade Act of 1974, the U.S. administration could finally negotiate effectively not only tariffs, but also nontariff barriers to trade (see discussion in chapter 4). While the actual accomplishments were somewhat minor, especially if compared to the subsequent Uruguay Round, the Tokyo Round agreements still symbolized a fundamental expansion of GATT responsibilities and member-state commitments. The agreements included a fundamental decrease in tariffs; a 33 percent tariff cut on industrial products on a weighted basis (38 percent on a simple-average basis) left industrial tariffs at about 5 percent on a trade-weighted basis (Lipson 1982, 424). In addition, the Tokyo Round extended multilateral regulations to cover many nontariff barriers to trade, including comprehensive codes on government procurement, customs valuation, technical barriers and standards, import licensing procedures, and subsidies and countervailing duties.[55]

The United States initiated the negotiations of nontariff barriers to trade for it was expected to improve the access of U.S.-based companies to foreign markets. The agreements were not only about nontariff barriers of other countries, however, but also about U.S. barriers, most particularly its trade remedy laws—for while U.S. trading partners supported the shift from import quotas to AD and CVD petitions, they also charged that the U.S. unfair-trade laws were inherently unfair in their application (*New York Times*, 11/3/1977, IV, 1, 4; Rhodes 1993, 128). Already at the Kennedy Round, which was concluded in 1967, U.S. trade negotiators agreed on an antidumping code that, if implemented, would have altered the practices governing AD investigations in the United States. Congress, however, refused to ratify the agreement (Winham 1986, 353).

In the Tokyo Round negotiations on subsidies and countervailing duties, the Europeans demanded that the United States insert a "material injury" test in both countervailing and antidumping legislation (Winham 1986, 353). The existing U.S. countervailing duty law included no injury test,[56] while the antidumping law simply required that imports be a cause of "injury," rather than "material injury" as required by the antidumping code

---

[55] The only agreement that GATT member-states initiated but failed to conclude was an agreement on safeguards. The failure of the safeguards negotiations was due to a disagreement between the Europeans, who wanted to introduce the right to apply safeguards selectively against import surges from one or two countries, and Japan and the Newly Industrialized Countries, the most likely targets of such safeguards, who strongly supported the customary GATT principle that remedies should apply uniformly to all exporters (Lipson 1982, 431; Winham 1986, 122).

[56] Such legislation was inconsistent with Article 6 of the GATT (1947), which stated that duty may not be levied unless the subsidy granted caused or threatened to cause "material injury" to a domestic industry in the importing country. But since the legislation was in effect before the United States entered the GATT, it was considered legal under the terms of the Protocol of Provisional Application (the "grandfather clause").

negotiated during the Kennedy Round. United States negotiators, in return for equally significant concessions made by the EC,[57] agreed to introduce the "material injury" test into the countervailing duty law and to modify the injury test in the antidumping legislation.[58]

With the conclusion of the Tokyo Round, the U.S. administration submitted the Trade Agreements Act of 1979 to Congress, in order to implement the international trade agreements. The "fast track" procedure of the Trade Act of 1974, which required both houses to vote on bills implementing international trade agreements without making amendments to them, weakened the ability of Congress to reject or modify obligations taken on by the administration at the international level, and therefore prevented Congress from reversing U.S. compromises at the Tokyo Round as had been the case with compromises made at the Kennedy Round. The arrangements in place nevertheless allowed Congress an effective voice. While the chance of having a majority voting against the bill was slim, Congress could still affect the content of the bill put for vote (Destler 1997, 9–12).

The countervailing and antidumping agreements, the major concessions that the United States had made in the multilateral negotiations, were the most contentious issues in the discussions between Congress and the administration over the content of the bill (Winham 1986, 220). Led by the steel industry, representatives of the potentially affected industries argued passionately against changing the definition of the term injury in the U.S. laws. They received wide support from members of

---

[57] The Antidumping Code negotiated during the Kennedy Round, which was used as the basis for the Tokyo Round negotiations, required that dumping had to be the "principal cause" of injury. In the Tokyo Round, the United States attained EC agreement that the Code on Subsidies and Countervailing Measures (SCM) and the Code on Anti-Dumping Practices would not require signatories to find that subsidies were the "principal cause" of material injury to a home industry, reducing the difficulty of proving such an injury (Winham 1986, 221). The SCM agreement also articulated—at U.S. insistence—what appeared to be substantially stricter rules on the use by signatories of subsidies (Grieco 1990, 60–63).

[58] Some argue that the economic deterioration of the United States—the United States suffered from a chronic trade deficit at the same time that the EC had become the largest trading entity in the world and Japan emerged as a significant economic force (Bergsten 1971, 634–35; Diebold 1974, 479)—directly affected U.S. bargaining position at the GATT, leading to significant compromises on its part (McRae and Thomas 1983, 58; Winham 1986, 11). However, the deteriorating economic performance of the United States seemed to have only indirect effects on the negotiations. The changing economic status of the United States did not affect its ability to dominate the negotiations. Rather, political developments and institutional transformations at the *domestic* level—possibly most importantly the "fast track" procedure—affected the nature and content of the negotiations, including the concessions U.S. negotiators could offer.

Congress who attempted to press the administration into concessions by, for example, introducing competing protectionist bills.[59]

In the end, Congress members accepted the inclusion of the "material injury" test in both the antidumping and the countervailing duty laws. At the same time, however, supporters of the steel industry succeeded in writing into law a definition of material injury as "harm which is not inconsequential, immaterial or unimportant," which rendered the inclusion of "material" less significant than originally intended (Winham 1986, 311–12; O'Halloran 1994, 102; Destler 1995, 150). They also introduced changes into countervailing duty procedures that would provide more effective and expeditious relief (Twiggs 1987, 71–72). Timetables were shortened and were mandated not just for AD and CVD cases taken as a whole but also for specific stages; importers would now have to post a deposit just three months (rather than a year) following a preliminary finding of subsidy (and injury), enabling effective trade restraints to be obtained more quickly; and negotiated settlements could now include price or quantity guarantees. The act also subjected the determinations of the ITC to judicial review, which provided domestic industries with a more effective legal basis with which to force the administration to act on AD and CVD litigation (Prechel 1990, 659; Destler 1995, 150; Goldstein 2002). The law was passed in the House 395–7 and in the Senate 90–4.

The 1979 act was the first in a long list of bills aimed to turn the trade remedy laws into useful protectionist tools. Adapting their strategies to the new institutional frame, protectionist industries invested their political capital in Congress in making unfair-trade laws even more lenient. The Trade Remedies Reform Act, introduced in 1984, intended to strengthen the unfair-trade laws and counter a variety of unfair foreign trade practices. At its center was an "industrial targeting" provision that would have allowed the U.S. government to impose countervailing duties in response to actions of foreign governments promoting particular export industries. Another provision, put forth by a coalition of fertilizer manufacturers and cement producers, would have allowed the consideration of foreign governments' indirect (upstream) subsidies to exports, not just direct grants, in dumping and countervailing duty cases (*National Journal,* 1/14/1984, 63). The bill drew the opposition of the Reagan administration as well as

[59] Senator H. John Heinz III, a member of the Senate Finance Subcommittee on International Trade and a leader of the Steel Caucus, introduced two bills: a Buy American bill (S. 533), and a bill (S. 538) that would have amended the countervailing duty law to "make it relatively easy to prove injury, although not as easy as the steel industry favors" (Twiggs 1987, 71).

internationally oriented firms and associations. A compromise version of the bill was passed by the House in late July (194 Democrats and 66 Republicans voted for the bill, 25 Democrats and 72 Republicans voted against), but was never voted in the Senate.

A weakened version of the Trade Remedies Reform Act was ultimately included in the Trade and Tariff Act of 1984. The same act, however, also weakened congressional supervision over the administration's handling of escape-clause cases. In conformance with a Supreme Court declaration in the *Chadha* case,[60] that congressional veto provisions violated the doctrine of separation of powers and were therefore unconstitutional, Congress substituted joint disapproval resolutions, which are subject to presidential veto, for the previous concurrent resolutions, which are not. Congress could enact a law changing a presidential escape-clause determination, but a two-thirds vote of both Houses would be required to override the president's veto of such a law (Jackson 1998, 183).[61]

Another, unsuccessful, effort to help industries by reforming unfair-trade laws was launched in 1986. Although the bill that passed in the House did not restrict imports directly, it revised section after section of general U.S. trade laws with the goal of making it easier for firms to qualify for import relief and more difficult for presidents to deny it to them. The bill also included a call for the transfer of authorities from the president to the U.S. Trade Representative, including the authority to make the final decision as to whether or not to impose import barriers recommended by the ITC in escape-clause cases (Destler 1995, 91). The omnibus measure passed the House 295–115. The White House denounced the bill as "pure protectionism," describing it as "the toughest trade bill since the Depression." The administration was particularly opposed to the provisions limiting its discretion in unfair-trade actions (*National Journal,* 3/22/1986, 709). In the Senate Finance Committee, the proposals under consideration were more moderate than in the House, and the bill eventually died as the committee failed to mark up its legislation.[62]

---

[60] Immigration and Naturalization Service v. Chadha, 462 U.S. 919 (1983).

[61] The Trade and Tariff Act of 1984 was supported by the administration since it included a provision extending the General System of Preferences (GSP), and a provision authorizing the negotiation of a bilateral free-trade agreement with Israel. The bill also expanded the president's authority to negotiate tariff-free trade pacts with other nations.

[62] The bill expired for lack of time on the legislative calendar, because of disagreements concerning how tough the legislation should be, and because the sense of urgency was lost once it was realized that trade had not become a presidential election campaign issue (*National Journal,* 5/17/1986, 1212; *National Journal,* 6/28/1986, 1590).

Two years later, the Omnibus Trade and Competitiveness Act of 1988 did pass.[63] An important aspect of this bill was an attempt by the chairman of the Finance Committee, Lloyd Bentsen (D-Texas), to remove the president's discretion in escape-clause cases, thus making the ITC's recommendation mandatory. "We have made it more difficult for companies to get protection," Bentsen said, "but if they pay the price, then I want more certainty that there is a reward" (*National Journal*, 7/25/1987, 1898). The administration, however, strongly opposed the provision. In the end, the bill reduced the president's discretion in some respects, but left him with some scope for choice. The president could, for example, deny an industry protection from imports on the grounds that such protection would hurt the poor, or national security, or businesses reliant on the import in question. An analyst at the *Economist* assured his readers that "[these options] ought to provide a free-trader with an excuse for almost any occasion" (*Economist*, 8/13/1988, 21). The bill also amended the substantive requirements of the escape clause, making it somewhat easier for firms to obtain relief, but it forced them to agree to a five-year plan to restore their competitiveness if they did so (*Economist*, 8/13/1988, 21). As for antidumping and countervailing duty laws, effective lobbying by domestic firms led to the introduction of "minor alterations of highly technical and little-understood provisions that had great potential for changing international commerce" (*National Journal*, 4/18/1987, 927). During the House and Senate conference, however, many of "the most egregiously protectionist antidumping provisions" in the original bill, including a Senate "exporters' sales price" provision and a House "private right for action" provision, were dropped or cleaned up (*National Journal*, 8/13/1988, 2126).[64]

---

[63] The trade bill, which was formulated by Congress, initially reflected particularly strong protectionist sentiments. These were later toned down, especially following the stock market crash of 1987, after which the Economic Policy Council sent Congress a long list of objections to parts of the bill and warned, "we should all take care not to repeat the error of the 71st Congress in 1930 by enacting protectionist trade legislation, which would harm rather than help the economy" (*National Journal*, 7/11/1987, 2823). See Schwab (1994) for a detailed analysis.

[64] When the bill reached Reagan, he vetoed it, mainly due to a "plant closing" amendment that required companies with a hundred or more employees to give sixty days' notice before shutting down a factory. The House overrode Reagan's veto by a vote of 308 to 113. However, the Senate voted (61 to 37) to uphold Reagan's veto. House Democrats then agreed to accept another version of the trade legislation without the plant closing notification. The new bill passed the House by a vote of 376 to 45, and the Senate by a vote of 85 to 11. On August 23, 1988, Reagan signed the new bill into law.

Adaptive Politics: Organizational Restructuring

Users of the escape-clause and unfair-trade laws attempted not only to change the substance of the laws, but also the institutional arrangements governing them. Most fundamentally, the Trade Agreements Act of 1979 that ratified the Tokyo Round Agreements required the president to submit to Congress a proposal to restructure the international trade functions of the executive branch. The congressional committees responsible for trade judged the Treasury to have been insufficiently aggressive in enforcing the unfair-trade statutes and to have provided inadequate protection to domestic industries. They thus explicitly demanded that administration of these statutes be transferred from the Treasury to Commerce. The committees believed that the Commerce Department would be more responsive than the Treasury to domestic producers.[65] This requirement led to a heated discussion in the administration. As a memo written by the Secretary of State and the Secretary of Treasury dramatically, and insightfully, declared, "Function follows form. The organization of our trade policy apparatus will shape that policy for years to come."[66]

The assistant to the president for reorganization, Richard Pettigrew, and Commerce officials were the only ones who supported the radical offer to centralize *all* trade and international economic functions, including the functions held by the Department of State, the Department of Treasury, and STR, either into a new department or into the existing Commerce Department. Transferring functions to Commerce, they argued, would increase the likelihood of faster and more rigorous enforcement, help satisfy congressional pressure, and locate import and export controls in the same place.[67] State and Treasury officials were passionate in their opposition:

> The proposal shifts responsibility for administrating all import relief mechanisms into one agency. In the best of circumstances that agency would come under a protectionist siege. But the proposal

---

[65] Memo, Jim McIntyre, Director of OMB, to president, 10 May 1979, Staff offices, DPS, Eizenstat #292, Jimmy Carter Library; *New York Times*, 3/26/1979, IV, 4, 5, see also Goldstein 1993, 202; Destler 1995, 150.

[66] Memo, Cyrus R. Vance, Secretary of State, and W. Michael Blumenthal, Secretary of Treasury, to president, 21 June 1979, Chief of Staff, Butler #137, Jimmy Carter Library.

[67] Memo, Jim McIntyre, Director of OMB, to president, 10 May 1979, Staff offices, DPS, Eizenstat #292, Jimmy Carter Library; Memo, Dick Pettigrew, Assistant to the President for Reorganization, to president, 4 May 1979, Staff offices, DPS, Eizenstat #292, Jimmy Carter Library.

places all administrative responsibility in an agency—Commerce—with a proven inability to resist protectionist forces. This shift in administrative responsibility foreordains a slide into protectionism.[68]

As an alternative, they proposed "a reorganization built around the establishment of a new U.S. Export Corporation based on the highly successful Eximbank model."[69] The Special Trade Representative, Robert Strauss, together with the director of the Office of Management and Budget (OMB), James McIntyre, also opposed the radical reorganization approach, fighting in particular for the preservation of the Office of STR.[70] They offered, instead, to divide the authority by centralizing all policy coordination and negotiation responsibilities in STR and all operational responsibilities, including antidumping and the countervailing duty functions, and import relief, in Commerce.[71]

It was the STR/OMB plan that was ultimately adopted. The Carter administration's reorganization plan, implemented on January 4, 1980, strengthened the Department of Commerce's authority, at the expense of the Treasury (Cohen 1988, 181–85). The plan turned the Department of Commerce into "the focus of nonagricultural operational trade responsibilities" and thus the chief administrator of import and export programs (Destler 1986, 99). Commerce's duties came to include the export promotion program, responsibility for enforcing legislated restrictions on U.S. business compliance with certain boycott regulations maintained by foreign countries, and responsibility for collecting government statistics on foreign trade and investment (Cohen 1988, 69–70). Most important, the authority to enforce the CVD and AD laws moved from the secretary of the treasury, who had held this authority since 1897, to the secretary of commerce.

---

[68] Memo, Cyrus R. Vance, Secretary of State, and W. Michael Blumenthal, Secretary of Treasury, to president, 21 June 1979, Chief of Staff, Butler #137, Jimmy Carter Library.

[69] Howard Gruenspect to Eizenstat, 18 June 1979, Staff offices, DPS, Eizenstat #292, Jimmy Carter Library; Memo, Cyrus R. Vance, Secretary of State, and W. Michael Blumenthal, Secretary of Treasury, to president, 21 June 1979, Chief of Staff, Butler #137, Jimmy Carter Library.

[70] "The objective [of the Office of Special Trade Representative] was to have the United States represented with a single voice for all of its trade interests: industrial, agricultural, as well as labor; representative of both the Congress and the President, and close enough to the President to be able to judge what is in the political best interests of the Administration and be able to coordinate all of the line agencies that are engaged in trade policy." Memo, Strauss to President, 11 May 1979, Staff offices, DPS, Eizenstat #292, Jimmy Carter Library.

[71] Memo, Eizenstat and Gruenspecht to president, 11 May 1979, Staff offices, DPS, Eizenstat #292, Jimmy Carter Library; Memo, Strauss to President, 18 May 1979, Staff offices, DPS, Eizenstat #292, Jimmy Carter Library.

The plan also strengthened the STR policy formulation mandate, at the expense of the Department of State.[72] The renamed Office of the United States Trade Representative (USTR) was now assigned the functions of "international trade policy development, coordination and negotiation," including responsibilities previously handled by the Department of State, involving the GATT, bilateral, commodity, and East-West trade matters, as well as policy responsibility for overseeing trade-remedy cases. The office also doubled in size to approximately seventy-seven professionals (Destler 1986, 99). Congressional insistence on an internal organization within the administration clearly paid off, as there is no doubt that the shift from Treasury to Commerce contributed to the high number of AD and CVD investigations and positive determinations after 1979.

In short, unfair-trade laws had a very different trajectory compared to the escape clause. While initially hesitant, declining industries soon followed the administration's encouragement and filed antidumping and countervailing duty law petitions. Their strategic repertoire expanded, however, beyond the mere usage of existing opportunities. The lack of discretion gave weight to the legal text governing the decision-making process of the ITC and the Department of Treasury. Declining industries, therefore, wisely utilized their political influence in Congress to change the substance of the law to their advantage. They also successfully fought for changing the institutional arrangements themselves.

---

[72] The respective responsibilities of the Office of the STR and the Department of State for certain trade policy issues caused a long-term debate between the two offices. The State Department position was that since it had responsibility for the conduct of U.S. foreign policy, and since trade policy was a basic element of foreign policy, it should have primary responsibility for trade policy issues. The STR, in State's judgment, had primary responsibility for negotiating trade agreements (other than commodity agreements), but only secondary responsibility for trade *policy* issues. The State Department, significantly, defined the debate in terms of the distribution of power between Congress and the administration: "We are firmly convinced that, in effect, STR's efforts [to take over the lead role within the Executive Branch in policy formulation and trade negotiations] threaten to erode the authority of the Presidency itself since the fundamental issue at stake here is the distribution of power between the Executive and the Legislative Branches. Presidential authority over the making of foreign policy, including the crucial field of foreign economic policy, must be fully maintained. . . . A shifting of leadership responsibilities of the sort STR is urging would, however, result in a loss of Presidential authority to the Congress." The STR, for its part, contended that Congress and the president share responsibility for trade policy, and that both had named the STR as the basic instrumentality through which this new Executive-Legislative partnership was to be carried out. The debate, partly due to congressional involvement, was resolved to the advantage of the Office of USTR. Memo, Dent (STR) to Seidman, January 24, 1976, Seidman papers, box 91, STR (3), Gerald R. Ford Library; Memo, Robinson (State) to Seidman, February 1976, Seidman papers, box 91, STR (6), Gerald R. Ford Library.

Section 301 under the Reagan Administration

Section 301 of the Trade Act of 1974 granted the president the authority to take retaliatory actions against a country that "maintains unjustifiable or unreasonable tariff or other import restrictions . . . which have the effect of substantially reducing sales of the competitive United States product." In the Trade and Tariff Act of 1984, Congress authorized the USTR to initiate investigations without waiting for a private petition or an order from the president. The 1984 act also broadened the definition of unfair trade practices to include discrimination against services, transfer of information, and foreign direct investment (Bayard and Elliott 1994, 28; O'Halloran 1994, 104–5).

This was a potentially powerful weapon against foreign practices that restricted U.S. commerce, but during the first decade of its existence it was hardly utilized. From 1975 to 1984, private firms filed thirty-eight Section 301 petitions, less than four per year on average.[73] Petitions typically led to consultations, at times under the auspices of the GATT. Prior to 1985, there was only one case in which the president took the unilateral retaliatory action authorized by law. In contrast, between 1985 and 1988, the administration processed twenty-three Section 301 petitions (almost six per year) and took retaliatory action three times. Since 1989, the president has taken no retaliatory action against a GATT/WTO member (see table 5.4).[74]

The shift in the relative prominence of Section 301 after 1985 was initiated by the Reagan administration. In the early 1980s, an overvalued dollar, declining industrial competitiveness, and the emergence of new (particularly East Asian) competitors brought an upsurge of the U.S. trade deficit. For the first time since World War II, manufacturing employment declined for three consecutive years between 1980 and 1982. In the same period, imports, which usually fall during a recession, actually grew by 8.3 percent, while exports declined by 17.5 percent (Pearson 1990, 26; Shoch 2001, 77). Over the next five years, the situation worsened. Total U.S. imports increased by almost 50 percent, rising from $257 billion in 1980 to $362 billion in 1985. Trade deficits nearly quadrupled in the six-year period beginning in 1980, soaring from $36 billion to $148 billion. The bilateral deficit with

[73] The analysis is based on USTR's "Section 301 Table of Cases," available at http://www.ustr.gov/reports/301report/act301.htm, and "Trade Policy Agenda & Annual Report of the President of the United States on the Trade Agreements Program," available at http://www.ustr.gov/reports/index.shtml.

[74] In many cases, of course, sanctions were avoided because of the willingness of the trading partner to change its practices (and see more below).

Table 5.4 Section 301 petitions and unilateral sanctions, 1975–2002

Year	Average per year (number of petitions)	Sanctions
1975–84	3.8 (38)	1
1985–88	5.8 (23)	3
1989–94	4.8 (29)	0
1995–2002	3.3 (26)	1[a]

Sources: USTR Reports, various years; USTR's "Section 301 Table of Cases," http://www.ustr.gov/reports/301report/act301.htm.

[a] Not a WTO member.

Japan accounted for about one-third of the total U.S. deficit (Cohen 1988, 207; Shoch 2001, 105–11).

During its first term in office, the Reagan administration embraced a defiant hands-off posture in response (Cohen 1988, 206; Destler 1995, 123–24). The priority was to fight inflation domestically, and exchange rates and trade policies were neglected (Milner 1990, 166). The Reagan administration not only refused to confront the source of the problem, it also seemed to be comparatively less inclined than previous administrations to offer remedies for the benefit of vulnerable industries.

The administration's indifference to the mounting trade woes of domestic agricultural and industrial sectors forced a change of strategy on the part of affected domestic industries. Faced with "nonproductive" meetings with senior administration officials, the industrial sector turned to Congress with a barrage of pleas for relief (Cohen 1988, 209). As Senator John Danforth (R-Mo) remarked, "The executive branch, which should be the place to manage specific trade problems, is now closed to industries seeking import relief. When the executive branch is closed for business, Congress is the only place to turn, and the remedy Congress offers is quota legislation" (quoted in Cohen 1988, 210). Effective threats of such quota legislation forced the administration to react, usually with an offer to initiate voluntary export restraints (VERs).

The cases of the automobile industry and the steel industry serve as two prominent examples for this type of dynamic. In 1980, the United Auto Workers and the Ford Motor Company filed for escape-clause relief. In its report, the ITC agreed that the industry had suffered serious injury but concluded that injury had been caused by factors other than imports. No relief was recommended. Soon after Reagan's election, several auto trade bills were introduced, including the Danforth bill, which proposed to limit auto imports from Japan to 1.6 million units annually until 1983. To block this legislation, the Reagan administration brokered an agreement with the Japanese to restrain their imports (Goldstein 1993, 231–33). In June 1984, in an escape-clause case of the carbon and alloy steel, the ITC ruled that imports were injuring the domestic steel industry and proposed a five-year import relief program for steel consisting of tariffs and quotas. The Reagan administration was concerned that tighter steel quotas might lead to Common Market retaliation against U.S. agricultural products, but needed to fend off quota legislation pending in Congress (Shoch 2001, 90). The administration thus sought voluntary restraint agreements with countries responsible for surges in U.S. steel imports. The intention was to devise agreements that would hold imports to 18.5 percent of the market (imports stood at 25 percent in 1984). Congress again intervened in favor of the domestic industry: the Trade and Tariff Act of 1984 included a "sense of Congress" resolution limiting steel imports to between 17 and 20.2 percent of the market, and authorizing the president to negotiate the necessary arrangements (*National Journal*, 1/28/1984, 147; Goldstein 1993, 225–26; Destler 1995, 84–88). The pattern that emerged, in short, was one in which the administration refused to attend to an industry's plea, as a result of which the industry appealed to Congress, which forced the administration into VERs.

By the mid 1980s, Congress's impatience with the administration led to unprecedented legislative activity. In 1985 and 1986, the number of bills concerned with "import restrictions" submitted in Congress increased quite dramatically, from 144 in the Ninety-eighth Congress (1983–84) to 277 in the Ninety-ninth Congress (1985–86). However, almost all of the attempts to enact trade-restricting laws failed. During the Ninety-ninth Congress, only 6 import-restricting laws passed, exactly the same number that had passed during the Ninety-eighth Congress.[75] This, again, suggests that for most members of Congress the primary objective was not to impose import quotas, but to capture the executive's attention that the international trade and monetary status quo was unacceptable (Cohen 1988, 210).

Partly due to congressional pressure, the administration at last devised a trade strategy in the end of 1985. The plan was aimed at opening markets abroad and staving off protection at home (Cohen 1988, 214; Destler 1995, 123–24). The new treasury secretary, James A. Baker III, who took control of trade policy, focused on the overvalued dollar as his first priority.[76] In addition, the Economic Policy Council (EPC), which Baker established and

[75] Data compiled by the author from "Thomas," available at http://thomas.loc.gov/, under the category of "import restrictions."

[76] In September 1985, Baker reached the so-called Plaza Agreement, with Japan, West Germany, Britain, and France, according to which these governments would sell dollars in currency markets, increasing the worldwide supply and thereby force a reduction in the value of the dollar (Destler 1995, 125; Dryden 1995, 311).

chaired,[77] crafted a novel approach to international trade relations, which emphasized unilateral pro-growth and export enhancing elements. It called for market-opening pressures accompanied by threats of retaliation in sectors in which U.S. firms were competitive. As part of this approach, the EPC recommended that the government should "self-initiate" (that is, without waiting for an industry petition) Section 301 cases against foreign trade barriers (Cohen 1988, 216; Feketekuty 1990, 94–95; Dryden 1995, 310; Destler 1995, 126–27). Following the EPC's recommendation, the USTR self-initiated an investigation into alleged unfair trade practices of Brazil (for walling off its computer market to outside suppliers), South Korea (for its laws forbidding non-Korean companies to enter the insurance market), and Japan (for its restrictions on the sale of foreign tobacco). The USTR self-initiated six additional cases in this manner during the Reagan administration.

The administration's self-initiation of these Section 301 cases symbolized its endorsement of "strategic" trade policy. (Others refer to it, more critically, as "aggressive reciprocity"). Such policy focused on fighting against the protection of foreign markets by demanding trade barriers for the home markets if foreign markets were protected (Milner and Yoffie 1989). As a strategy for opening foreign market, this policy was compatible with trade liberalization. However, it could also be utilized for protectionist purposes, such as attaining a government-managed bilateral trade *balance* instead of a surplus determined by market forces (Keohane 1986, 4). Immediately, therefore, a conflict emerged over how to employ Section 301, with some attempting to restrict it while others tried to expand its protectionist potential.

The most significant changes to Section 301 were introduced by Congress in the Omnibus Trade and Competitiveness Act of 1988. The act strengthened Section 301 authority through the imposition of shorter time limits for action (which limited the president's discretion by preventing him from quietly dropping suits); and an expanded definition of unfair trade practices abroad (including refusal of opportunities for the establishment of an enterprise, denial of intellectual property protection, export targeting, denial of workers' rights, and foreign government tolerance of anticompetitive activities). One important debate evolved around the location of authority. Congress transferred to the USTR the authority to initiate investigations of unfair trade practices and order sanctions when necessary, which had previously been in the hands of the president. The motive behind this transfer of

---

[77] The EPC was a cabinet-level, interagency coordinating body, which effectively absorbed the preexisting Trade Policy Committee (Cohen 1988, 90).

authority was, as always, to increase the USTR's importance and power, and thus reduce the likelihood of trade benefits for foreigners being exchanged for nontrade benefits (Bello and Holmer 1990, 51). However, the president retained control over the timing and method of retaliation. Thus, in the end he kept more authority than Congress had wanted.

The question of discretion was another source of contention. Many members of Congress, of both parties, pointed to the president's discretion to take action as the main source of the failure of Section 301 (Bello and Holmer 1990, 57–58). Senator George J. Mitchell (D-Maine) argued: "The history of Section 301 is a history of administration after administration of both parties refusing to implement the law. Instead, this president [Reagan] and his predecessors have used the wide discretion provided in the law to deny or to delay taking action sometimes for close to a decade."[78] The administration, however, strongly opposed any mandate to retaliate under Section 301. The final bill took a moderate approach, limiting the scope of the mandate to retaliate to those Section 301 cases involving a violation or denial of benefits under a trade agreement or a breach of any other agreement. Even in those cases, the bill contained a limited national economic interest exception (Bello and Holmer 1990, 64).

Congress also introduced new "Super" and "Special" 301 provisions. The Super 301 amendment required the USTR, in the following two years (1989 and 1990), to identify and produce a list of trading partners engaged in generic or systemic unfair trade practices, and then to seek the removal of the discriminatory measures by negotiating changes with the targeted countries. If negotiations failed within nineteen months, the president then would be required to retaliate against the offenders. The principal, although by no means only, target of Super 301 was Japan (Preeg 1995, 79).[79] Special 301 actions focused specifically on intellectual property protection, and allowed the USTR to identify countries that did not provide adequate protection to intellectual property and to impose sanctions against them.

---

[78] *Presidential Authority to Respond to Unfair Trade Practices: Hearings on Title II of S. 1860 and S. 1862* Before the Senate Committee on Finance, 99th Cong., 2d sess., 1986, 11, cited in Bello and Holmer (1990, 58).

[79] Super 301 was formulated in the Senate as a more moderate alternative to Representative Richard A. Gephardt's (D-Missouri) amendment, which was included in the House bill and was strongly supported by organized labor. The Gephardt amendment required the president to take retaliatory trade action against countries that had large trade surpluses with the United States (exporting to the U.S. more than 175 percent of the value of imports from the U.S.) and that were judged to engage in unfair trade practices (*National Journal*, 4/18/1987, 927; Bello and Holmer 1990, 76–83).

Super 301 under the Bush and Clinton Administrations

Under Section 301, private companies filed petitions in reference to specific practices. Super 301, in contrast, forced the administration into the politically sensitive task of naming trading partners engaged in unfair trade practices. A strong camp in the Bush administration, led by Chief Economic Adviser Michael Boskin and Treasury Secretary Nicholas Brady, opposed the targeting of any state, and were supported by State and Defense department officials who were fearful of jeopardizing the strategic relationship with Japan (Shoch 2001, 139). However, USTR Carla Hills' more pragmatic, and relatively aggressive, position won. Hills named Japan for three practices, India for two, and Brazil for one.[80] Taiwan and South Korea had edged themselves off the list with some well-timed concessions (*Economist*, 3/27/1993, 69). The European Community was not named, possibly because it had made clear that it would not negotiate under a procedure it considered illegal (*Economist*, 5/5/1990, 32). Noting "substantial progress in obtaining improvements in intellectual property protection from various trading partners," Hills declined to name any "priority" countries under the Special 301 provision of the trade act. Rather, she created a "priority watch list" of eight countries (*National Journal*, 6/17/1989, 1562). A year later the administration agreed not to name Japan in return for (minor) trade concessions, which included all three of the practices identified the year before. Brazil too made concessions and was subsequently removed from the list. India remained on the list for protecting its insurance industry and keeping out foreign investment (*Economist*, 5/5/1990, 32; *National Journal*, 5/5/1990, 1099). However, India refused to negotiate, and in the end the U.S. government decided not to retaliate, possibly because it feared that India would have taken the case to the GATT, which would have probably ruled that the U.S. action had been illegal (*Economist*, 3/27/1993, 69).

Super 301 expired at the end of 1990, but President Clinton promised to resurrect it in his presidential campaign in 1992. Once again, the principal target was Japan. Once in office, however, Clinton's interagency trade policy team devised an alternative strategy for organizing the U.S.–Japan economic relationship. Instead of explicit unilateralism, concerns were

---

[80] *The Economist* found Hills' list to be cleverly chosen. On Japan, for instance, she picked the timber trade, which appealed to the constituency interests of two members of the Finance Committee. Japan's other "categories of sin" were satellites and supercomputers, both of which depended on public procurement and thus were open to remedy by government fiat. Brazil and India, in turn, were picked largely to avoid charges of Japan-bashing (*Economist*, 6/3/1989, 30; *Economist*, 5/5/1990, 32).

brought forward under a bilateral negotiating framework (Shoch 2001, 175). The negotiations with Japan were a central aspect of Clinton's more general strategy of "export-led growth," which included aggressive policies of export promotion and an intensified pursuit of international market-opening initiatives and agreements, as a way to raise domestic demand and lower unemployment (Shoch 2001, 171–72).

When the negotiations with Japan failed, Clinton headed off congressional legislation renewing Super 301 by renewing the provision administratively, although in a milder form: instead of listing erring countries, the administration would list trade practices that posed obstacles to trade (Bayard and Elliott 1994). Shortly after, the White House released its list of countries erecting egregious trade barriers, singling out Japan as the worst offender. At the same time, administration officials said that they were not, for the moment, contemplating any new sanctions against Tokyo. Clinton reinstituted Super 301, again by executive order, in 1994 for a two-year period, and extended it in 1995 to 1996 and 1997. On April 1999, Super 301 was again reinstituted by executive order for the years of 1999–2001. It has not been renewed since.

Reaction of Congress

Inevitably, a crucial element in the shift from a selective to conditional regime of protectionism was the new role Congress took upon itself in managing trade practices, as already indicated throughout this chapter. Under the regime of selective protectionism, Congress was at the center of protectionist activity, willingly, if selectively, imposing quantitative restrictions on imported goods. Under the regime of conditional protectionism, in contrast, Congress concentrated on reformulating safeguard and unfair-trade laws and on overseeing the implementation of these laws by the administration.

Selective Legislation

Significantly, after 1974 Congress shied away from addressing protectionist demands of "special interests." The reference by scholars to "a new wave of protectionism" during this period is often based on the increased number of trade bills submitted in Congress (but see Nivola 1986, 577; Pearson 1990, 25). Indeed, there were numerous attempts to introduce "selective" measures after 1974. These included bills raising duties (on steel and plastic containers, hand tools, candles and tapers, sugar, shrimp, copper); imposing quantitative limitations (mushrooms, shrimp, meat, steel, automobiles, textiles and apparel, softwood lumber, tobacco, footwear, fresh-cut flowers); requiring labeling and changing rules-of-origin (dairy products, palm oil, meat, mushrooms, textiles and apparel, canned tuna, wood); requiring the exclusion of specific products from multinational trade negotiations and/or from the GSP (textiles and apparel, copper, glass products); imposing price support (milk, tomatoes); introducing "Buy-American" and domestic content laws (automobiles); and introducing more general import surcharge laws, aimed at Japan, Taiwan, South Korea, and Brazil. As I have already indicated, however, while the impressive increase in the number of restrictive trade bills reflects a rise in protectionist *sentiments*, it does not show a corresponding rise in protectionist *practices*. Of the hundreds of such bills introduced in Congress only a small number were enacted into law (see table 5.5).

As a general rule, the major trade laws passed by Congress in the 1970s and the 1980s were liberal in their orientation. The delegation of authority to reduce tariffs and negotiate nontariff barriers to trade were extended to the administration in 1974, 1979, and again in 1988. Congress ratified the Tokyo Round Agreements in the Trade Agreements Act of 1979 and the Uruguay Round Agreements in the Uruguay Round Agreements Act of 1994. The comprehensive trade restrictions proposed in 1984 and 1986 were not adopted. Even when restrictive measures were introduced into comprehensive trade laws, which was a common and effective strategy during the regime of selective protectionism, most of the "specific cases" were eventually eliminated in the conferences. In the Trade and Tariff Act of 1984, for example, amendments favoring producers of copper, bromine, wine, footwear, ferroalloys, and dairy products were deleted or neutralized

Table 5.5 Number of "import restrictive" bills in Congress, 1975–94

Congress	Years	Import restrictions submitted	Import restrictions passed
94th	1975–76	210	2
95th	1977–78	318	8
96th	1979–80	127	5
97th	1981–82	137	5
98th	1983–84	144	6
99th	1985–86	277	6
100th	1987–88	247	12
101st	1989–90	157	10
102nd	1991–92	172	16
103rd	1993–94	134	12

Source: Compiled by the author from "Thomas" http://thomas.loc.gov/ under the category of "import restrictions."

in the House-Senate conference (*National Journal*, 9/29/1984, 1841; Destler 1995, 84–88). The selective cases that were introduced to the Omnibus Trade and Competitiveness Act of 1988, such as lamb import quotas and sugar duty drawbacks, were similarly dropped in the House and Senate conference (*National Journal*, 3/5/1988, 631).

The underlining *logic* behind the introduction of selective legislation also changed. Often, it came as a reaction to what Congress perceived to be an inadequate response by the administration, and was thus a way to force the administration into action. The wave of laws submitted in 1985 was motivated not only by objective economic conditions but also by Reagan's hands-off attitude to monetary and trade issues, and reflected Congress's attempt to attract the administration's attention.

Congressional support of the textile and apparel industries can be partly explained by the fact that the particular characteristics of international competition in those products—textiles and clothes are rarely dumped, rarely subsidized, and it was difficult to prove injury across the industry— limited the industry's ability to utilize the escape-clause or unfair-trade laws as effective alternative strategies. It was by way of congressional pressure that the Multi-Fiber Agreement (MFA) of 1974 was extended in 1977 and again in 1981 (Aggarwal 1985, 143–66; Cline 1990, 11). Congress also backed the textile industry during the Tokyo Round negotiations, passing a bill to exclude all textiles from tariff reduction negotiations. Carter, however, vetoed the bill (Destler 1986, 61–62; Twiggs 1987, 54). In addition, Congress attempted, on three different occasions, to impose quotas on imports of textiles and apparel. All three bills, however, were promptly vetoed by the president—two by Reagan and one by George H. W. Bush.[81]

---

[81] The Textile and Apparel Enforcement Act of 1985 was initially introduced in order to strengthen the administration's position in the negotiations concerning the renewal of the MFA, which was due to expire in 1986, and to prevent the inclusion of textiles and apparel in the GATT negotiations. The bill would have cut back imports of textiles and apparel by rolling back imports to levels based on 6 percent growth since 1980, and would have replaced the existing system of bilateral negotiations with explicit and comprehensive import licenses. The bill passed both the House and the Senate but was vetoed by Reagan. The original motivation for the bill was, however, satisfied: the congressional vote on overriding the veto was delayed until after the date of the MFA's expiration, thus putting added pressure on the White House during the negotiations on the new MFA (Cline 1990, 210). In 1987, the textile and apparel industries once again succeeded to obtain protective legislation. The Textile and Apparel Trade Bill of 1987 provided for comprehensive global quotas (i.e., a single quota for imports of a product from all sources) on imports of textiles, apparel, and footwear. The level of textile and apparel quotas would be constrained to a growth of only 1 percent annually, with the footwear quota frozen at the 1986 level. The bill introduced a sharp departure from past practices under the MFA, in which only imports from developing countries and Japan

Conditional Legislation

Many of the bills introduced in Congress that aimed at the narrow concerns of particular industries were not "protectionist" in the traditional sense but were instead concerned with providing fair trade to industries. Such bills included requests to conduct new investigations if the president denied ITC affirmative recommendations for import relief (nonrubber footwear, and bolts, nuts, and large screws of iron and steel), or if the secretary of treasury waived countervailing duties (honey, sugar, high-carbon ferrochromium, metal fasteners, fish, leather, meat, shoes, milk protein products). Congress also "referred" cases to the administration (dairy products, steel, cattle, milk protein products, mushrooms) and requested bilateral negotiations with other countries (steel, automobiles, nonrubber footwear, potatoes, copper, machine tool industry, mushrooms, coffee). Congress referred cases to the administration even when the industries asked Congress for restrictive legislation. In the case of the mushroom industry in 1976, for example, Congress did not hold hearings on restrictive bills, but instead passed a resolution calling on the president to negotiate with representatives of foreign countries in an effort to obtain bilateral agreements.

As described above, Congress paid most attention to amending safeguards and unfair-trade laws. Amendments included changing the procedures in escape-clause investigations, strengthening adjustment assistance, reaffirming support for vigorous enforcement of unfair-trade laws, and strengthening antidumping and countervailing duty laws. Especially after 1988, Congress used unfair-trade claims to improve domestic exporters' access to foreign markets. This was accomplished through congressional efforts to revive, strengthen, extend, and/or enhance the operation of Section 301 (generally and in connection to specific cases, such as with automobiles and auto parts, semiconductors, livestock, meat, cheese, beer to Canada, rice to Japan, and seafood to France).

In short, Congress has fundamentally shifted its trade policy activities since the mid 1970s: while reluctant to assert its constitutional power to impose product-specific trade barriers, Congress instead focused on strengthening unfair-trade measures. Protectionist legislation now concentrated

---

had been restricted, by subjecting all sources of imports in the restrictions, including Canada and Europe (Cline 1990, 224–25). Reagan vetoed this bill as well, and Congress failed to override the veto. The Textile, Apparel and Footwear Trade Act of 1990 closely resembled the legislation that had been introduced in 1987. The bill passed the House and the Senate, but was again vetoed, this time by President Bush.

mainly on instructing and overseeing the administration, ensuring that it used its new powers in ways that were sufficiently attentive to domestic concerns. As one journalist observed in 1985, "Congress usually avoids the political dilemma of industry-by-industry trade aid requests by letting the executive branch decide whether an industry deserves protection. Although it may yet heed cries for help from the textile and shoe industries, Congress now appears ready to let the Reagan Administration continue handling the sensitive question of protectionist aid, perhaps with changes in the executive branch mechanisms for awarding relief" (*National Journal*, 11/9/1985, 2524). This was an indirect outcome of the institutional arrangements in place and the new opportunities they provided for pressure groups and for the administration, as I describe below. Even when pressure for selective legislation existed, the administration now had the power to "pacify" Congress and to prevent import quotas by suggesting alternative solutions, such as VERs.

Evaluating New Protectionism

The increased activity and higher rates of affirmative decisions in trade remedy cases have led scholars to label the 1980s as a period of "new protectionism" (Nivola 1986, 577; Nivola 1993; see also Strange 1979; Smith 1994) and interpret the reaction of the U.S. government to protectionist demands as evidence of a reverse in the historic shift toward free trade (Nivola 1986; Pearson 1990). However, other studies convincingly show that the administration's reaction to heightened protectionist sentiments did *not* lead to heightened protectionism (Destler and Odell 1987; Milner 1988; Goldstein 1993). Rather, the new type of measures *curbed* protectionism so that demands, when met, did not threaten the general process of trade liberalization.

First, legislated import quotas, the most disrupting manifestation of protectionism, were no longer a viable practice. Congress, for the most part, did not enact patently protectionist statutes. The few bills that had features of selective protectionism and were passed in Congress, such as the textile bills, were blocked by sustained presidential vetoes. It is important to view the administrative measures addressing protectionist demands—in particular, the active marketing of AD remedies in the late 1970s and the self-initiation of Section 301 cases in the mid 1980s—as precisely the means that prevented legislated solutions.

Second, the administration's major tools for restricting imports— including safeguards, antidumping and countervailing duties, as well as "voluntary" restraint agreements—were not as effective as the legislated import quotas they prevented and had only a limited impact on the volume of trade (Milner 1988, 11). Following conventional measures,[82] antidumping and countervailing duty positive determinations resulted in the imposition of a low level of duties, covering only a low percentage of total imports, with no negative effect on trade imports as a whole. In the fiscal year 1992, for example, the trade-weighted average AD duty imposed was only 5.5 percent, and the trade-weighted average CVD imposed was only 5 percent. In the same year, AD orders covered only 0.61 percent of imports ($3.2 billion out of a total of $513 billion), and CVD orders covered only 0.7 percent ($3.6 billion out of $513 billion) (CBO 1994, 58–59). Measured differently, revenues from AD duties made up only 1.0 percent of total revenues from all import duties, and revenues from CVD duties constituted only 1.1 percent (CBO 1994, 59). Based on data for each antidumping case filed between 1980 and 1988, Thomas J. Prusa (1996) found that AD duties substantially restricted the volume of trade *from named countries*. However, he also found that there was substantial trade diversion from named to nonnamed countries. Because of the diversion of imports, the *overall* volume of trade continued to grow even for those cases that resulted in duties.

Not all of the trade restrictions that resulted from AD/CVD cases took the form of duties. Many more, estimated at around additional 45 percent, were superseded by bilateral agreements (CBO 1994, 59). Voluntary export restraints were also reached to offset an initiation of protectionist legislation in Congress. VERs at various points of time governed imports of textiles, specialty steel, footwear, motorcycles, machine tools, consumer electronics, automobiles, and semiconductors. Importantly, exporting nations preferred VERs to either quotas or tariffs. This was so because such agreements were often equivalent to a global cartel, especially in industries with high entry barriers and a limited number of suppliers. Through upgrading, controlled markets, and transshipment, VERs yielded high prices for the importing consumers and high profits for the exporting industries (Goldstein 1993, 221–22). In addition, VERs could be targeted to individual producers without disrupting the entire trading system, which a universal quota system would (Yoffie 1983). Finally, VERs have not been that restrictive in their requirements and less restrictive than previous arrangements (Bhagwati 1988, 56; see also Destler and Odell 1987). All this made VERs a poor substitute for tariff increases and made scholars conclude that "VERs

---

[82] The debate over the impacts of nontariff barriers to trade often focuses on how to measure those impacts. See CBO 1994; Destler 1995, 210–11.

may be the most liberal of possible American options" (Goldstein 1993, 223). Hence, by choosing administrative arrangements, including VERs, "the negotiating countries may well have opted for the least damaging way of responding to protectionist demands that could not be successfully rejected outright" (Bhagwati 1988, 57). The new restrictions did not stop the flow of trade and allowed the administration, as well as Congress, to resist even tighter protection (Destler and Odell 1987, 1; see also Yoffie 1983, 174–75; Goldstein 1986, 162; Dryden 1995, 211, 271–72).

Third, and independent of the actual level of duties, the *logic* behind safeguards and unfair-trade laws was also more hospitable to free trade than the practices characterizing selective protectionism. For it is not only the comparatively low impediment to trade that should be emphasized. A similar level of tariffs may have a different effect on the process of trade liberalization, depending on the goal or logic behind the higher duties and the legitimacy and legality of the measure.

In the regime of selective protectionism, Congress imposed tariffs and import quotas in order to protect declining industries from import penetration. In contrast, in the regime of conditional protectionism the administration pursued *fair* and *strategic* trade policy, combating unfair trading practices of *other* countries (Pearson 1990; Nollen and Quinn 1994). The objective was to impose further liberalization on foreign markets, by prohibiting trade practices that provided unfair advantage to foreign producers in the U.S. market, or that caused unfair disadvantage to U.S. producers in the foreign market, *not* to protect uncompetitive U.S. producers nor to keep the American market closed (Goldstein 1993, 216; see also Milner and Yoffie 1989). The shift in practices from import quotas to safeguard remedies and unfair-trade laws, and then to Section 301, reveals a systematic trajectory toward greater emphasis on the liberalization of foreign markets and lesser emphasis on the protection of the American market. The aim was to establish fair competition, rather than no competition at all.

Embodying the idea of *strategic* trade policy, Section 301 was unique with its emphasis on "export politics" as the preferred solution to correct the trade deficit, rather than shielding the American market from imports (Destler 1995, 127). In contrast to studies on AD/CVD cases and VERs, several studies have found that Section 301 brought effective outcomes.[83] However, they also

---

[83] Michael Ryan (1995) finds that of forty cases in which the USTR pursued market-opening negotiations with Japan, Korea, and Taiwan, over the 1976–90 period, only three resulted in no action, compared to thirty-seven instances in which the United States won some change in foreign trade practices. In an impressively thorough and cautious study, Bayard and Elliott (1994, 64) conclude that "U.S. negotiating objectives were at least partially achieved

found that the outcomes adhered to the logic of fair access, rather than protectionism. Bayard and Elliott (1994, 59) conclude that the USTR has generally been conscientious in using Section 301 to reduce obstacles to trade and has avoided any temptation to use it as a protectionist tool. Concretely, the USTR chose cases in which agreed international rules were at issue (Noland 1997; Ryan 1995); formal actions were more correlated with the existence of formal barriers to trade than to bilateral trade imbalances, suggesting that the USTR did not follow the logic of narrow reciprocity (Noland 1997); and the market opening that had been achieved was extended to producers from all nations, not just the United States, thereby strengthening, not undermining, the multilateral trading system (Ryan 1995). In addition, the USTR generally chose cases in which U.S. producers were highly competitive and hence could exploit the sought-after market opening (Ryan 1995).

Fair and strategic trade policies did not disrupt the general process of trade liberalization as much as congressional protectionist measures did for other reasons as well. In contrast to legislated quotas, implementing antidumping and countervailing duty laws or VERs did not require compensation, and thus removed the threat of retaliation and avoided lingering disputes. Since unfair-trade laws were, for the most part, consistent with GATT laws,[84] trading partners generally accepted the legality of the rulings. The lack of discretion granted a layer of legitimacy: the U.S. government claimed that affirmative determinations should not be read as evidence for an "outbreak of trade protectionism" in the United States, as it had no discretion in accepting them (*National Review*, 10/11/75, 1431).

In sum, under the regime of conditional protectionism U.S. administrations addressed the needs of protectionist industries, but under conditions that reduced the inevitable contradictions between the general process of trade liberalization and protectionist exceptions. This was achieved by following a protectionist logic that was largely compatible with the GATT's notions of fair competition and open access.

---

about half of the time (35 of 72 cases)" and that "Section 301 appears to have been a reasonably effective tool of American policy." However, Noland (1997) finds that Section 301 practices did not have a significant, distinct impact on the level of exports or investment or on the growth of export and investments. This suggests that even if Section 301 led to changed behavior in particular sectors, the effects were too small or too random for an econometric model to capture.

[84] Section 301, in contrast, violates several norms associated with the international trade regime. It is discriminatory, for it singles out particular countries for their unfair trade practices; and it calls for unilateral action, since the United States is the sole judge and jury in a foreign nation's case (Milner 1990, 163–64).

Discussion

The institutional arrangements that characterize the regime of *conditional protectionism* emerged out of internationalists' opposition to *selective protectionism*, as I describe in chapter 4. To end congressional dominance over unilateral protectionist measures, business internationalists and supporters in the administration advocated the strengthening of administrative tools for granting relief. In this chapter I showed that the new set of institutional opportunities and constraints offered by the modified trade remedy laws successfully transformed the political strategies of domestic industries. The steel industry, along with many other industries, was persuaded by the administration not to seek congressional legislation and to instead file petitions for remedial trade action under the escape-clause, countervailing duty, and antidumping provisions.

The increased use of the trade remedy laws transformed U.S. trade practices in significant ways. The relocation of authority from Congress to the administration meant a shift in the location of decision making away from where protectionists had access and a high degree of influence. While protectionist interest groups maintained their influence in Congress, this was no longer the main locus of decision making. Restrictive legislation, which had been central to the regime of selective protectionism, was rarely utilized. Congress, instead, took upon itself the amending of unfair-trade laws and regulations, as well as some of the institutional arrangements themselves, to increase protectionists' chances for positive determinations, and to otherwise supervise the administration's activity.

In its turn, the administration's response to heightened protectionist sentiments focused on preventing dumped and illegally subsidized imports into the U.S. market and on penalizing discrimination against U.S. exporters. These measures constituted a step in the direction of liberal trade, for they allowed state officials to address protectionist pressures in a manner that did not interfere with the general process of trade liberalization. I showed that the decisions of several successive administrations were shaped less by social pressures and more by the orientation already inscribed in the executive, itself based on structural constraints and bureaucratic responsibilities. Consequently, there was a significant variation across administrative measures: where discretion to reject positive determination was granted—to the president in escape-clause and Section 301 cases, and to the secretary of treasury in CVD cases—decisions were only loosely based on legal obligations and were often informed by the bureaucratic responsibilities of the various agencies taking part in the deliberations and the hierarchical distribution of authority among them. Consequently, macroeconomic and foreign policy considerations prevailed, leading to an internationalist bias restrained only by rare threats on the part of Congress to override a specific decision. In contrast, when an administration had no discretion and decisions were left to quasi-judicial bodies, a major determinant of the outcome was the legal text itself. In the struggle over legal wording, Congress could water-down provisions agreed on by GATT member-states but did not reject international agreements altogether. The rate of success in "legalized" cases was therefore higher than in the "discretionary" ones.

The war over words between the GATT and Congress suggests that negotiations at the international level began having an increased influence on domestic policymaking—largely thanks to the "fast track" procedure. Once the United States launched negotiations over nontariff barriers to trade, international obligations had the potential of more effectively dictating U.S. domestic policy. During the regime of conditional protectionism, however, this has proven a relatively empty threat. Congress has often managed to modify the most objectionable concessions U.S. negotiators had made.

In short, the new institutional arrangements weakened the situational position of protectionists and strengthened the relative influence of state actors so that, in spite of protectionists' adaptive political strategies that transformed some limitations into opportunities, trade policies were ultimately internationally oriented. The shift in the 1970s, like the shift in the 1930s, was *not* a shift in the substantive orientation of the state as a whole. Congress maintained its protectionist reservations, as did some state officials. Rather, globalizing policies were possible because of institutional transformations that shifted authority to the more "internationalized" segments of the state.

The evidence offered in this chapter challenges historical institutionalists' contention that institutions rarely meet initial expectations and plans—even historical institutionalists who agree that institutions originate in political action deny that the moment of institutional making has an enduring impact on the nature of the institutions in later periods (Thelen 1999, 383–84; Thelen 2003; Mahoney 2000; see also Rothstein 1992; Pierson 2000a, 483). It also challenges rational choice institutionalists, who often analyze institutional design in a way devoid of power relations and struggles, and therefore assume that the outcome is functional and beneficial for the participating actors (Shepsle 1989; Koremenos, Lipson, and Snidal 2001; Rosendorff and Milner 2001). Instead, *pace* historical institutionalism, the period between 1974 and 1994 demonstrates that the outcomes of institutional transformations may be what the creative agents expected: thanks to the new institutional arrangements, protectionist measures, when taken, did not threaten the emerging project of globalization. *Pace* rational choice institutionalism, these outcomes have hardly reflected a mutually beneficial arrangement. Instead, the new institutions allowed a biased distribution of benefits in favor of the internationalists and at the expense of protectionist interests. Finally, unforeseen developments should not be attributed to a lack of foresight on the part of the designers or to an independent evolution of the institutions (Rothstein 1992, 52; Pierson 2000a, 483). Rather, it was the result of *ongoing* political struggles. Protectionists managed to somewhat counterbalance the trade-liberalizing trend by constantly modifying their political strategies in a way that allowed them to improve their position within the institutional context. The analysis here makes a strong case for how "adaptive politics" occasionally allows a modified redistribution of benefits within a given institutional setting and may even lead to a change of the institutions themselves (Thelen and Steinmo 1992; Thelen 2004). Still, being "adaptive," it could never seriously undermine the globalizing project advanced by the institutions in place.

The regime of conditional protectionism lasted until 1994. It was then itself challenged and replaced with a new regime, which I call *legalized multilateralism*. This is the subject of the next chapter.

CHAPTER SIX

LEGALIZED MULTILATERALISM, 1994–2004

The process of trade liberalization in the United States is a story of political struggles and institutional shifts, both at the domestic *and* the international levels. Until the 1990s, the more challenging site of struggle for U.S. protectionist industries was at the domestic level. While internationalists had the upper hand, protectionists did gain some important concessions, and they could trust the U.S. administration to successfully secure those concessions in the international negotiations. The ability of the United States to impose protectionist exceptions on others stemmed from its economic position: the size of its market made access to the United States valuable enough for other countries to accept such limits. In chapter 3, I showed that the institutional arrangements of GATT reproduced this inequality, allowing the United States to exercise its economic and extra-economic resources to achieve biased trade agreements. Hence, the institutional arrangements of GATT largely worked to the advantage of the United States. Still, by the 1970s, U.S. negotiators in the multilateral trade negotiations pushed for greater legalization (Hudec 1993). Their attempts failed in the Tokyo Round but succeeded in the Uruguay Round, which was signed in 1994.[1] In addition to

---

[1] The Uruguay Round was launched in 1986 and concluded on December 15, 1993. The Uruguay Round Agreements were subsequently signed on April 15, 1994, in Marrakesh, Morocco, by 108 countries.

finally creating a formal international organization—the World Trade Organization—member-states also agreed to greatly strengthen the dispute settlement mechanisms that governed trade disputes. Why the push for legalization? Did it affect the globalization project? Particularly, did it affect the political opportunities of protectionist industries?

In this chapter I argue that legalization was a desired component considered necessary for a new phase of multilateral trade liberalization. Since the establishment of the GATT, in 1947, the scope of issues governed by the international trade agreements gradually widened—moving from tariffs to nontariff barriers (NTBs) to trade. In the Uruguay Round, U.S. negotiators wanted the GATT to also include market access for services and investment and to regulate intellectual property rights. Compared to tariff reduction, which was relatively easy to implement, agreements covering NTBs often required complicated domestic legislation and implementation. One major complaint against the GATT was its inability to ensure effective implementation of the international trade agreements. Businesses that supported the introduction of services, investment, and intellectual property to the legal framework of GATT were rightly concerned that without a more effective enforcement mechanism many countries would fail to implement the new agreements. The GATT dispute settlement mechanisms were not up to the task. The legalization of the WTO was designed to solve this problem.

Scholars who argue that the legalization of disputes maintained, or even enhanced, U.S. power, are therefore correct: thanks to the strengthened procedures, U.S. internationalists now had better control over domestic legislation and economic practices in other countries, and they gained some important victories that improved their access to foreign markets (Raghavan 2000; Garrett and Smith 2002; Iida 2004). However, such accounts often ignore the heavy price paid by U.S. protectionists. For the legalization of the WTO amounted to a delegation of authority from the U.S. administration to the WTO. As a result, many decisions that the United States could until then make unilaterally were now supervised at the international level. Further, legalization weakened the control of member-states over the decisions made. Rather, panelists were now the ultimate judges. Consequently, U.S. ability to determine the content of decisions was greatly compromised. Finally, the enhanced legalization also led to greater compliance at home. In short, the new dispute settlement mechanisms constrained the ability of the U.S. government to apply controversial protectionist practices at home, as other member-states successfully challenged U.S. trade policies that violated international obligations. These changes amount to a shift from the regime of conditional protectionism to a new regime that I call *legalized multilateralism*. Globalization has finally gone global.

In this chapter I provide a detailed description of the organizational transformation from the GATT to the more formalized and legally effective WTO, which brought trade liberalization to a third phase in the United States. I first analyze the conditions that permitted an international agreement on strengthened dispute settlement procedures and Congress's ratification of the new procedures. I then review the major features of the new dispute settlement mechanisms, as they affected the U.S. position. I show that since 1994, member-states have relied heavily on the adjudication procedures to challenge alleged violations by the United States; that decisions of the WTO panels have consistently affirmed principles and imposed practices of free trade, even when the United States was the respondent; and that WTO dispute settlement proceedings have led to further liberalization of U.S. trade practices and laws. I substantiate these claims by describing the fate of protectionist measures of both selective and conditional kinds that were common in the United States—global import quotas, voluntary restraint agreements, unfair-trade laws, and Section 301. In addition, I describe the fate of politically sensitive "social protectionist" laws, which have become a new major cause for mobilization. I show that the new dispute procedures led to the further curbing of those protectionist practices. While quite effectively curbing the demands of traditional protectionists, the regime of *legalized multilateralism* also saw the rise of new political actors, particularly labor and environmental interests, who developed new strategies in response to the now international opportunity structures. I describe how the new institutional environment, combined with new political strategies, again altered Congress's role in governing international trade relations. In the last section I offer an analytical explanation as to how the legalization of the WTO, by creating new relations of influence, made this new stage of trade liberalization possible.

The Uruguay Round: The "New Issues"

Facing a mounting trade deficit prompted by a strong dollar, the Reagan administration initiated a new round of multilateral trade negotiations, which was launched in 1986.[2] The administration had one major purpose in

---

[2] See also chapter 5 for the economic conditions at that time.

initiating the talks: introducing the so-called "new issues" into the regulatory umbrella of the GATT. These new issues included trade in services, foreign investment, and intellectual property rights. The goal was to resolve the trade deficit problem by providing expansion opportunities to those U.S. sectors that had the potential of being internationally competitive but that were restrained by domestic regulations and other barriers imposed by other countries (Secchi 1997, 65).[3]

The service sector—including banking and finance, transportation, construction, telecommunications, management consulting, advertising, education, and entertainment—was a particularly promising endeavor. In contrast to the trade deficit in goods, which kept growing (in 1982, the United States suffered a $35 million trade deficit), the service industries had a positive trade balance (in 1982, it amounted to $15.6 million).[4] In an effort to convince them to support the new round and the inclusion of the "new issues" to the negotiations, members of Congress were told that U.S.-based service companies clearly had the competitive edge to take advantage of expansion opportunities abroad.[5] Services, however, were tightly regulated in many countries, and only an inclusion of services in the international trading system would allow "liberalization" of the kind that had been negotiated for manufactured goods (Preeg 1995, 37). As David R. MacDonald, Deputy USTR, reasoned:

> We see great potential growth opportunities for U.S. exporters of services, many of which represent the most dynamic sectors of our economy. However, having a competitive product or even the best product on the market is not enough. The United States will not be able to reach its full export potential unless we are able to deal effectively with a wide range of barriers that confront many of our service industries. . . . [T]he most serious barriers are of an international

---

[3] Investment, services, and intellectual property rights have played an important role also in bilateral and regional negotiations during that period. An agreement with Mexico has been strongly advocated by companies like American Express and Kodak (Mayer 1998, 41–42, 125), and the agenda for NAFTA included eliminating barriers to trade for all goods and services, eliminating barriers to investment and providing greater security for investors, and establishing new rules for intellectual property (Mayer 1998, 109).

[4] U.S. Department of Commerce, Bureau of Economic Analysis, National Income and Product Accounts Tables, Table 4.2.5, Exports and Imports of Goods and Services by Type of Product.

[5] Statement of David R. MacDonald, Deputy USTR, U.S. Congress. May 24, 1982, Hearings before the House Committee on Ways and Means, *Trade in Services and Trade in High Technology Products*, 14.

nature and it is in international negotiations that solutions will have to be found.[6]

The administration supported negotiations over foreign investment for similar reasons. Here, too, American companies had a clear competitive advantage:

> First and foremost, financial services are an area of enormous importance to the United States economy. Our financial companies accounted for over 7 percent of GDP in 1993—more than $450 billion in revenues. U.S. firms are global leaders in scores of financial industries with enormous worldwide potential—mutual fund management, asset securitization, investment banking—to cite but a few. We have a very strong competitive advantage in this burgeoning area.[7]

And here, too, possibilities for further expansion have often been blocked by "host" governments. As C. Fred Bergsten, then a senior associate at the Carnegie Endowment for International Peace, explained to members of Congress: "The basic problem is that host countries to foreign direct investment . . . are increasingly active in manipulating the investment flows to promote their national economic, social, and political interests."[8] The solution, here as in the case of services, was by reaching a multilateral agreement.

> We cannot do it unilaterally. The only effective way is to negotiate a new international GATT for investment which would seek to keep Governments' hands off the international investment process, the same way that the GATT itself has sought . . . to keep Governments' hands off international trade flows.[9]

The last issue, intellectual property rights (IPR), was a response to U.S. industries' concern about the growing costs of inadequate protection for

---

[6] Statement of David R. MacDonald, Deputy USTR, U.S. Congress. May 24, 1982, Hearings before the House Committee on Ways and Means, *Trade in Services and Trade in High Technology Products*, 14.

[7] Testimony of Robert E. Rubin, Secretary of the Treasury, U.S. Congress, June 8, 1995, Hearings before the Senate Committee on Banking, Housing, and Urban Affairs, *Financial Services Negotiations*.

[8] Statement of C. Fred Bergsten, U.S. Congress, July 30, 1981, Hearings before the Senate Committee on Foreign Relations, *U.S. Policy Toward International Investment*, 2.

[9] Statement of C. Fred Bergsten, U.S. Congress, July 30, 1981, Hearings before the Senate Committee on Foreign Relations, *U.S. Policy Toward International Investment*, 6–7.

patents, trademarks, copyrighted material, and other IPR, particularly in newly industrialized Asian countries. The computer, pharmaceutical, motion picture, publishing, and apparel industries all claimed to be seriously affected. The U.S. International Trade Commission, based on industry surveys, estimated the annual loss to U.S. industry at $40 billion (Preeg 1995, 63). The administration hence concluded that "there [was] a need for vigorous efforts to increase the level of domestic and international protection."[10]

Achieving the consent of Congress, however, was only the first stage in a very long process. In the Uruguay Round negotiations, a bloc of Third World countries, led by India and Brazil, strongly resisted inclusion of the new issues, in particular the issue of investment.[11] They also objected to any negotiations on services, though they were willing to consider negotiations on a dual track basis, so that retaliation in regard to services could not affect exports of manufactured goods.[12] They probably had the strongest case against the introduction of IPR into the GATT, as intellectual property

---

[10] Statement of Harvey E. Bale, Jr., Assistant USTR for Trade Policy and Analysis, U.S. Congress, July 31, 1986, Hearings before the Senate Committee on Foreign Affairs, *Status of Intellectual Property Protection.*

[11] USTR Clayton Yeutter's recounting to Congress of an exchange he had with the Argentinean representative, who opposed the inclusion of the new issues, shows the dismissive attitude developing countries have often suffered in diplomatic negotiations:

I responded by saying that the last time I looked, Latin America had some major debts. We had been in Punta del Este at that time for about 4 days, and I hadn't had time to read any newspapers, but I assumed there might still be a few debts to pay. If so, it seemed to me that Latin America had a need to shift some of its financing burden from the debt side to the equity side, the equity side meant investment. Unless all of that investment could be generated within Latin America, I suspected there was a need for some foreign investment in that part of the world, too, and so, negotiations in the GATT to improve the investment climate would be in order. And then I said perhaps I have missed what occurred in the last 4 days, and maybe all of Latin America's debts have been paid, all of Latin America is now rich and doesn't need foreign investment any more. But if that is really not the situation, maybe we ought to sit down and have a negotiation.

Statement of Clayton Yeutter, USTR. September 25, 1986, Hearings before the House Committee on Ways and Means, *Results of the GATT Ministerial Meeting held in Punta Del Este, Uruguay,* 8.

[12] Statement of Clayton Yeutter, U.S.TR. Sept. 25, 1986. Hearings before the House Committee on Ways and Means, *Results of the GATT Ministerial Meeting held in Punta Del Este, Uruguay,* 6. There were also, of course, disputes among the major trading partners. The EC, for example, insisted on its right to maintain its restrictions on imports of foreign television programs under a "cultural exclusion" that would prevent it from having to make binding commitments to weaken or remove European local content restrictions for television and motion pictures (*Inside U.S. Trade,* 5/21/1993).

protection could itself be considered a barrier to trade. In all three cases, India and Brazil were forced to compromise when the United States threatened to call off the entire round if these particular issues were not included (Dryden 1995, 334; Dunkley 2000, 46). By threatening to employ unilateral means, the United States even prevailed in the intellectual property rights discussions. In the midst of the negotiations, the U.S. administration aggressively pursued strengthened protection for IPR through the enhanced Special 301 provision of the 1988 Omnibus Trade Act (see chapter 5). In particular, retaliatory import restrictions were levied against Brazil, and threatened against India and China (Preeg 1995, 67). In the end, therefore, the United States prevailed, and the Uruguay Round Agreements included an Agreement on Trade in Services (GATS), an Agreement on Trade-Related Investment Measures (TRIMs), and an Agreement on Trade-Related Intellectual Property Rights (TRIPs).

But the introduction of the new issues came with a cost. In return for the significant commitments taken on by developing countries, U.S. negotiators promised to open up the U.S. market in areas of particular export interest to developing countries, including agriculture and textiles. Developed countries agreed to "tariffy" agricultural quotas, and then to cut those tariffs and reduce other market access restrictions to agricultural imports (Finger and Nogues 2002). They also agreed to abolish the Multi-Fiber Agreement governing trade in textiles and clothing since 1974, so that textiles and clothing would be integrated into the GATT. The Uruguay Round Agreements included other provisions that had negative implications for American protectionists. In the Agreement on Safeguards, for example, developed countries agreed to prohibit the use of Voluntary Restraint Agreements. Existing VRAs were to be phased out within four years, with each country allowed only one "grandfathered" exception. Given the widespread use of these practices in the United States—the imports of textile, apparel, steel, and other sectors were largely governed by such bilateral agreements—this represented a significant narrowing of domestic industries' range of possible actions in their attempts to restrict imports. Many antidumping and countervailing duty cases, in particular, were resolved by reaching "voluntary" agreements with the countries involved. At the same time, of course, the Uruguay Round Agreements maintained a skewed flexibility, still very much in favor of American interests. Changes in unfair-trade provisions, for example, were quite limited, and U.S. negotiators managed to make an exception to the antidumping provisions, so that the standard-of-review of the judicial panels, which did not require deference to national laws, would not apply to them (see below).

The Uruguay Round: The Dispute Settlement Understanding

At the international realm, dispute settlement mechanisms provide procedures through which states can resolve their disputes under the auspices of an international organization by filing a petition to a judicial body. GATT dispute mechanisms, however, had become throughout the years disturbingly ineffective (Hudec 1975; Hudec 1993; Jackson 2000). While interstate disputes were initially adjudicated by the member-states themselves, since 1955 disputes were referred to a panel of three to five experts acting on their own capacity rather than as representatives of states (Jackson 2000, 181). A final report issued by the panel was then submitted to the GATT Council (composed of all member-states) for approval. But effective legalization was constrained by the principle of consensual decision-making, which "gave defendants the ability to drag their feet at every stage of the process" (Hudec 1993, 54). The most persistent problem of delay had been refusals to agree to create a panel to investigate the complaint. Problems also arose in the process following formal creation of the panel. There were deadlocks over terms of reference, over choosing panelists, and over defining procedures. Most disturbingly, there were the increasingly common cases of governments blocking the adoption of the report in the council (Hudec 1993, 54). Finally, there was a potential problem of enforcement even when a country did not block the ruling against it: while the GATT could authorize the contracting parties to suspend concessions, this happened only in one case, and the country in question, the Netherlands, did not act on that authorization (Jackson 2000, 182). Member-states relied, instead, on the more vulnerable force of organized normative pressure (Hudec 1975, 175). While historically member-states showed a very high level of compliance with negative rulings, the 1980s brought with it a decrease in that rate (Hudec 1993; Hudec 1999).

Of course, the United States, too, readily used the weakness of the procedures to its advantage. Like other states, the United States often blocked the creation of panels and blocked the adoption of panel reports—it was the United States that set the precedent of blocking a panel report in the *DISC case*, in which a panel ruled against U.S. tax practices. Worse, the United States used its privileged position to intimidate countries into withdrawing their challenges and showed lower levels of compliance than most·other countries (Hudec 1993, 305). Hence, while arguing that the system as a whole was much more effective than the credit it usually received, Hudec offers U.S. behavior as the exception to this general rule (Hudec 1993, chap. 11).

In spite of the ability of the United States to exploit the deficiencies of the system, the U.S. government has insisted on the need to strengthen these dispute settlement procedures (Hudec 1993). During the Tokyo Round, U.S. negotiators managed to strengthen the dispute settlement procedures covering the agreements that regulated nontariff barriers to trade. The new rules contained language that appeared to create an automatic right to have panels appointed without the consent of the defendant. Due to the EC insistence, however, the reforms of the basic GATT article governing dispute procedures (Article XXIII) were much more restrained (Hudec 1993, 55–56). While taking the organization in the direction of greater legalization (Hudec 1999, 4), these changes hardly achieved radical improvements. In fact, events in the early 1980s had quite disastrous effects to the reputation of the system. Five complaints initiated by the United States against the EC, in particular, have "made it clear that the Tokyo Round dispute settlement reforms had been much oversold" (Hudec 1993, 130). The delays and obstructions during the procedures, the poor quality of the rulings, and the refusal of the EC to implement the decisions against it cost the GATT dearly in its reputation.

In the Uruguay Round, U.S. negotiators again insisted on the need to strengthen the dispute settlement procedures. At stake now was also the implementation of the "new issues." Agreements on services, foreign investment, and intellectual property rights required the signatory governments to make substantive, and politically sensitive, changes in their domestic legislation and economic practices. While diplomatic negotiations enabled the United States to impose these rules on other countries, they were useless in ensuring implementation. Implementation could have possibly been enforced by unilateral means—Section 301 was designed exactly for this purpose—but it so clearly violated GATT rules that the U.S. administration hesitated before using it to challenge the EC and at least in one case chose not to retaliate in the fear that the affected country, India, would challenge the retaliation in GATT (see chapter 5). Hence, a more reliable system of *international* trading disciplines and procedures was the only potentially effective solution (Rosenthal and Vermylen 2000).

The U.S. proposal to strengthen the dispute settlement mechanisms initially met with strong resistance from other member-states. The EC and Japan, in particular, favored a more conciliatory process of negotiations and resented the American rule-oriented inclination.[13] But the EC and

[13] Peter Kuijper, Director of the WTO Legal Affairs Division, interview with the author, July 2001. See Hudec (1980) for a review of the tension between the legalistic and nonlegalistic orientation of the GATT; see also Preeg 1995, 35, 77–78.

Japan reconsidered their opposition when the U.S. Congress adopted the extended version of Section 301, providing a stronger unilateral alternative to the multilateral adjudication of alleged unfair trading practices of others (see chapter 5). The implicit message was that if the United States was dissatisfied with international dispute resolution mechanisms, it would act unilaterally. A greatly strengthened and broadened GATT dispute settlement procedure was now seen by other countries as a necessary means to induce the United States to restrain its unilateral approach (Hudec 1993, 230–31; Hudec 1999, 13; Preeg 1995, 77–78, 103).[14]

The Understanding on Rules and Procedures Governing the Settlement of Disputes (also known as the Dispute Settlement Understanding or DSU) eliminated the veto power that parties had enjoyed. Instead of requiring a consensus decision of the council for each step of the process—a consensus that could be blocked by the respondent—all steps were now to be taken automatically, subjected only to a consensus decision *not* to do so. Panels could be appointed to hear a complaint without the defendant's consent. Panel rulings could be given legal effect by the council without the losing party's consent. If a ruling of violation was not complied with, retaliation could be ordered, again without the defendant's consent. Retaliation outside the WTO was no longer acceptable (Hudec 1993, 194). The result was that panel reports came into force as a matter of international law in virtually every case (Jackson 2000, 185). The quid pro quo was an appellate process: both parties had the right to appeal to a panel of three experts drawn from a permanent roster of seven. Although the agreement still provided for consultations prior to the establishment of a panel, the core of the procedure was now unquestionably judicial. According to the DSU standard-of-review, moreover, a panel had the authority to determine for itself the facts and the law of the case, and was not required to defer to an administering authority's assessment of the facts or interpretation of the covered agreements (Jackson 2000).

The Dispute Settlement Understanding was the most significant of various other organizational changes that accompanied the decision to finally establish, almost fifty years after the failed attempt of the ITO, a formal

---

[14] Neoliberal institutionalists argue that states support the legalization of interstate agreements because of the expectation that legalization would bring greater cooperative gains by resolving collective action problems more efficiently (Abbot and Snidal 2001). The Uruguay Round negotiations show how problematic this rationalist perception can be, for while it is correct to read EC and Japan's support of a strengthened dispute mechanisms as based on an expectation of greater cooperative gains, these were considered gains only in light of the alternative of unilateral American action.

organization to govern international trade relations—the World Trade Organization.

The Uruguay Round Agreements in Congress

The agreements concluded in the Uruguay Round had to be ratified by the U.S. Congress. The implementing legislation, the Uruguay Round Agreements Act (URAA) of 1994, was strongly endorsed by the most politically influential business groups—the Business Roundtable, the National Association of Manufacturers (NAM), and the U.S. Chamber of Commerce. Together, they established a powerful coalition called Alliance for GATT Now that cooperated closely with the Clinton administration (Rupert 2000, chap. 3). The alliance's chairman was Jerry R. Junkins, the CEO of Texas Instruments, one of the largest U.S. electronics companies. Companies that took a leading lobbying role included Boeing (aerospace), Monsanto (agricultural biotechnology), and Warner Lambert (pharmaceutical). Other active companies included Caterpillar (construction, mining, and forestry machinery), General Electric (electronics), Abbot Laboratories (pharmaceutical), and American Express (financial services). Supporting associations included the Pharmaceutical Research and Manufacturers of America and the Motion Picture Association. Clearly, the "new issues" brought new and powerful firms into the GATT-oriented constituency (Drake and Nicolaidis 1992) and their contribution to the lobbying efforts helped to guarantee congressional support.

Even the "old guardians" of protectionism—including the textile, steel, and semiconductor industries—reluctantly supported the bill, after being coaxed by the administration (see more below). There were other actors and groups, however, who strongly opposed the Uruguay Round Agreements, in particular the Dispute Settlement Understanding. Those included a coalition of labor, environmental, and consumer-protection activists led by Ralph Nader's Public Citizen; business associations, like the U.S. Business & Industrial Council; and conservative public figures such as Newt Gingrich, Ross Perot, Jesse Helms, and Pat Buchanan. A year earlier, these same forces almost led to the demise of NAFTA (Mayer 1998). Now they warned that the WTO would undermine U.S. sovereignty and threaten domestic laws. The DSU, they argued, would turn the WTO into a Supreme Court of trade, controlled by faceless bureaucrats in Geneva making decisions directly affecting American policy in virtual secrecy (*Economist*, 5/7/1994, 29; *Wall Street Journal*, 4/29/1994). However, this opposition was too weak to make a real impact, and the new DSU was included in the URAA of 1994 practically untouched, other than adding a process of domestic review of WTO rulings.[15]

During these political battles in Congress, U.S. administration officials explained, time and again, why it was in the U.S. national interest to support more effective legal procedures. They insisted that the stronger dispute settlement mechanisms would increase the disciplinary measures available against other countries, thus allowing U.S. products and services better access to foreign markets. They also insisted that it would *not* have the same effect on the trade laws and practices of the United States. They repeatedly asserted that the DSU was not a threat to American sovereignty and that the WTO would have no power to modify U.S. law, since no substantive changes in WTO rules could apply to the United States without congressional approval (*Wall Street Journal*, 4/29/1994). In his testimony before the House Ways and Means Committee, United States Trade Representative Mickey Kantor expressed it most clearly:

> The dispute settlement understanding creates more effective dispute settlement processes. . . . We will benefit from this system because we bring more cases than any other country under the dispute settlement mechanism of the GATT. We've won 80 percent of those cases, Mr. Chairman, and we were frequently frustrated . . . as other countries used their ability to block under the GATT, to inhibit the ability of the U.S. to take these rulings and to force countries to change their policies which in effect kept U.S. products out of their markets. While the new system includes improvement, the system does not dictate changes in U.S. law. Only Congress and the executive branch decide whether to implement panel recommendations and how to implement them. The WTO agreement, the dispute settlement understanding and panel reports cannot change U.S. law.[16]

[15] A panel of five federal judges was to review all rulings by the dispute-resolution panels that rule against the United States and decide, for each such ruling, whether the WTO had "exceeded its authority" or whether panelists had conflicts of interest that had created a biased panel decision. Three such rulings within a five-year period would trigger a vote in Congress on withdrawing from the WTO, and the president could either approve or veto that resolution. This was a concession given by the administration to Robert Dole, the Republican Senate leader, whose support of the URAA was pivotal and who sought assurances that WTO panels would not infringe on American sovereignty by issuing arbitrary rulings against U.S. laws (*Washington Post*, 11/24/1994).

[16] Testimony of Michael Kantor, U.S. Congress, June 10, 1994, Hearings before the House Committee on Ways and Means, *World Trade Organization*.

These sentiments were echoed by supportive think tanks and business associations. Economic analysts at the American Enterprise Institute (AEI), for example, applauded the agreement for bringing "the rule of law" to international trade, and the Heritage Foundation circulated a paper that declared that the WTO would "expand the sovereignty of American citizens" by reducing trade restrictions on the free choices available to businessmen and consumers (*National Review,* 6/13/1994). In spite of such assurances, the impact of the DSU on U.S. domestic laws soon became apparent.

The Dispute Settlement Understanding: General Review

An analysis of DSU cases initiated between January 1995 and December 2004 that involve the United States as a respondent reveals three important characteristics.[17]

First, member-states challenge alleged U.S. violations under the WTO dispute settlement mechanisms far more frequently than they did under the old GATT system. Between 1948 and 1989, a total of 52 cases (Hudec defines "cases" as the number of government measures that have been made the target of one or more legal "complaints" [Hudec 1999, 155]) were filed against the United States, an average of 1.2 per year (Hudec 1993, 297).[18] Between 1995 and 2004, in contrast, the United States was the respondent in 74 cases (88 complaints), an average of 7.4 per year.

Of course, this dramatic increase in complaints applied also to cases not involving the United States. Between 1948 and 1989, a total of 236 complaints were filed, an average of fewer than 6 per year (Reinhardt 1996). Between 1995 and 2004, in contrast, a total of 324 complaints were filed, an average of more than 32 per year.[19] Although the contrast is not as extreme

[17] Of the 324 cases that were initiated between 1995 and 2004, I here analyze only those that involved the United States, mostly as a respondent (at times, I look at the cases of the United States as a plaintiff, as a point for comparison). The United States was the respondent in 88 complaints, and the complainant in 80 cases. Data on GATT dispute settlement is based on Hudec 1993; Reinhardt 1996. Data on the WTO dispute settlement is based mostly on information provided by the WTO website http://www.wto.org/english/tratop_e/dispu_e/dispu_e.htm, complemented by more comprehensive reviews in GAO June 2000, August 2000, July 2003; USTR annual report 2004; Destler 2005.

[18] I do not calculate here the cases between 1989 and 1994 because in 1989 the principles of the new dispute mechanisms were already agreed on, so states' behavior was influenced by the new system as much as the old one (Hudec 1993).

[19] The number of complaints has decreased since the late 1990s, but it is still too early to know whether this is an act of self-restraint in the context of the Doha Round negotiations or a more permanent development.

if we differentiate the GATT era into separate periods—as the number of complaints gradually increased—it remains very clear that 1994 was a turning point in the popularity of legal disputes (Hudec 1993; Hudec 1999, 16).

The rise in the number of disputes was partly due to the increase in WTO's jurisdiction. In the Uruguay Round, many existing agreements were tightened and numerous new ones were signed. In addition, a "single undertaking" principle obliged member-states to sign all of the agreements. The greater number of issues covered by international agreements also increased the scope of issues that were vulnerable to legal challenges (Hudec 1999; Busch and Reinhardt 2002). The increased number of disputes was also the result of growing confidence in the system (Hudec 1993, 290, 362; Petersmann 1994, 1205; Jackson 1998, 59–60; Busch and Reinhardt 2002, 462). The new procedures promised an effective handling of disputes and hence encouraged member-states to give the system a try. Once the first disputes were concluded successfully, the confidence in the system grew even more and the number of disputes rose accordingly.[20]

Second, WTO panelists consistently affirm principles and impose practices of free trade, even when the United States is the respondent. The rate of success under the DSU, as was also the case under the GATT, is exceptionally high. Holmes, Rollo, and Young (2003, 17) calculate that between 1995 and 2002, complainants won in 88 percent of cases that reached a final ruling.[21] Because petitioners always complain that the defendant *violated* GATT/WTO-governed trade liberalizing rules, this impressively high rate of success clearly reflects an orientation in favor of liberal principles. This "enduring pro-plaintiff bias" (Busch and Reinhardt 2002, 470) applied in affirming liberal commitments, as well as in narrowing GATT *exceptions* to trade liberalization, such as unfair-trade laws. Panels rarely ruled that a respondent's use of such exceptions had been legal. In the few cases in which exceptions have not been ruled as GATT-inconsistent, the panels rarely

[20] There is also, one might argue, "snowball" logic to judicial disputes that diplomatic negotiations do not have. In diplomatic negotiations, states may choose not to make demands from other countries because this would surely involve reciprocal concessions. For example, the United States may choose not to ask the EC to reduce its subsidies to Airbus so it doesn't have to offer concessions regarding Boeing. By contrast, in judicial proceedings, a party can demand that another party comply with international rules, with no direct impact on its own practices. Of course, often the challenged state retaliates in kind. This, at times, prevents the initial petition. At other times, however, it can cause an escalation that serves the project of trade liberalization in a way that restrained negotiations do not.

[21] Winning is measured as any case in which any of the respondent's rules were found to be inconsistent with the WTO on any of the counts (Holmes, Rollo, and Young 2003). According to Hudec's calculations (1993, 278), the rate of ruling in favor of the complainant under GATT was also very high—77 percent—although lower than under the WTO.

approved them as such. In a dispute involving computer equipment (DS62),[22] for example, the EC lost to the United States when the panel determined that the Uruguay Round Agreements had not explicitly covered the practices. In a case in which the United States lost an attempt to challenge Japanese trade practices (DS45), the ruling relied on lack of evidence, not on permitted exceptions. In cases involving a conflict between trade-related and non-trade-related issues, such as environmental laws, states trying to protect domestic legislation consistently lost (see below).

The rate of success was high even when the United States was the respondent, although lower than the general rate of success. Under the WTO, the United States lost 74 percent of the time. This was a much higher rate than before the dispute settlement procedures were strengthened—under the GATT, the United States lost in 61 percent of the cases that reached a final report (Hudec 1993, 303–4). Also, decisions against the United States did not occur more often when a rich country was the complainant, as would be reasonable to expect. Indeed, developed countries challenged the United States more often than developing countries: developed countries initiated forty-three of the total of seventy-four cases against the United States (58 percent), while developing countries initiated only twenty-nine of the cases (39 percent). Two cases were jointly initiated. Of the eighty-seven countries involved in cases against the United States, sixty were developed countries (69 percent) and only twenty-seven were developing countries (31 percent)(see also Hudec 1993, 295; Horn, Nordstrom, and Mavroidis 1999).[23] At the same time, developing countries that do take advantage of the system fare *better* than the average—while the U.S. total rate of loss is 74 percent, its rate of loss when the plaintiffs are developing countries is a high 86 percent. This higher rate of success of developing countries in challenging the United States probably reflects the fact that developed countries (in particular, the EC) initiate cases that are much more complicated (some

---

[22] DS numbers refer to the numbers given to the cases by the WTO. See http://www.wto.org/english/tratop_e/dispu_e/dispu_e.htm.

[23] Most active in challenging the United States were the EC (27 cases); Canada (12); Brazil (7); Japan, Mexico, and India (6 cases each); and Korea (5). Other countries that initiated cases were: Argentina, New Zealand, Australia (2 cases each); and Colombia, Chile, Pakistan, China, Switzerland, Norway, Venezuela, Costa Rica, Germany, Philippines, Italy, Thailand, and Antigua and Barbuda (1 case each). There is a gap in the level of activity of developed and developing countries also more generally. Leitner and Lester (2004, 181) calculate that, as of July 2003, developed countries initiated 60 percent of the cases and developing countries initiated 37 percent of the cases; 2 percent were initiated jointly by developed and developing countries. Developed countries were the defendants in 59 percent of the cases, and developing countries in 41 percent of the cases (see also Holmes, Rollo, and Young 2003, 21).

would say, speculative). Still, the data clearly shows that developing coun-tries do not fare less well than developed countries.

A look at the phase of early settlements reveals another interesting devel-opment. Hudec (1993) has convincingly argued that under GATT the bias in favor of the United States rested not in the formal rulings but in the ability of the United States to make countries withdraw their cases before a formal ruling, and without the United States offering any concessions in return. The United States, Hudec (1993, 303) concludes, "emerge[d] as the unruly defendant most difficult to bring to court." But this, too, has changed with the shift from the GATT to the WTO. Under the GATT, the United States managed to force "inaction" in 44 percent of the cases. Under the WTO, the rate of inaction went down to 35 percent. It should be noted that there is *no* difference here between developed and developing countries; the number of cases initiated by developing countries that the United States managed to "inact" is slightly *lower* than the general average: 32 percent. The only stage in which developing countries fare less well than average is early settlements; as Busch and Reinhardt's careful analysis shows (2003a; 2003c), this is the stage at which developing countries are most vulnerable to biased conces-sions. Compared to the 9.5 percent of early settlement, the United States set-tled with developing countries in 12 percent of the original complaints.

Finally, the WTO dispute settlement procedure led to a change in U.S. domestic practices and laws, always in the direction of greater liberalization. Although the administration declared that the WTO could not impose its determinations on the U.S. government, the high rate of compliance with these decisions contradicts this assertion.[24] The White House always chose to comply with the ruling and urged Congress to do the same when compli-ance necessitated congressional action. Here, again, we can see a difference in U.S. behavior under the GATT and the WTO. Under the GATT, the U.S. rate of compliance was 71 percent, but it was only 60 percent in the 1980s (Hudec 1993, 305).[25] In contrast, under the DSU, the U.S. rate of compliance

[24] See also Jackson 2000. A similar conclusion holds for other countries, including the EC and Japan. There were, of course, examples where countries preferred to suffer retaliation rather than comply. In one particularly contentious case, the panel and the Appellate Body both found that an EC ban on importation of hormone-treated beef was inconsistent with its international obligations. When the EC did not take sufficient steps to comply with the rul-ing, the WTO authorized the suspension of U.S. trade concessions to the EC in the amount of $116.8 million per year (DS26, DS39). For strategies to circumvent compliance, such as ex-ceeding the prescribed "reasonable" period of time, see Garrett and Smith 2002, 3.

[25] In his analysis, Hudec emphasizes the fact that even in the 1980s, when the number of "failures" (no compliance) increased, more than 80 percent of the cases were still being "suc-cessfully disposed of " (that is, complied with, either partially or fully)(Hudec 1999, 8). At the same time, Hudec makes painfully clear that this was not the case with the United States.

Table 6.1 Dispute settlement activity against the United States, 1948–2004

U.S. Respondent	No. of finalized cases	Settled	Inactive	U.S. won	U.S. lost	U.S. complied(*)
Pre-DSU 1948–1989	52	12%	44%	39%	61%	71% 60% in 1980
DSU 1995–2004	63	9.5% (6)	35% (22)	26% (9)	74% (26)	76% (21)
DSU Initiated by developing countries	25	12% (3)	32% (8)	14% (2)	86% (12)	100% (8)

(*) The numbers do not match because not all finalized cases have exhausted the schedule for compliance.

Sources: GATT cases from Hudec 1993, DSU cases complied by the author from the WTO website <http://www.wto.org/english/tratop_e/dispu_e/dispu_e.htm>, complemented by more comprehensive reviews in GAO June 2000, August 2000, July 2003; USTR annual report 2004; Destler 2005.

was 76 percent. And, again, developing countries fared better than developed ones. The rate of compliance of the United States in cases where developing countries were the plaintiffs is a surprising 100 percent. This suggests that compliance had little to do with who the complainant was and much to do with what compliance required (Busch and Reinhardt 2003b), and, as I show below, who in the U.S. government had the power to comply.

In short, at the same time that the DSU improved the ability of the United States to impose trade liberalizing rules on others, it also weakened the United States' ability to block challenges of others (see summary in table 6.1): it litigated many cases, lost in most of them, and complied with most of the negative rulings. This had an important effect on the ability of the U.S. government to maintain those "selective" and "conditional" types of protectionism declared illegal by the WTO panelists' interpretation of the international rules. Although U.S. administrations maintained their dominance in the diplomatic negotiations, and therefore preserved skewed flexibilities on behalf of their protectionist industries, they found their ability to disregard international obligations weakened by the strengthened legal procedures. The DSU accelerated the demise of policies protecting textiles and apparel, weakened the ability of domestic industries to use unfair-trade laws, and reversed the unilateral dimension of Section 301. Finally, the DSU also threatened social protectionist laws.

Textiles, Apparel, and the Demise of Selective Protectionism

The textile and apparel industries were exceptional in their ability to maintain, in spite of the general shift to conditional protectionism, benefits of the selective kind. Thanks to their ability to mobilize Congress in their favor, the textile and apparel industries could successfully pressure the administration to exclude them from the trade liberalizing process under the GATT, and the administration negotiated with other countries to renew the Multi-Fiber Agreement (MFA) in 1977, 1981, and 1986. When the textile and apparel industries found that the U.S. negotiators agreed, in the Ministerial Meeting launching the Uruguay Round, to phase out the MFA, they convinced Congress to initiate, in 1985 and again in 1987, import-quotas legislation (see chapter 5). But this time their influence in Congress was not a strong enough deterrent, and Reagan vetoed both laws.

Once the textile and apparel trade associations realized that they could not prevent the elimination of the MFA, they focused instead on negotiating the structure of the phasing-out process, so as to minimize its effects.[26] Following the demands of the U.S. textile and apparel industries, U.S. negotiators asked that the phasing-out process last no less than fifteen years and that the bilateral textile quotas of the MFA be converted to global quotas during the phasing-out period. But the trading partners opposed this plan, and U.S. negotiators had to soften those demands as well. The final agreement, the Agreement on Textiles and Clothing (ATC), set a ten-year transitional period by the end of which the textile and apparel sectors would be "fully integrated" into the GATT, meaning in particular that all quantitative restrictions inconsistent with the GATT would be abolished. United States negotiators succeeded in including conditions for the pace of integration favorable to the American industries. The transition was to happen gradually, in four stages (the day the agreement entered into force, and then after three, four, and three years), during each of which a certain percentage of the products covered by the MFA would no longer be subject to quotas (16 percent immediately, 17 percent after three years, 18 percent after four more years, and finally, 49 percent by the tenth year of the agreement). The quotas on the remaining products would be enlarged at progressively accelerated rates. Moreover, members were generally free to choose the categories they wanted to integrate, in effect allowing them to leave the most sensitive products for the latest phase. In spite of these concessions, the *Wall Street Journal* declared that one of the GATT winners had been U.S. retailers, and that the American textile industry had lost (*Wall Street Journal*, 12/1993).

Not long after it became evident that U.S. negotiators would give concessions to developing countries by liberalizing the textile and apparel sectors,

---

[26] Robert DuPree, ATMI, interview with the author, June 2001; Larry Martin, American Apparel and Footwear Association (AAFA), interview with the author, June 2001.

the American Apparel Manufacturers Association (AAMA) altered its political strategies. In 1990, the AAMA did not support a third attempt, initiated by the association representing textile manufacturers, to pass protectionist legislation.[27] Instead, the apparel sector focused on tightening U.S. country-of-origin rules, that is, the rules that determine the country of origin for apparel products. The AAMA wanted to ensure that apparel imports would be governed by strict rules of origin, so that trade preferences granted to importing countries would not be abused by third parties (for example, through transshipment). The shift was undoubtedly affected by new economic strategies, mainly offshore production in Latin American countries,[28] but was also heavily influenced by what the AAMA perceived as new constraints on its political leverage.

The American Textile Manufacturers Institute (ATMI) maintained its traditional stand longer, but it too eventually changed its political strategies.[29] Like the AAMA, ATMI also focused on country-of-origin rules. In order to give incentives to non-American apparel producers to use American textiles, ATMI wanted rules of origin that would allow imported apparel to be free of duty only if it had been produced from American textiles. ATMI eventually supported the Uruguay Round Agreements Act of 1994, after the administration had agreed to include in it a number of elements which the U.S. textile industry believed would help offset the damage done by the tariff cuts and the phasing-out of the MFA,[30] as well as a favorable amendment to the rules of origin.[31] Under previous U.S. Customs practices, country-of-

[27] Larry Martin, AAFA, interview with the author, June 2001.

[28] New economic strategies included mergers, brand managing, outsourcing, and contracting out. Most companies, however, also concentrated on moving production offshore. The ones who continued to produce domestically were those producing high-end clothing (whose production was not labor intensive) and unique products (Larry Martin, AAFA, interview with the author, June 2001).

[29] These strategic changes were long debated within ATMI. It was only in the 1990s that a group of moderates that "favored negotiation with the Administration rather than a hard nosed strategy" moved to the center of the association. The opposition, led by Roger Milliken, became a distinct minority, and Milliken was ultimately removed from the Board of Directors. Roger Milliken eventually left ATMI in 2000 (Cass Johnson, ATMI, interview with the author, June 2001).

[30] The URAA modified the impacts of the phasing out of the MFA by requiring that quotas on the least import-sensitive textile products be phased out first. In addition, the administration of the program was delegated to the Committee for the Implementation of Textile Agreements—an interagency government body that the textile industry believed had a good "understanding" of the U.S. industry. The legislation also provided for sanctions against those countries that did not open their markets sufficiently, and it extended the authority of the U.S. government to impose unilateral textile and apparel quotas (*Textile World*, 11/1994).

[31] Robert DuPree, ATMI, interview with the author, June 2001.

origin status could be claimed by countries in which minimal processing, such as cutting, was done. The new legislation required the country of origin of textile and apparel products to be the country in which an apparel product was actually assembled or a textile product was actually manufactured. These new rules of origin provided further benefits for producers in Mexico, where producers were more likely to buy fabric from U.S. manufacturers and where U.S. textile companies already owned textile and apparel companies (*Wall Street Journal*, 9/30/1994). Rules-of-origin provisions were also at the heart of ATMI's support of NAFTA,[32] and continued to be the primary concern of the apparel and textile industries in the debates regarding the Caribbean Basin Initiative (CBI) and trade relations with China.[33]

In short, the textile and apparel industries in the United States maximized their leverage within the contours of the WTO agreement by forcing concessions on the administration in its drafting of the URAA and by modifying provisions regarding country-of-origin rules. They could not, however, prevent the eventual phasing out of quotas, and the focus on the rules of origin symbolized, in effect, a dramatic political defeat on the part of the domestic textile and apparel industries. Moreover, even this more limited strategy was somewhat curbed due to challenges from other countries, which used for this purpose the new Dispute Settlement Understanding.

Modifications by the United States to rules of origin provisions made in the URAA of 1994 and the Trade and Development Act of 2000 were challenged in two cases initiated by the EC (DS85, DS151). The Europeans complained that the provisions adversely affected their textile exports to the United States, since they were no longer recognized in the United States as being of European origin, and thus lost the quota-free access to the U.S. market that they had previously enjoyed. In both cases, in order to avoid a negative decision the United States struck a deal with the EC, essentially making certain exemptions of textile products from the applicability of the modified U.S. rules. In a third case challenging the same provision, this time initiated by India (DS243), the panel and the Appellate Body both ruled in favor of the United States. Of four other textile and apparel cases,

---

[32] The Bush administration agreed to a "triple transformation test": to benefit from NAFTA's provisions, apparel would have to be made in North America from North American cloth that had been produced from North American fiber.

[33] The debate surrounding the CBI concerned whether duty-free products needed to contain fabric made in the United States, as demanded by ATMI, or also regional fabric, as agreed by AAMA. As for China, ATMI was against the Permanent Normal Trade Relations (PNTR) and the accession of China to the WTO, arguing against Chinese "illegal transshipment" practices. AAMA, in contrast, supported both (Robert DuPree, ATMI, interview with the author, June 2001; Destler 1995, 227).

not related to rules of origin, the United States resolved one dispute without a ruling,[34] and lost in three. In the first case, initiated by Costa Rica, the panel ruled against quantitative restrictions the United States imposed on underwear (DS24). Since the contested measure had expired a month before the report was adopted by the Dispute Settlement Body, in March 1997, there was no need for compliance. In the second case, initiated by India, the panel ruled against U.S. safeguards on wool shirts (DS33). The United States had lifted the measure against imports from India in December 1996, before the issuance of the final report of the panel was issued. In the third case, initiated by Pakistan, the panel found that transitional safeguard on cotton yarn was not justified under the ATC (DS192), and the United States eliminated the limit on those imports from Pakistan.

In short, due to the Uruguay Round Agreements, the textile and apparel industries finally had to abandon the Multi-Fiber Agreement, and rely instead on less effective strategies, such as country-of-origin rules. Even those rules, however, were often challenged under the DSU. The industries' attempt to rely on exceptions allowed by the ATC was also unsuccessful. These outcomes suggest the final erosion of selective protectionism. The political influence of these industries over Congress lost some of its effectiveness once trade decisions were made by the administration and, even more so, once the administration agreed to (re)incorporate the industry negotiations into the GATT/WTO. The ability of the administration to block congressional action—reflected in the vetoing of import quotas and in the negotiations during the Uruguay Round—forced the industry to devise new economic and political strategies. It still relied on Congress to change the wording of the rules of origin, but the new demands generally did not clash with the interests of other U.S. corporations and did not endanger international negotiations. The new rules of origin, moreover, were now open to challenge at the WTO. To a certain extent, by relying so heavily on congressional action, the textile and apparel industries were able to sustain protectionist support for a few more decades, but were ultimately left behind.

Unfair-trade Laws and the Threat to Conditional Protectionism

By the late 1970s, antidumping (AD) and countervailing duty (CVD) laws became the most effective tool against surges of imports from foreign countries (for reasons I discuss in chapter 5). Although GATT rules generally

---

[34] The United States agreed to remove safeguard duties it imposed on Indian wool coats (DS32).

sanctioned domestic unfair-trade laws—countries were allowed to impose duties on imported goods when domestic industries had been injured due to unfair trade practices of foreign competitors—WTO members had been complaining against the discriminatory formulation and implementation of the rules by the U.S. administration. The Tokyo Round Agreement on Antidumping was modified quite radically by Congress in the Trade Agreements Act of 1979, so U.S. unfair-trade laws were again bitterly contested in the Uruguay Round negotiations.

Predictably, the steel industry strongly opposed any changes to the U.S. unfair-trade laws. This objective was secured when, in an attempt to win approval of a Senate extension of fast-track authority, United States Trade Representative Mickey Kantor sent a letter to Senator Ernest F. Hollings (D-SC), declaring the administration's commitment to "a Uruguay Round agreement which preserves our antidumping and countervailing duty laws as effective remedies against unfair trade practices."[35] Kantor then made it "abundantly clear" to other countries that "this was a crunch issue as far as the U.S. was concerned."[36] Accepting U.S. domestic political reality—the U.S. administration would have lost crucial support in Congress for the final Uruguay Round deal if the antidumping laws were compromised—the trading partners did not insist on a wholesale dismantling of American AD and CVD laws (Dryden 1995). Member-states did secure U.S. agreement on substantial changes, aimed at curbing practices that had tilted the process in favor of domestic protection seekers. These provisions were not as substantial as antidumping reformers had sought, but they did make it significantly more difficult for domestic petitioners to obtain protection under the antidumping statute.[37] Similarly, most changes that were introduced into the Agreement on Subsidies and Countervailing Measures did not challenge existing U.S. procedures, but they did make it more difficult to win and keep countervailing duty actions.

In order to win the steel and semiconductor industries' support of the URAA in spite of those compromises, the administration promised to minimize the impact of the Uruguay Round changes by enacting "the strongest possible antidumping and countervailing duty laws, consistent with our obligations under the GATT."[38] Hence, ambiguities in the multilateral agreement were resolved in the URAA in favor of the petitioning

[35] The letter is reprinted in *Inside U.S. Trade*, 2 July 1994, 15 (cited in Destler 1995, 231).

[36] Interview in *Inside U.S. Trade*, Special Report, 24 December 1993, 4

[37] For the changes made by the Antidumping Code, see Destler 1995, 241–42.

[38] AISI testimony. U.S. Congress, February 8, 1994, Hearings before the House Committee on Ways and Means, *Uruguay Round Trade Negotiations*.

industry.[39] This was in spite of strong opposition from U.S. domestic companies and subsidiaries of foreign firms that used imported products, as well as from major U.S.-based multinational corporations, which were worried that changes in U.S. law that made it easier to bring antidumping cases would trigger copycat legislation abroad (*National Journal,* 7/9/1994, 1630). The implementing language "changed some words in highly technical but critical ways, in effect . . . easing the ability of domestic industries to show injury" (*National Journal,* 7/9/1994, 1630). According to Destler (1995, 242), supporters of AD laws appeared to have won back in Washington most, but probably not all, of the ground they had lost in Geneva.

Another source of concern for the steel industry was the new dispute settlement procedures. According to the American Iron and Steel Institute (AISI), in cases under the GATT dispute settlement procedures that had challenged AD or CVD positive determinations, the United States had lost only when the panelists had accorded the administering authorities very little deference, or had considered information that had not been part of the administrative accord. The steel industry therefore insisted on a special rule of deference, and U.S. officials negotiated a special provision in the Antidumping Agreement that declared that as long as a national antidumping proceeding established the facts properly and evaluated them in an "unbiased and objective" manner, its evaluation could not be overturned by a WTO panel (Rosenthal and Vermylen 2000, 874). While expressing concern that "GATT panels (historically hostile to U.S. trade laws) will have potential new authority to issue binding decisions that could overturn the dumping and subsidy laws passed by Congress," and given the agreed standard of review, the steel industry did not object to the new DSU.[40]

The impact of the DSU on U.S. unfair-trade laws was put to a test when, in 1997, with steel imports reaching a new record of 31 million tons (representing about 23.8 percent of the U.S. market),[41] the AISI, together with United Steelworkers of America (USWA), launched an aggressive AD and CVD assault.[42] Altogether, sixteen investigations were launched in 1997, thirty-one in 1998, and forty-four in 1999. Many of the petitions resulted in affirmative determinations by the Department of Commerce and the U.S.

---

[39] For details on the changes made, see Destler 1995, 242.

[40] AISI testimony. U.S. Congress, February 8, 1994, Hearings before the House Committee on Ways and Means, *Uruguay Round Trade Negotiations.*

[41] In 1998, imports into the United States increased further, to 41.5 million tons, or 30 percent of the market. By January 1999, foreign steel imports were estimated to account for roughly one-half of the U.S. market. For an excellent review of the steel industry's economic conditions and its political response from 1959 to the 1990s, see Hall 1997.

[42] The industry also lobbied Congress, and see the results below.

ITC. This time, however, countries affected by these affirmative decisions confronted the U.S. administration by filing petitions to the WTO. Often, they succeeded in forcing the United States to change previous determinations and even laws.

Overall, thirty-eight cases were filed between 1995 and 2004 against the United States in AD/CVD-related cases. Of the fourteen CVD-related cases against the United States, it lost in *all* six cases with a ruling (seven cases are pending or inactive and one case was resolved without a ruling). Of the twenty-four AD-related cases, the United States lost in ten of the cases and prevailed in two (three cases were resolved without a ruling and nine cases are inactive or still pending).[43]

In three of the AD cases in which the United States lost—one regarding Korean stainless steel plate and sheets (DS179), one regarding Indian steel plate (DS206), and one regarding Canadian softwood lumber (DS264)— the complaining countries argued that the United States had not correctly followed WTO procedures in specific determinations, and the WTO panels recommended that the United States bring the antidumping duties imposed into compliance with the international agreements. In two other cases—one regarding Korean semiconductors (DS99) and another regarding Japanese hot-rolled steel products (DS184)—the complaining countries challenged the legality of the regulations themselves, and the WTO panels ruled that the United States had to change its AD regulations to make them consistent with the WTO Antidumping Agreement. Finally, in four cases (consolidated into two at the appeal), the complaining countries challenged U.S. legislation addressing unfair-trade laws and the WTO panels ruled that the legislation was WTO-illegal and should be repealed. In the first case (DS136, DS162), the WTO ruled that the Unfair Competition Act of 1916, which allowed U.S. companies to privately sue foreign companies for anticompetitive practices in the U.S. market, was illegal. In the second case (DS217, DS234), the WTO ruled that the so-called Byrd Amendment of the Continued Dumping and Subsidy Offset Act of 2000 (PL 106–387), which directed payment of any antidumping and countervailing duties to the companies that had pursued the cases rather than to the U.S. Treasury, violated WTO rules by illegally subsidizing U.S. companies.

In short, the WTO proved to be an efficient site for challenging positive determinations made by the Department of Commerce, administration

---

[43] Of the 3 cases resolved without a ruling, two were resolved after the Department of Commerce agreed to revoke the AD order (DS63, DS89). The third case was resolved due to a suspension agreement that established a predetermined floor price for the imported Mexican tomatoes under dispute (DS49).

regulations, and even congressional laws. Furthermore, the rate of compliance with negative decisions was impressive. In all the cases in which a panel ruled against the United States and compliance required an administrative action, the administration consistently complied. In the AD cases requiring revision of duties (the Korean stainless steel case and the Indian steel plate case), the Department of Commerce followed the panel's ruling and amended its final determinations.[44] The Department of Commerce also complied when ordered to change its regulations governing the AD and CVD determinations. In the case of the Korean semiconductors, the department replaced a "not likely" standard with a "necessary" standard, thus making it more difficult to rule against revocation of old determinations.[45] In the case of the Japanese hot-rolled steel, the Department of Commerce amended its regulations regarding the treatment of sales to affiliated parties in calculating dumping margins—the so-called "99.5 percent" rule that had been rejected by the Appellate Body.

When compliance necessitated congressional action, the White House consistently urged Congress to comply with the ruling. In a testimony before the House Committee on Ways and Means in February 26, 2003, United States Trade Representative Robert B. Zoellick stated:

> The United States should also live up to its obligations under WTO rules. . . . We recognize that each matter [in which compliance is required] involves sensitive interests. Yet America should keep its word, just as we insist others must do. As the largest trading nation, the WTO rules serve U.S. interests. We will work closely with the Congress to determine approaches to resolve these issues.[46]

But Congress was reluctant to follow rulings that would negatively affect domestic interest groups, hence compliance became less predictable when it required congressional action. In reaction to the ruling regarding the Byrd Amendment, the office of USTR stated, "The United States has been a

---

[44] In the case regarding Canadian softwood lumber, Canada and the United States are still negotiating the terms of implementation.

[45] Using this modified standard, the Commerce Department then reconsidered the case and found that the continued application of the dumping order was *necessary* to offset dumping and, accordingly, did not revoke the antidumping order under dispute. Korea, in reaction, requested the matter to be referred to the original panel. This compliance panel proceeding was terminated when the United States finally revoked the antidumping order at issue (WTO July 2001; GAO July 2003).

[46] Statement of Robert B. Zoellick, U.S. Congress. February 26, 2003, House Committee on Ways and Means, *President Bush's Trade Agenda*.

leader in supporting rules-based dispute settlement in the WTO. Therefore, in this case as in others, the United States will seek to comply with its WTO obligations."[47] President Bush's budget proposal for fiscal year 2004 urged repeal of the law, saying it amounted to a "corporate subsidy" and provided a "double-dip" benefit to industries that had already benefited from the increased prices on competing import goods resulting from countervailing tariffs. But Senator Robert C. Byrd and sixty-seven of his colleagues (twenty-three Republicans, forty-three Democrats and one independent) sent a letter to Bush calling on him to support the amendment despite the WTO ruling. "In our view," the letter stated, "the WTO has acted beyond the scope of its mandate by finding violations where none exists and where no obligations were negotiated" (*Washington Times*, 6/14/2003). The United States had to comply with the ruling no later then December 27, 2003, but failed to do so. In November 2004, the WTO authorized affected countries to impose about $150 million in trade sanctions on the United States in retaliation (*New York Times*, 11/27/2004). Consequently, EC, Canada, and Japan imposed additional duty of 15 percent on certain U.S. products, which covered a total value of trade of $28 million (EC), $11 million (Canada), and $52 million (Japan), respectively. So far, the U.S. Congress failed to amend the law.

To comply with the WTO ruling regarding the Act of 1916, Congress had to pass a law that would repeal the act and terminate ongoing cases before U.S. courts. Several bills to that effect were introduced in the 107th Congress, but they did not get to the stage of being discussed in Congress and became void when Congress adjourned in November 2002. Only in the final days of the 108th Congress, more than four years after the appellate body delivered its ruling, did both the Senate and the House finally pass the Miscellaneous Trade and Technical Corrections Act of 2004, which contained the repeal of the 1916 Antidumping Act (PL 108–429). Although the bill does not have a retroactive effect—Senate Finance Committee Chairman Charles Grassley (R-IA) stated that terminating pending cases would set a "dangerous precedent" (*Washington Monitor*, 8/4/2000)—it was nevertheless welcomed by Japan and the EC.

How did the steel industry react to these legal defeats? The negative decisions by the WTO panelists and the compliance at home made the steel industry conclude that "the whole area of binding dispute settlement has ultimately proven to be quite trade law weakening."[48] AISI protested that

---

[47] See http://www.ustr.gov/releases/2003/01/2003–01–16–statement-wto.PDF, U.S.TR Press Release, January 16, 2003.

[48] AISI official, confidential, interview with the author, June 2001.

Table 6.2 Antidumping and countervailing duty cases, 1980–2003

Years	AD average of petitions per year	AD acceptance rate	CVD average of petitions per year	CVD acceptance rate
1980–94	50	0.5	20	0.58[a]
1995–2003	36	0.5	7	0.38

Sources: AD and CVD cases initiated from January 1, 1980, until December 31, 1999, are reported in http://ia.ita.doc.gov/stats/caselist.txt; USTR Annual Reports, various years.

[a] For the years 1986–94.

"Japan, Korea and other countries whose producers have engaged in unfair trading have tried to achieve through the WTO dispute settlement system what they could not achieve through multilateral negotiations," and urged the U.S. administration to "defend aggressively the trade laws enacted by Congress from this ongoing effort by unfair traders to use the WTO dispute settlement process to undermine America's fair-trade rules."[49] The steel industry initiated congressional bills that would make unfair-trade laws more effective.[50] The industry also tried to prevent the further weakening of unfair-trade laws in future international trade negotiations by agreeing to support a new round only on the condition that there be no new negotiations on AD/CVD laws. This strategy, too, failed when American negotiators at the Ministerial Meeting at Doha, Qatar, in November 2001 allowed future negotiations on antidumping measures.

The ability of foreign countries to effectively challenge positive determinations by using the DSU might have contributed to a decline in the use of unfair-trade laws. The average number of AD investigations between 1980 and 1994 was fifty per year. The average number of AD investigations between 1995 and 2003, in contrast, was thirty-six per year. Similarly, the average number of CVD investigations between 1980 and 1994 was twenty per year, while the average between 1995 and 2003 was seven per year. The average rate of success in CVD cases declined from 58 percent (1986–94) to 38 percent (1995–2003); the acceptance rate remained 50 percent for antidumping decisions (see summary in table 6.2).

In short, trade remedy laws, which were common practices under conditional protectionism, were quite effectively challenged under the Dispute Settlement Understanding: gains won at the administrative level were constantly eviscerated by the WTO dispute settlement process. As a result of positive decisions by the WTO panelists, the U.S. administration and

[49] AISI, May 10, 2001, Public Comments on WTO, Ministerial Conference in Doha, Qatar.
[50] See chapter 5 for several such legislative efforts.

Congress were forced to modify the biased components of the laws. The reduced number of AD and CVD investigations since 1995 is plausibly a secondary reaction to the same source of threat.

Section 301 under Legalized Multilateralism

Section 301 of the Trade Act of 1974, as amended in 1988, gives the president authority to take unilateral retaliatory actions against foreign countries that either violate trade agreements or otherwise maintain laws or practices that are unjustifiable or restrict U.S. commerce. In contrast to the AD and CVD provisions, Section 301 was not meant to prevent imports from entering the United States but rather to ensure access of U.S. exports to foreign markets. Since the goal of Section 301 was further liberalization, it was not, as such, inconsistent with the project of free trade. Other governments, however, complained about the unilateral dimension of this section.

As mentioned above, the primary incentive for other countries to strengthen international dispute settlement mechanisms was what they had interpreted as the growing tilt toward unilateralism on the part of the United States, symbolized by Section 301. They were therefore willing to accept a stronger dispute settlement mechanism only if the United States would commit to bring Section 301 disputes to the WTO (*National Journal*, 3/26/1994, 729). But when members of Congress expressed concern that the Uruguay Round Agreements would constrain future use of Section 301, the administration assured them that this would not be the case, promising that "we will continue to be able to use U.S. trade law, including Section 301, to enforce our international trading rights" (*National Journal*, 2/19/1994, 427). In spite of this promise, Section 301 ultimately lost its unilateral orientation.

Initially, the United States continued to use Section 301 unilaterally, despite the commitments made in the Uruguay Round. The first Section 301 case after 1994 involved Japan's alleged failure to purchase American autos and auto parts.[51] Negotiations on automobiles and auto parts, which accounted for nearly two-thirds of the $60 billion U.S. trade deficit with Japan, dragged on for twenty months and finally broke off in May 1995. An affirmative determination under Section 301 followed, and the United States threatened to impose punitive import duties of $5.9 billion. In response,

---

[51] On U.S.–Japan trade relations during the 1990s, see Shoch 2001.

Japan filed a complaint with the WTO arguing that Section 301 was inconsistent with the DSU's prohibition on unilateral action in resolving trade disputes (DS6). This was the sixth case brought to the WTO and the third against the United States, and domestic opponents used the occasion to express their position on the WTO. Robert C. Byrd (D-WV), for example, declared, "I cannot conceive of continued U.S. commitment to an organization that would reward blatant discrimination and the perpetuation of sanctuary behavior." Greg Mastel, senior fellow at the Economic Strategy Institute, warned, "If the WTO cannot address these big issues, it's not going to become a credible policeman of world trade" (*Washington Report*, 6/1995). Prior to the formation of a panel, however, the United States and Japan reached an agreement on measures to deregulate the replacement parts and accessories market in Japan. On the basis of this agreement, the United States terminated its Section 301 investigation and Japan ceased to pursue the establishment of a dispute settlement panel.

The next opportunity for the United States to challenge Japan's trade practices came when Kodak, an American company, complained that Japan discriminated against imported film (Dillon 1999). Kodak alleged that its Japanese market share had been artificially depressed by a complicated web of collusion between Japanese film manufacturer Fuji, film wholesalers, camera shops, and government bureaucrats. This time, instead of using the unilateral sanctions available under Section 301, the U.S. administration decided to bring the case to the WTO (DS45). The decision to go to the WTO and to defer a final decision concerning the use of sanctions under U.S. trade law heralded an important shift in U.S. trade policy away from the use of unilateral sanctions.

This voluntary shift has become a WTO-sanctioned legal obligation when the EC complained against the legality of the section itself (DS152). In a petition filed in 1998, the EC argued that in applying Section 301 and related sections of the U.S. Trade Act of 1974 the United States breached an understanding that in exchange for other Uruguay Round participants agreeing to automatic adoption of WTO panels, the United States would abandon its policy of taking unilateral action against foreign trade barriers (*National Journal*, 6/10/1995, 1398). The WTO panel found that the disputed sections were inconsistent with the WTO dispute settlement rules, because, if considered alone, they gave the United States discretion to make certain determinations before the completion of panel proceedings. The panel held, however, that this inconsistency had been removed by the Statement of Administrative Action accompanying the URAA, and by U.S. representations to the panel that the administration would base any Section 301 determination on a dispute settlement finding. The panel stated that should these U.S. representations be repudiated, its findings of conformity between the provisions in the sections and U.S. international obligations would no longer hold. Thus, while technically ruling against the EC, the panel explicitly determined that the United States was obliged to present all future 301 cases before the WTO.

Even before this damning WTO decision, Section 301 increasingly lost its unilateral edge. From 1975 to 1994, only 28 percent (twenty-seven out of ninety-five) of the Section 301 cases initiated resulted in one or another form of negotiation under the auspices of the GATT (including consultations, delegation to multilateral negotiations, and fourteen cases of dispute panels). From 1995 to 2003, in contrast, the United States asked for consultations under the WTO in 65 percent of the cases (seventeen out of twenty-six cases). Of the seventeen cases, eight were resolved through consultations and agreements, and nine were ruled by a WTO panel. With the exception of a 2001 case against Ukraine, which is not a WTO member, all the cases not referred to the WTO were resolved through bilateral agreements, without the imposition of unilateral retaliatory sanctions.[52] In short, from a symbol of "aggressive American unilateralism," the section turned into a mere first stage in a legal process situated in the international realm (*Economist*, 5/5/1990, 32; Ryan 1995). Since 2000, the year the panel report was adopted by the Dispute Settlement Body, the USTR also radically decreased its level of activity. The average number of petitions between 1985 and 1994 was 5.2 per year. The level of activity remained practically the same between 1995 and 1999, an average of 4.8 per year. In contrast, there was only 1 investigation in the year 2000, 1 investigation in 2001 (against a non-WTO member), and no investigations since (see table 6.3).

It is important to note, however, that the WTO did not constrain the ability of the United States to fight against what it viewed as discriminatory practices of other countries. In all the 301 cases brought by the United States to the WTO but one (the Kodak case), it won WTO approval. Thus, on the one hand, the new dispute mechanisms constrained *unilateral* American action. On the other, it provided effectiveness, as well as international legitimacy, to its methods of disciplining foreign countries and thus provided more effective remedies for those American industries interested in opening foreign markets to their products.

---

[52] For list of cases, see http://www.ustr.gov/reports/301report/act301.htm, USTR's "Section 301 Table of Cases."

Table 6.3 Section 301 petitions and bilateral consultations, 1975–2004

Year	Average per year (Number of petitions)	Rate of cases referred to consultations
1975–1994	4.75 (95)	0.28
1995–2004	2.6 (26)	0.65

Sources: USTR Reports, various years; USTR's "Section 301 Table of Cases," <http://www.ustr.gov/reports/301report/act301.htm>

Labor, the Environment, and Social Protectionist Laws

At the same time that traditional protectionist industries seemed to have been successfully co-opted into the system—industries like textiles and steel endorsed the URAA—new actors emerged who opposed the drive to free trade for a different set of reasons. Their concern was not with "the balance to be struck *among* U.S. commercial interests, but the proper balance *between* these interests and others" (Destler and Balint 1999, 9). Prominent among the new actors were environmental and citizen rights groups. Their opposition stemmed largely from the fear that international trade agreements would have a destructive effect on U.S. domestic laws and practices. But their concern crossed national boundaries—their opposition to NAFTA, for example, was also due to the effect the agreement would have on Mexico (Mayer 1998). Organized labor in the United States joined this coalition and adapted arguments along similar lines. While still warning that free trade agreements would lead to unemployment, suppression of wages, and job insecurity, labor unions also decried labor conditions outside the United States and warned that free trade agreements undercut labor standards.[53]

This political opposition has been vocal and surprisingly effective in the debates on NAFTA and extensions of the fast track procedure (see more

---

[53] In the debate over NAFTA, labor's early focus was on the cost to American jobs, but later it emphasized the plight of the Mexican workers and the environmental degradation that surrounded them (Mayer 1998, 72). This, however, was not the first time that the issue of labor conditions outside of the United States was part of the political debate. "In 1984 . . . Congress included in the extension of trade preferences for developing countries a provision to deny them to any country that 'has not taken . . . steps to afford internationally recognized worker rights to workers in the country.' Labor also won inclusion of 'worker rights' as the fourteenth of sixteen 'principal trade negotiating objectives' in the Omnibus Trade and Competitiveness Act of 1988 authorizing U.S. participation in the Uruguay Round trade talks. [In the URAA of 1994], Congress called on the president to 'seek the establishment in . . . the WTO of a working party to examine the relationship of internationally recognized worker rights' to the existing international trade regime (Destler and Balint 1999, 22, footnotes omitted).

below). It was also prominent in the discussion on the DSU. The introduction of the new dispute resolution mechanisms alarmed political activists, who feared that "social" domestic laws and regulations would be reversed by WTO panelists because of indirect barriers to trade these laws at times created (Destler and Balint 1999). During the debates preceding the passage of the URAA, Ralph Nader's *Public Citizen* led a coalition, which included environmental groups and organized labor, in a fight against the WTO. The *Citizens Trade Campaign* emphasized two issues. First, they warned against the prospect of the loss of U.S. sovereignty and the ability of international panels to change domestic laws unfavorable to trade liberalization but which "protect our environment, ensure imported foods are safe, defend family farms and protect workers' rights" (an ad in the *Washington Post,* 8/12/1994). A second concern was the undemocratic nature of the new binding dispute mechanisms, including the lockout of the press and the public from WTO tribunals and deliberations; the suppression of briefs and other documents presented by governments that were parties to disputes; the denial of citizens' right to petition; the absence of conflict-of-interest standards for the tribunals' panelists; and a prohibition on any independent appeals of WTO tribunal decisions (*Washington Post,* 8/12/1994). "The WTO pact is more than an economic document," Nader informed readers of *The Nation.* "It is a system of international governance with powerful legislative, executive and judicial authority over member nations. As such, any evaluations of the WTO regime should use the democratic yardsticks we apply domestically" (*The Nation,* 10/10/1994).

Article XX of the GATT (1947) does provide exceptions for measures "necessary to protect human, animal or plant life or health" (section [b]) or "relating to the conservation of exhaustible natural resources" (section [g]). Such measures are permissible, however, only provided that they do not constitute a means of arbitrary or unjustifiable discrimination between countries where the same conditions prevail, or a disguised restriction on international trade. Under the GATT, member-states systematically failed to convince panels to use those measures.[54] Predictably, disputes under the WTO had similar results. In the two cases in which free trade and U.S. environmental interests came into conflict, the WTO ruled against the United States.[55]

---

[54] Canada lost in an attempt to justify prohibition of the exportation and sale for export of certain herring and salmon, Thailand lost in an attempt to justify prohibition of the importation of cigarettes, and the United States failed in an attempt to prohibit the importation of tuna caught with dolphin-unfriendly nets from Mexico.

[55] There were two additional Article XX cases, which did not involve the United States as a respondent. In the *EC-beef hormones* case (DS26, DS48), the United States complained against a EU ban on imported beef containing hormones. The Appellate Body ruled against the EC, holding that it failed to demonstrate a scientific risk associated with hormone-treated

In the Clean Air Act case (DS2, DS4), Venezuela and Brazil challenged regulations of the U.S. Environmental Protection Agency (EPA), which established a baseline for determining acceptable levels of contaminants in gasoline and set up separate requirements for various countries. The panel, ruling against the United States, upheld the claim that the EPA gasoline standard was discriminatory and ordered the United States to change its rules on imported gasoline. Although United States Trade Representative Kantor, in reaction to the decision, said the U.S. government had the "discretion" to decide how or whether a WTO ruling would be implemented, that "WTO panel reports have no force under U.S. law" (*Washington Post,* 1/24/1996), and that "the results of this dispute will not and cannot compromise the Clinton administration's commitment to our environmental laws" (*Wall Street Journal,* 2/21/1996), the administration has eventually revised the EPA requirements for imported conventional gasoline, to bring them into compliance with the ruling.

In the *Shrimp-Turtle* case (DS58), India, Malaysia, Pakistan, and Thailand challenged a 1989 amendment to the U.S. Endangered Species Act that required countries that export shrimp to the United States to use a special device on their shrimp nets to protect sea turtles from drowning. The United States argued that the measure was a justifiable restriction on importation under GATT's Article XX(g). The appellate panel's ruling determined that the WTO dispute settlement process must take into account policies other than those that are merely "trade liberalizing" (Jackson 2000, 197), and granted a general endorsement of the idea that trade barriers, under certain conditions, *could* be permissible to protect the environment. The panel also granted environmental organizations the option of filing legal briefs in the case, a practice not previously allowed. However, the panel made the standards for determining that a measure was not an unjustifiable discrimination exceedingly difficult to meet, rendering its general assessments empty. Consequently, the panel ruled that the U.S. measure did not qualify for an exception. Responding to the ruling, United States Trade Representative Charlene Barshefsky promised that the decision "does not suggest that we weaken our environmental laws in any respect, and we do not intend to do

---

beef. The *EC-Asbestos* case (DS135) is the most recent environmental case and so far the only one that upheld a health regulation that restricted trade as a justifiable exception. Canada challenged a French decree banning the manufacture, sale, and imports of all forms of asbestos. Canada argued that the asbestos in question posed no risk under properly controlled use. The Appellate Body considered the ban to be a legitimate means of pursuing the objective to "halt" the spread of asbestos-related health risks, which had a clear scientific basis in studies of the toxicity of asbestos (Garrett and Smith 2002, 25).

so" (*Washington Post*, 10/13/1998). But the National Association of Manufacturers and other business associations supported the ruling and urged the U.S. government not to "lose sight of the national interest" in its "desire to protect the relatively narrow though not necessarily illegitimate concerns of individual interest groups."[56] Eventually, the Department of State issued revised guidelines aimed at implementing the ruling.[57]

Congress's New Multilateral Engagement

The regime of legalized multilateralism, as we have seen, shifted the site of activity from the domestic to the international. This greatly affected Congress, which was forced to revise its core protectionist activities. In the previous institutional shift, from selective to conditional protectionism, Congress's main concern changed from providing import quotas and other selective measures to improving protectionists' position in the administrative processes. In the shift from conditional protectionism to legalized multilateralism, Congress again changed its focus. Adapting to the new authority shift, Congress's new objective was supervising the procedures of the DSU, as well as the content of particular decisions. In addition, responding to the demands of social protectionist forces, Congress fought to improve social protectionists' position in the diplomatic negotiations.

Since the 1990s, Congress has done little to support the textile and apparel industries, other than securing favorable rules-of-origin in multilateral or bilateral agreements. The predicament of the steel industry, especially following the crisis of 1997, led to more intensive congressional activity. Legislative initiatives to impose import quotas (e.g., The Stop Illegal Steel Trade Act of 1999) were never put to vote, but other laws did pass, including the Emergency Steel Loan Guarantee Act of 1999 (PL 106–51), which provided $1 billion in loan guarantees to American companies in the steel and oil industries, and the Byrd Amendment (that was later successfully challenged at the

[56] NAM, "Comments of the NAM on the WTO Dispute Settlement Proceeding Regarding U.S. Shrimp-Turtle Laws," 1998; cited in Destler and Balint 1999, 36.

[57] Malaysia argued that the new guidelines had failed to comply with the rulings and the matter was referred to the original panel. The panel concluded that the revised guidelines as applied by the U.S. authorities were legal, *as long as* the ongoing serious good faith efforts to reach a multilateral agreement remained satisfied. The panel noted that should any one of the conditions referred to cease to be met in the future, the recommendations of the DSB may no longer be complied with (WTO July 2001; GAO July 2003).

WTO). More commonly, following practices of conditional protectionism, members of Congress attempted to make unfair-trade and safeguard laws more effective (e.g., the Fair Trade Law Enhancement Act of 1999 and the Import Surge Response Act of 1999). In addition, some bills were aimed at constraining the administration in its multilateral trade negotiations, by calling on the president to abstain from renegotiating international agreements governing AD and CVD measures (in 1999), or expressing the sense of Congress that the USTR should oppose any changes that would weaken existing AD and safeguard laws at the WTO round of negotiations (in 2001). But these bills, too, were not voted on.

While abandoning old objectives, members of Congress found alternative, albeit much less effective, means of intervention. Unsurprisingly, the DSU has become a major source of frustration.[58] On behalf of domestic industries, Congress offered statements condemning specific WTO reports against U.S. practices, or general criticism aimed at the DSU panelists. The Trade Act of 2002 (PL 107–210), for example, included a statement that "the recent pattern of decisions by dispute settlement panels . . . to impose obligations and restrictions on the use of antidumping, countervailing, and safeguard measures by WTO members . . . has raised concerns." As we have seen, Congress has also strongly resented the obligation to change domestic legislation to adhere to DSU rulings.

Congress was also concerned with whether the DSU followed what would be considered "effective adjudication" in domestic courts (Helfer and Slaughter 1997). One complaint focused on the improper judicial activism of WTO panelists. In addition to their expansionist tendencies—panelists rarely admitted that a dispute was beyond their jurisdiction—panelists were also accused for "making" law, rather than merely applying it, and consequently, for "politicizing" the system (Charnovitz 2002, 232–34). Senator Charles Grassley (R-Iowa) hence remarked, "I wonder to what extent the WTO dispute settlement panels create new law that is not agreed to among the parties. I worry about this because we don't know, if we don't have a new

---

[58] At the same time, Congress has also been active in urging the administration to take advantage of the DSU and to file consultation requests on behalf of specific industries. In the Trade Act of 2002, the first trade negotiating objective was to "further strengthen the system of international trading disciplines and procedures, including dispute settlement." The mandatory once-in-five-year-vote on whether or not to withdraw the approval of the United States from the agreement establishing the WTO reflected, if anything, a bipartisan acceptance of the dispute settlement processes. In 2000, the resolution to withdraw failed by 56 to 363. In 2005, the resolution failed by 86 to 338.

round of negotiations now for some time, panels then might begin to fill in some of the details that the member states ought to deal with."[59] Another concern was how to "open up the process more and make it more transparent."[60] Members of Congress, but also the Office of the USTR, called for a prompt release of panel findings, for measures for enhancing the input of citizens and citizen groups, for providing the opportunity to file amicus briefs in dispute settlement proceedings, and for opening those proceedings to public observation.[61] Finally, some members of Congress reiterated the concern that the WTO weakened the ability of the U.S. government to protect health, safety, and the environment, but also that it weakened the ability of U.S. states, and their citizens, to make other laws. Senator Henry Sanders (D-Alabama), for example, raised the prospect that state-originated divestiture campaigns, as the one originated against South Africa, would be illegal under the WTO.[62]

While these half-hearted attempts on behalf of the old guardians had little effect on the trajectory of trade liberalization, actions on behalf of the new opposition seemed more consequential. Here the focus was not on disputes but on negotiations. Realizing that the locus of decision-making has gradually shifted to the international level, labor and environmental groups fought for integrating their concerns into the international trade agreements. Procedurally, this required that a "fast track" legislation, in which Congress formulates the U.S. trade objectives, would include such issues. In 1991, when President Bush asked for a two-year extension of fast track authority to negotiate the free trade agreement with Mexico, the coalition of unions, environmental organizations, and other citizens groups forced the Bush administration to design an "action plan" on labor and environmental issues. The president was "committed to working with the Congress to ensure that there is adequate adjustment assistance and effective retraining for dislocated workers," and promised to "develop and implement an expanded program of environmental cooperation in parallel with the free trade talks" and "expand U.S.–Mexico labor cooperation."

---

[59] Charles Grassley, U.S. Congress, June 20, 2000, Hearings of the International Trade Subcommittee of the Senate Finance Committee, *World Trade Organization Dispute Settlement*.

[60] Ibid.

[61] Statement, Charlene Barshefsky, USTR, U.S. Congress, June 20, 2000, Hearings of the International Trade Subcommittee of the Senate Finance Committee, *World Trade Organization Dispute Settlement*.

[62] Henry Sanders, U.S. Congress, March 30, 1998, Hearings before the Subcommittee on International Economic Policy and Trade of the Committee on International Relations House of Representatives, *WTO—Dispute Settlement Body*.

The president also promised to appoint environmentalists to the trade advisory committees and committed himself to formulating a plan to clean up the border (Mayer 1998, 90). However, the Bush administration followed up on only a few of those promises (Mayer 1998, 111). As a presidential candidate, Clinton promised to supplement NAFTA, which he generally supported, with additional agreements on labor and the environment (Mayer 1998, 165). The result, again, was disappointing. Rather than creating new international standards in the realm of labor and the environment—a kind of a regional "social charter"—the commitment was merely to ensure "national enforcement of national laws" (Mayer 1998, 168–69, 178). In spite of the weak concessions given to labor and the environment, NAFTA was ratified by Congress. A few years later, however, this same coalition almost managed to force the administration to include labor and the environment as future negotiation objectives. In this they failed, but the dispute over this issue paralyzed the system for years. Twice, in 1994 and 1997, the Clinton administration sought a new fast-track authority, and in both times it failed to reach a formula of labor and environmental objectives that would gain the support of the labor and environment coalition, as well as the business-based free-trade groups, including ECAT, the U.S. Chamber of Commerce, the National Association of Manufacturers, and the National Foreign Trade Council, which were militantly opposed to the inclusion of such standards (Destler 1997, 18; Shoch 2000, 121–28; CRS 2002, 17–19). In September 1998, a Republican-sponsored proposal, containing no strong labor and environmental provisions, was also defeated by fast-track opponents (Shoch 2000, 121, 136). Only in 2001 did the Bush administration manage to get a fast track authority, renamed trade promotion authority (TPA)(Destler 2005, 331–42). The Bipartisan Trade Promotion Authority Act of 2002, included in the Trade Act of 2002, had as negotiating objectives numerous, but substantively weak, references to the labor and the environment. Those included the objective "to seek to protect and preserve the environment and enhance the international means of doing so, while optimizing the use of the world's resources"; "to promote respect for worker rights and the rights of children consistent with core labor standards of the ILO"; "to seek provisions in trade agreements under which parties . . . strive to ensure that they do not weaken or reduce the protections afforded in domestic environmental and labor laws as an encouragement for trade"; and "to promote universal ratification and full compliance with ILO Convention . . . Concerning the Prohibition and Immediate Action for the Elimination of the Worst Forms of Child Labor."

On the Institutional Logic of Rulings and Compliance

The institutional changes introduced in the Uruguay Round transformed, once again, protectionist practices in the United States. Under the new regime of *legalized multilateralism*, contested practices, such as voluntary restraint agreements, trade remedy laws, and social protectionist measures, were quite effectively curbed by the enforceable obligation to follow international agreements. Domestic exceptions to trade liberalization have become more difficult to practice and the process of trade liberalization has been further intensified. Strengthened dispute settlement mechanisms forced a heightened liberalization in the United States—in a way that diplomatic negotiations could not—because the distribution of influence between IO officials, member-states, and their domestic constituencies under the DSU favored those supporting trade neoliberalization at the expense of those who opposed it. In particular, the strengthened authority of WTO judicial panels led to the delegation of authority from the national to the international level, the judicialization of interstate relations, and the structural internationalization of the state.

Delegation of Authority to the International Level

Due to the greater scope of the multilateral trade agreements, a larger number of U.S. laws and practices fell under the organization's jurisdiction. Due to the strengthened dispute settlement mechanisms, U.S. practices that violated any of this increased number of obligations could now be effectively confronted in the nonvoluntary international setting of the DSU, where the United States could no longer block the establishment of panels or the adoption of negative rulings. Hence the DSU expanded the organization's jurisdiction and led to a (partial) delegation of authority from the U.S. government to the WTO, which now held an improved authority to interpret and enforce the international agreements. As the dramatic increase of the number of complaints against the United States clearly demonstrates, policies and practices that were in the past under the exclusive jurisdiction of the U.S. government have now been effectively supervised at the international level.[63]

---

[63] A relocation of authority from the national to the international level occurs also in diplomatic negotiations, or any other form of international cooperation. Hence, a delegation of authority from the U.S. government had already occurred with the establishment of the GATT in 1947, but, especially in the case of developed countries, it had only limited effect on restraining domestic policies incompatible with international rules.

But the DSU has not merely shifted authority from the domestic level to the international one. In addition, it has also transformed the relations of influence in the two locations.

Judicialization of Interstate Relations

At the international level, the logic of power underlying judicial proceedings was quite different than the one underlying diplomatic negotiations. In international trade negotiations, outcomes were biased in favor of countries with the largest economies, most particularly the United States (Curzon and Curzon 1973; Finlayson and Zacher 1981, 591–92; McGillivray 2000; Wilkinson 2000; Steinberg 2002; Jawara and Kwa 2003; and see chapter 3). The United States could effectively press other countries to sign agreements that were against their perceived interests. In particular, the United States could impose painful liberalization on poor countries, while at the same time maintain protectionist practices at home. United States negotiators systematically blocked the inclusion of noncompetitive sectors, such as the textile and apparel industries, subsidized many of its agricultural producers, and prevented significant modification of its trade remedy laws.[64] This was not necessarily the case in the legal disputes. First, the dispute settlement process provided poor or otherwise marginalized member-states better access to the site of decision making, particularly an improved ability to challenge grievances against them. As the high number of challenges to U.S. policies initiated by developing countries demonstrates, the DSU provided poor countries an opportunity, which they did not have in diplomatic negotiations, to raise issues of concern to them and to effectively express their voice.[65] Second, the dispute settlement process provided relatively equal chances of prevailing in the dispute. This was because the DSU made the gap in resources between the disputing countries less dominant in shaping the final outcome. In diplomatic negotiations, the outcomes largely reflect the unequal distribution of economic and political resources among states, which clearly benefits the United States. In judicial proceedings, in contrast,

[64] This slightly changed with the "fast track" authority, as I argued in chapter 5, for it gave U.S. negotiators leverage against Congress that they often used to sacrifice protectionist interests for the sake of greater trade liberalization of other countries.

[65] Not only the formal parties of the dispute are heard. Any WTO member can become a third part in a dispute, by indicating that it has an interest in the subject matter (Jackson 2000, 187).

third-party adjudication, relatively available information, and adherence to formal rules make such resources less salient (Loungnarath and Stehly 2000; Bown 2004; Smith 2004, 543). Of course, rich countries are still in an advantageous position. They have better access to information and legal expertise and better administrative capacity. Furthermore, they are better able to afford the costs of litigation and have a greater capacity to suffer retaliation (in cases of noncompliance with a negative decision); they also have the benefit of having the substantive legal rules that determine decisions reflecting their interests (Smith 2004, 548; Bown and Hoekman 2005; cf. Michalopoulos 2001, 167; Busch and Reinhardt 2002, 467; Busch and Reinhardt 2003a; Reinhardt 2000, 19). And yet the fact that the rate of success of developing countries in challenging the United States was higher than the rate of success of developed countries suggests that this inequality of resources has little effect on panelists' decisions. In short, legalization introduced an equalizing element to trade relations among states; poor member-states now have a better chance to successfully challenge practices of their trading partners, including the United States, and ensure their adherence to international obligations.[66]

However, at the same time that the DSU made member-states more equal, it also rendered them much less influential. In diplomatic negotiations, decisions are made by the contracting parties and are largely determined by the unequal distribution of resources among participating states. By contrast, in legal proceedings, decisions are made by panelists—legal experts who are not affiliated with nation-states and whose basis for consideration are the international agreements. With the strengthened dispute settlement procedures, WTO panelists have thus

---

[66] The analysis here concentrates on interstate relations. However, it is important to identify also private economic actors that play behind the scenes. In particular, some of the cases in which developing countries challenged the United States are, in effect, cases in which multinational businesses mobilized governments of poor countries to represent their interests. In the dispute between Antigua and the United States on the prohibition of Internet gambling and betting (DS285), for example, the forces behind the case were international gambling companies that located themselves in Antigua and Barbuda, in particular the U.S. company, World Sports Exchange (Krajewski 2004). Similarly, the *EC-banana* cases (DS16, DS27) were brought by Ecuador, Guatemala, Honduras, Mexico, and the United States, but the main potential beneficiary of the case was Chiquita Brands, an American company, which has large investments in banana import licenses in Europe and wanted to control shipments of Latin American bananas (*Wall Street Journal,* 11/17/1995). This is in line with the conclusion of the analysis here that to identify the beneficiaries of the new system we need to look not at nation-states as coherent units but at the internationalists and protectionists of each country.

gained substantial influence over legal decisions and remedies. Consequently, substantive decisions now depend less on the relations of power among member-states and more on the logic inscribed in the organization itself.[67]

The content of this inscribed logic has reflected the formal rules and inherited orientation imposed on, and internalized by, WTO panelists. These factors have directed WTO panelists toward a rigid free-trade ideology. The General Agreement on Tariffs and Trade of 1947 and subsequent agreements identified and continuously expanded the trade-liberalizing responsibilities of member-states and treated permitted deviations as exceptions that should be minimized. Under the DSU, these agreements were the sole legal corpus for resolving disputes because the standard-of-review provided no space for national and/or extratrade considerations (Dillon 1999, 208–9; Jackson 2000, 200; Rosenthal and Vermylen 2000). The legal procedures provided panelists only limited authority to ignore legal obligations or to provide exceptions in "hard" cases, which granted further influence to the international agreements. The WTO panelists, for their part, "have been unabashedly expansionist" (Dillon 1999, 198; Smith 2003), never acknowledging a lack of jurisdiction and rarely refusing to deal with a case on the grounds that international agreements did not provide an answer to the debate (see more below).[68] Moreover, panels have

---

[67] The role of the Secretariat also slightly changed. Traditionally, the Secretariat provided information and mediated disagreements, but did not have much influence over the resulting compromises. After 1994, some WTO officers began spending a large part of their time providing legal information (historical cases and precedents) and legal analysis to the panelists, and came to have far greater influence over the outcome. For example, officials working for the "Rules Division" in the WTO Secretariat, which is the office responsible for antidumping and countervailing duty laws, were, in 2001, spending approximately 70 percent of their time on the dispute settlement (WTO Rules Division officials, confidential, interview with the author, July 2001; see also Jackson 2000, 190).

[68] I do not suggest that panelists' decisions are fully constrained by the legal text. On the contrary, international trade agreements are particularly vague and leave great flexibility of interpretation. Indeed, defenders of domestic unfair-trade laws have not only criticized the regulations but also expressed concern that individual panelists are ideologically biased in favor of trade liberalization (a confidential interview with the author, May 2001). WTO officials, however, strongly deny any suggestion that panelists might be biased or, another common complaint, that they might have latent conflicts of interest. The main counterargument conveyed by WTO officials is that panelists are chosen by the parties to the disputes (Peter Kuijper, Director of WTO Legal Affairs Division, interview with the author, July 2001). The political or ideological motivations behind the panelists' decisions, however, are beyond the scope of this research. Instead, the analysis here emphasizes the structural and institutional constraints that create a process that is *inherently* biased, independently of possible ideological biases of individual panelists.

relied on information and legal analysis provided to them by WTO officials who have been committed, due to their institutional position, to free-trade ideology. Finally, bias was also rooted in the rules of access. The dispute settlement mechanism improved member-states' access by providing an effective site for the resolution of interstate debates. Yet to have a standing, a state has to have a complaint based on an alleged breach of international obligation. Consequently, only disputes over trade liberalization are permitted to enter the process, and states practicing protectionist measures are always in the defensive. Those interested in defending protectionist actions can never use the legalized system to their advantage since as respondents they can never win—they can only not lose. As a result of these layers of inscribed logic, the panel's rulings were consistently oriented toward trade liberalization, as can be seen by the disproportionately high rate of success.

These two qualities of the DSU offer an important insight. At the same time that the judicialization of interstate relations introduced a potential for equality in the international process, the relative autonomy of biased WTO panelists turned this potential into an *equalized ability to impose trade-liberalizing rules on others* but also an *equalized difficulty to defend protectionist measures at home.* Consequently, while allowing proliberal actors—in the United States and elsewhere—to more effectively impose their will on other countries, the DSU imposed further constraints on protectionist actors. In the same way that the shift at the domestic level from Congress to quasi-judicial bodies in the administration reduced the influence of protectionist actors relative to business internationalists, here the WTO judicial proceedings restricted the influence of the United States and enhanced the influence of other states. In the same way that the shift at the domestic level from Congress to the administration reduced the influence of pressure groups and increased the influence of state officials, here the WTO judicial proceedings granted great influence to the panelists over the final outcome, at the direct expense of the member-states. The ability of panelists to act independently of member-states has led to decisions that are based less on political pressures and more on the bureaucratic orientation of the panelists, which explains the liberal bias found in the decisions. The restricted ability of the United States to use its economic and political resources explains why this bias is applied in a consistent manner, independently of whether the United States is the respondent or the plaintiff in the case. It is for this reason that while the U.S. government could still dictate biased exceptions on behalf of its industries in the agreements themselves, it could no longer easily disregard concessions it had granted.

The Structural Internationalization of the State

The relocation of authority to the WTO also affected the distribution of authority at the *national* level, by strengthening those state agencies with substantive and institutional links to the international organization. In the United States, the legalization of the WTO empowered the Office of the USTR, which represents the U.S. government in WTO negotiations and disputes, at the expense of other departments, such as Commerce, whose decisions could now be challenged at the WTO, which necessitated the involvement of the USTR. Importantly, it also lessened the role of Congress, whose laws could also be challenged. I call this process the "structural internationalization of the state," to make explicit that the states are now more attuned to the world economy (McMichael 1996), and that the change has been made possible by institutional means.[69] As a result of the delegation of authority to the international level and the complementary hierarchical reshuffling at the domestic level, the political influence of domestic social forces has also changed (see also Goldstein and Martin 2000; Keohane, Moravcsik, and Slaughter 2000, 458). While maintaining influence over some agencies, like Congress, domestic actors with protectionist agenda found that their political base of support had been subordinated both to the international organization and to internationally linked domestic agencies.

It is this structural internationalization of the state that explains the high rate of compliance in the United States, for it meant that the authority to decide whether to comply with WTO rulings was often in the hands of agencies that supported adherence to international obligations. When requiring an action of Congress, which is more accessible to protectionist interests, adherence to WTO rulings was resisted. While the number of cases is still too small to gauge the extent to which the strengthened enforcement mechanisms introduced in the DSU could force Congress into compliance, it seems that Congress often chooses to postpone the implementation of unwanted results, but faces difficulties in attempting to disregard negative rulings.

---

[69] Of course, the empowerment of the USTR was only the most recent transformation that led to the structural internationalization of the state, for the institutional changes introduced in 1934, 1947, and 1974 all contributed to the same process.

Discussion

The WTO was established as part of the Uruguay Round Agreements that concluded eight years of multilateral trade negotiations. The new organization presides over a scope of issues broader than what has been traditionally under the jurisdiction of the GATT, including trade in services, foreign investment, and intellectual property rights. This enlarged scope of intervention has been accompanied by a particularly significant institutional transformation: the strengthening of the organization's dispute resolution system. A more effective dispute settlement mechanism has been a double-edged sword; while allowing member-states to challenge protectionist violations of others more effectively, it has made member-states just as vulnerable to judicial challenges to their own practices. In spite of the dominant position of the United States in the international realm, the impacts on U.S. trade policies followed the same pattern. The legalization of the WTO has therefore established a new institutional regime, followed by new trade policies and practices: while internationalists gained better access to foreign markets, protectionist measures have been constantly, and effectively, challenged. Some measures, such as voluntary restraint agreements, were undermined in the international negotiations; many others were declared illegal by WTO panelists. This is not to suggest that protectionism has been completely eliminated, and even less so that opposition to free trade has stopped. Since the early 1990s, however, the vanguard of an anti–free trade (and antiglobalization more generally) movement has not been the industries, but rather labor, environmentalists, as well as consumer and human rights groups. The (adaptive) strategies of this new coalition responded to the new institutional context of legalized multilateralism by concentrating less on domestic laws, and more on the substance of international agreements.

The differences in the outcomes between diplomatic negotiations and judicial proceedings and the impact those international judicial proceedings had on U.S. domestic politics demonstrate that institutions matter also at the international level, and challenge neorealist expectations that the balance of power alone, regardless of the institutional setting in place, would determine outcomes. Rather, institutions have the capacity to shape the situational position of member-states and the level of autonomy of IO officials, and thereby the very substance of policy outcomes. GATT diplomatic negotiations capture quite well the neorealist image of decisions and compromises reflecting the disparity of resources between the member-states. But this is not the case with judicial proceedings, where decisions are made by panelists relatively independent of member-states and where, I argue, U.S. dominance is more effectively circumscribed. While resources, such as legal expertise and effective means of retaliation held by rich countries, place those countries at a distinct advantage, legalization made the gap between member-states less relevant. At the same time, legalization lessened member-states' input, and concentrated authority in the hands of the relatively autonomous WTO panelists.

Legalization led to intensified trade liberalization because of the structural-legal context in which WTO panelists made their decisions. The leveling of states' influence, in turn, assured that this bias would be applied relatively indiscriminately. Stated differently, member-states that made claims compatible with the trade-liberalizing WTO agenda were now better positioned than those who made claims incompatible with it, in a way that often counterbalanced other sources of inequality. Of course, globalization could and was advanced by means of diplomatic negotiations, not only judicial disputes. But negotiations meant that developed countries could use their bargaining leverage to protect some of their industries, sectors, or workers from the general process. Legalization made this possibility less attainable. No sector, issue, or condition—once introduced into the international trade agreements—could be ignored. In other words, if diplomatic negotiations put globalization rules in place, judicial proceedings introduced more effective commitment and better compliance.

The strengthening of the dispute settlement mechanisms was the outcome of American pressure, itself derived from U.S. interest in legalized intervention in other countries' domestic policies and practices. The U.S. administration insisted, however, that the DSU would not be able to transform the policies of the United States *without the consent of the administration or of Congress.* While technically correct, this assertion ignored the fact that the DSU transformed the process of decision-making in a way that decreased the need for Congress to get involved in trade issues and made the administration more attentive to international expectations for compliance. Contested policies and practices that were in the past excluded from international negotiations—including voluntary restraint agreements, unfair-trade laws, Section 301, and social-protectionist laws—were (re)introduced. Moreover, the contestation occurred not as part of diplomatic negotiations where the United States could employ its economic and political resources to force consensus compatible with its interests, but in a legalized setting, which was better protected from such pressures. This legalized setting provided access to grievances against U.S. protectionism, and panels repeatedly ruled against those practices. Since most trade practices have long been under the jurisdiction of the administration and not Congress, the United States, in spite of previous promises to the contrary, adhered to negative rulings. It was only in rare cases, and probably only for a limited time, that Congress could block compliance.

By the end of 2004, seventy years after the original institutional turn, U.S. trade policies and practices were stripped, to an impressive extent, from protectionist tilts of the traditional types. "Voluntary" restraint agreements were rarely in practice, antidumping and countervailing duty laws and regulations were under constant scrutiny, and Section 301 no longer functioned as a means for unilateral imposition of sanctions. Of course, this is not the end of protectionism. Previous turning points illustrate the relentless ability of domestic industries to abandon obsolete strategies and then devise, within the new institutional conditions, more effective ones. Institutional transformations, however, tend to have broader effects, which change the political game in fundamental ways and go beyond the seemingly trivial changes of sites of decision making. In the concluding chapter, I analyze what implications the institutional shifts described in this book had on politics in the United States and abroad. I describe what I find to be the core characteristics of the institutional trajectories and draw from these some conclusions regarding the alleged weakening capacity of states and their possible loss of sovereignty.

CONCLUSION

Globalization as an Institutional Project

In the previous chapters I offered an account of the evolution of free-trade policies and practices in the United States. I showed how changes in the institutional arrangements in place caused a gradual shift toward free trade by substantively transforming the matrix of influence of state and nonstate actors. Supporters of liberal trade—among them exporters, users of imported goods, investors in foreign markets, and U.S.-based multinational companies—undermined protectionist opposition by modifying those domestic and international institutional arrangements that were harmful to their expansionist interests. Among a variety of biased arrangements that shaped the political leverage of interested groups and state officials, I emphasized the distribution of authority among various political bodies and agencies, the level of discretion and legalization of those agencies, and the differentiated access to them. I identified three consecutive regimes of trade policy in the United States that, as an outcome of internationalists' strategic maneuverings, were biased in favor of globalizing rules. Protectionist practices persisted, but each new set of institutions assured, more effectively than before, that only protectionist measures that did not interfere with the general process of trade liberalization were imposed.

Before the 1930s, export opportunities were impeded because Congress kept tariffs high and often refused to ratify bilateral trade agreements.

Following a practice of "reciprocal noninterference" (Schattschneider 1935, 145), members of Congress supported each other's protectionist provisions, leading to a cycle of increased demands and measures. In 1934, however, the emergency situation created by the Great Depression elevated the interest in export opportunities, and Congress agreed to share its authority over tariff setting with the executive. Under the regime of *selective protectionism*, which lasted until 1974, the division of authority between Congress and various administrations—and, in the executive, the privileged position of the Department of State—allowed administrations to reduce domestic tariffs in return for the reciprocal reduction of tariffs that had blocked the entrance of U.S. companies to foreign markets. At the same time, however, Congress arranged "pockets" of special protection for declining sectors. The institutional arrangements of the GATT reproduced the inequality of economic and political resources among states, and therefore had little effect on the domestic political processes in the United States.

During the postwar economic boom, the *selective* arrangements suited the interests of both internationalists and protectionists. In reaction to the recession of the late 1960s, however, economic actors developed new interests, which could not be addressed in the existing institutional context. Protectionists' extensive demands clashed with internationalists' increased dependence on production and sales in foreign markets. The more vulnerable internationalist-oriented U.S. businesses became, the less they could tolerate protectionist practices at home. By buying-off the most influential industries among the protectionists, internationalists passed the Trade Act of 1974. The act permitted the administration to negotiate nontariff barriers to trade without the need for congressional ratification. The act also modified the trade remedy laws, as a result of which protectionist claims were channeled from Congress to the administration. Under the regime of *conditional protectionism*, Congress discontinued its practice of imposing product-specific trade barriers, and the administration made protectionist measures available mostly to those industries that could demonstrate injury and provide evidence of unfair trade practices of foreign importers. Decisions to impose protectionist measures were administered according to relatively strict legal and bureaucratic rules and were quite effectively insulated from social pressures. Consequently, the extent to which protectionist intervention disrupted the general process of trade liberalization was effectively minimized.

In the 1990s, nonmanufacturing interests in the United States, including intellectual-property owners, service providers, and U.S. investors in foreign countries, lobbied for the legalization of the WTO, in order to effectively supervise other countries' domestic implementation of international agreements. Since 1994, under the regime of *legalized multilateralism*, the World Trade Organization has been authorized to supervise the compatibility of domestic laws and practices with member-states' international obligations. The strengthened dispute settlement mechanisms shifted authority from the U.S. administration to the WTO. At the dispute settlement setting, the relative autonomy of panelists meant that decisions reflected the logic inscribed in the organization itself rather than members' political influence. The new dispute settlement mechanisms strengthened the authority of internationally oriented agencies at the domestic level as well. As a result, U.S. protectionist industries have become extremely vulnerable to legal challenges of other countries—member-states have legal means to contest American protectionist provisions and measures, WTO panelists regularly rule in favor of such liberal challenges, the U.S. administration willingly complies with negative rulings, and Congress cannot effectively offset such threats. Seventy years after the Reciprocal Trade Agreements Act of 1934, import quotas, high tariffs, voluntary export restraints, and measures to counteract unfair trade measures are all vulnerable to domestic and international censure. Protectionist measures for manufacturing industries, while still available, had to closely follow international obligations, which at times reduced them to little more than ad-hoc and temporary actions.

The empirical evidence, as summarized above, reverses numerous scholarly postulations commonly made about the current process of globalization. At the most fundamental level, the number of liberalizing trade laws and regulations in the United States as they have been defined and redefined over the years together with the some thirty-thousand pages of the WTO Agreement and its appendices (Jackson 2000, 179) suggest that rather than a dismantling of the political framework, globalization entails a replacement of one set of policies with another. The management of free trade—like the management of free capital, the implementation of austere macroeconomic management, and other neoliberal practices—requires as many laws, regulations, and enforcement mechanisms as closed markets. This offers a very different image than the common view of globalization as a system in which economic actors act free of political chains (Ohmae 1990, 1995; Reich 1992; Strange 1996; Greider 1997; Albrow 1996).

These political and legal components of globalization have not merely been a reflection of or reaction to changed economic activity (Sklair 1991; Arrighi 1994; Block 1996; Strange 1996; Mann 1997; Sassen 1998). Rather, political transformations were necessary to permit global economic practices in the first place. These political transformations had international as well as domestic dimensions. A global economy requires interstate cooperation, and the United States, with the support of other industrialized countries, embarked on a political project of imposing global rules on other countries (Gilpin 1975; Helleiner 1994; Gowan 1999). The establishment of the GATT in 1947 and the subsequent creation of the WTO were fundamental in bringing about convergence of liberal trade practices among trading partners. Other international organizations fulfilled a similar function—the International Monetary Fund, for example, imposed structural adjustment reforms such as privatization and deregulation and structural policy prescriptions designed to promote "good governance" or efficient institutions on developing countries (McMichael 2003; Babb and Buira 2005). But a global economy also requires domestic support. It is at the domestic level that interstate cooperation is made possible—where international agreements are initiated, ratified, and complied with. While this is generally the case, it is even more so with dominant states, which determine the agenda of international rules and obligations.

Domestic support, even in the United States, was not a trivial affair. Rather, for internationalists to prevail they had, and still have, to engage in a costly struggle. These struggles have not been (only) ideological contestations with the so-called antiglobalization or alternative-globalization groups, which are the focus of scholarly literature today (Keck and Sikkink 1998). Rather, these were struggles between two groups of economic actors: those who were to benefit from open markets and those who were to lose from increased international competition. I showed that the most consequential of the struggles between internationalist and protectionist interest groups in the United States were those over the institutional arrangements in place. To make trade liberalization possible, internationalists first defined the setting in which disputes over substantive policies would take place. Since Congress was too susceptible to protectionist influence, they fought to transfer authority to the executive; when the measures of various administrations themselves became a barrier in the way of even greater liberalization, internationalists fought to transfer authority to the international organization.

While many scholars who analyze the domestic processes of globalization have shown the role of domestic institutions in *mediating* between global economic processes and national policy outcomes (Milner and Keohane 1996; Weiss 1998, 2003; Swank 2002; Kahler and Lake 2003; Campbell 2003), only the literature on the "structural transformation of the state" suggests that state institutional arrangements have themselves been *negotiated* and *transformed* to facilitate the project of globalization (Cox 1987; McMichael 1996; Jessop 2002; Brenner 2004). Robert Cox (1987, 1992), most prominently, describes a restructuring of the hierarchy of state apparatuses; he specifically notes a shift in power away from those agencies most closely tied to domestic social forces and toward those that were in closest touch with transnational forces. Philip McMichael (1996) has similarly described the budgetary cuts in agencies and ministries, such as education, agriculture, health, and social services, which were responsible for the majority of the citizenry, and the parallel expansion of those agencies, such as the financial and trade ministries, concerned mostly with the sectors connected with global enterprises. In this book I present a case in which such institutional transformations were not the outcome of structural economic processes, as Cox and McMichael suggest, but rather facilitated them. Trade liberalization in the United States is hardly an isolated incident. This was clearly the case of economic transformations in Europe, where the triad of the European Parliament, the European Court of Justice, and the European Commission, advanced economic policies and brought about economic trends of unimaginable magnitude. The literature on the diffusion of neoliberalism in Southeast Asia, Latin America, and Central Europe—to which I referred in chapter 1—suggest that this was also the case elsewhere. Globalizing transformations were often preceded by political struggles, institutional changes, and biased policies.

As a way of conclusion, in the rest of this chapter I identify the particular features that characterize globalizing institutions and identify the implications this has for two prominent questions in the literature on the politics of globalization—the evolving imbalance between state power and global capital, and the relations between sovereign states and international organizations. I then reflect on what future research the findings of this study invite, including comparative analyses and study of current developments. It is with some comments about current developments that I conclude.

Institutionalization as Bureaucratization and Judicialization

The trajectory of trade policy formation illustrates how the institutional transformation of domestic and international political entities shaped the scope and pace of global economic processes. The structural transformations of states and international organizations, which have so far been analyzed as an outcome of global processes, are instead at the core of those processes. The political struggles aimed at introducing biased institutional arrangements suggest that "the globalization project" (McMichael 1996) contains a political agenda of putting in place institutional arrangements hospitable to globalizing policies.

The institutional arrangements that internationalists could reasonably expect to be biased in favor of globalizing policies share a particular set of characteristics that are important to identify. First, the new sites of authority systematically excluded dissenting (here, protectionist) voices from the process of decision making. Protectionists' *situational position*, and hence their political leverage, drastically weakened with the shift of authority from members of Congress, who were attentive to regional interests and popular sentiments, to civil servants in the executive and to panelists at the WTO.

More than the weakening of protectionists' situational position, however, it was the decrease in nonstate actors' *general* access and the increased (relative) *autonomy* of state officials and WTO panelists from external pressures, of either protectionists or internationalists, that allowed the prioritization of liberal trade policies. With the shift of authority from Congress to quasi-judicial state agencies that administered the trade remedy laws, and then to WTO judicial panels, the scope of external political influence decreased and officials made decisions based largely on preferences inscribed in the agencies themselves. Since autonomy was granted to agencies whose bureaucratic assignments and structural constraints led them to support liberal trade principles, this guaranteed that internationalist interests would prevail over protectionist ones.

This increased level of autonomy from external pressures was largely an outcome of the bureaucratization and judicialization of the policymaking process. At the domestic level, the new institutional arrangements channeled policymaking authority away from direct political struggles in Congress to bureaucratic and quasi-judicial bodies in the administration. At the international level, the new institutional arrangements channeled debates away from diplomatic negotiations, where member-states could deliberate, challenge, and renegotiate international agreements, to WTO judicial panels, where third-parties imposed interpretations and required the implementation of existing agreements.

Bureaucratization and judicialization characterize not only trade liberalization, but other aspects of the process of globalization as well. At the domestic level, we find the depoliticization of central banks (Polillo and Guillen 2005) where monetary policy is shifted from politicians to insulated committees (the bank's board) with a set of rules to guide their decisions.

Even privatization brings bureaucratization. The privatization of infrastructure, such as telecommunications, stripped the executive, which controlled the pricing and access of those companies when they were state-owned, of all authority. At the same time, however, privatization often came along with the creation of independent regulatory agencies that, while regulating and supervising the companies, were insulated from politics (Jensen and Mertaugh 2005). At the international level, the European Union is probably the most unequivocal example of a transnational process of both judicialization (the European Court of Justice) and bureaucratization (the European Commission).[1] Also, outside Europe, scholars of international relations have noted a general process of legalization. International tribunals, including not only the European Court of Justice and the World Trade Organization but also the International Criminal Tribunal, the Law of the Sea Tribunal, and the World Bank's Inspection Panel proliferate, become increasingly more active, and preside over increasingly more comprehensive issues (Martin 1994; Romano 1999; Goldstein et al. 2000). Whereas in the past disputes between governments and foreign investors were expected to be resolved by way of negotiations, countries now allow foreign investors to take disputes to formal arbitration tribunals. NAFTA's Chapter 11 similarly allows foreign investors to file formal legal complaints against the "host" governments.

The globalization of finance is of particular interest to the discussion here, as "financialization" (Krippner 2005) competes with trade liberalization as a major feature of globalization. While how exactly the globalization of finance occurred is still debated, scholars have convincingly shown that, as in trade, rather than a "pure" economic development, political intervention was required—governments have created a regulatory structure for this international economic activity (Kapstein 1994, v; Helleiner 1994; Abdelal 2007). But the politics of trade and the politics of finance were different, for two main reasons. First, in contrast to trade liberalization, which triggered domestic political struggles, there was hardly any domestic opposition to the liberalization of finance. Second, and partly as a result of the previous point, while trade liberalization was based on reciprocity and therefore required either bilateral or multilateral agreements, the liberalization of finance could be conducted unilaterally (Helleiner 1994, 18). By the middle of the 1980s, four states—the United States, the United Kingdom, Germany, and Japan—liberalized capital flows across their borders (Abdelal 2007).

---

[1] On the European Court of Justice, see Weiler 1994; Stone Sweet 1998; Garrett, Kelemen, and Schulz 1998; Slaughter et al. 1998; Alter 2001; on the European Commission, see Schneider 1995; Kerremans 1996; Garrett and Tsebelis 1996; Pollack 1997; Schmidt 2000.

Just as in trade, however, the liberalization of capital movements in *other* countries first necessitated institutional transformation, particularly increased jurisdiction and strengthening of international organizations. The most important initiatives originated in the EU, the Organisation for Economic Cooperation and Development (OECD), and the IMF (Abdelal 2007; see also Helleiner 1994, 157–63). A 1988 directive issued by the Ministerial Council obliged EC members to remove all restrictions on the movement of capital among member states, as well as between members and nonmembers; in 1989 the OECD's Code of Liberalization of Capital Movements was amended to oblige members to liberalize virtually all capital movements; and in the mid 1990s the IMF management sought to give the Fund mandate over the liberalization of capital flows so it could promote capital liberalization (Abdelal 2006; Abdelal 2007).[2] Crucially, Abdelal's (2007) account shows that it was the bureaucracies of the organizations, rather than member-states, which pushed for the globalization of finance. The case of finance is therefore yet another illustration for the institutional foundations of the globalization project.

To conclude, the essence of the institutional project of globalization has been a project of shifting authority, both at the national and the international levels, away from *politicized* sites of decision making, such as Congress and diplomatic negotiations, where decisions are determined to a large extent by political debates and struggles. Authority was put, instead, in *bureaucratic* and *judicial* sites, where exogenous voices and political deliberations are effectively filtered out.[3] This feature of the institutional transformation of states and international organizations provide a new angle to rethink the questions of state power and state sovereignty.

The Strengthening of the State?

Analysts of the political dimension of globalization have struggled over the question of how the global market economy affected the nation-state, in particular its ability to regulate the domestic economy and maintain social

---

[2] The plan failed, partly due to the opposition of U.S. Congress.

[3] Scholars of globalization have identified practices of political exclusion that characterize politics in the age of globalization (Hirst 1994; Held 1996; Castells 1996; Young 2000). It is important to emphasize, however, that the exclusion of the weak has been the result of the bureaucratization of the state and of existing international organizations, rather than solely the outcome of new forms of transnational governance (Pierre and Peters 2000), or of decisions bypassing political authorities (Strange 1996).

and welfare policies in the face of business opposition (Held et al. 1999; Paul, Ikenberry, and Hall 2003; Kahler and Lake 2003). This has been intensely debated, with claims ranging from declarations of the "death of the state" to assertions about the ability of states to fight back and resist or, alternatively, actively shape global structures.[4] "Globalists" argue that the capitalist world economy forms a global structure that transcends the sovereign state, rendering it virtually powerless to make real policy choices (Ohmae 1990, 1995; Camilleri and Falk 1992; Reich 1992; *Daedalus* 1995; Strange 1996; Albrow 1996; Falk 1997; Greider 1997). Many of those critical of the "globalist" argument do not contest the possibility that a process of globalization would result in the weakening of the state but rather criticize "globalists" for overemphasizing current global processes, arguing that existing global linkages remain too weak to transcend or even constrain states (Zysman 1996; Hirst and Thompson 1999; Rodrik 2000). Others question the implied link between strong globalization and weak states. They accept the current intensity of globalization and its disciplinary power but argue against the view that this necessarily entails the demise of the nation-state (Sassen 1998, 195). They suggest, instead, that the state has remained sovereign by transforming its role and organizational structure in a way that is compatible with the new structural necessities (Rosenau 1980; Strange 1996; Cox 1996; Hoogvelt 1997). This transformation has been part of a process in which states have become "increasingly attuned to, conditioned and restructured by the pressures emanating from the global economy" (Gill 1992, 276). New roles for the state suggested by scholars include "coordinating different forms of governance and ensuring a minimal coherence among them" (Jessop 1997, 576), as well as stabilizing and enforcing the rules and practices of a global society (Cerny 1997, 257–58). Opposed to this view are those scholars adhering to the institutionalist analysis of the state, who hold that states may adapt to (Weiss 1998), resist (Garret 1995; Weiss 1998), and even take advantage of (Evans 1995) the structural conditions imposed from above (see also Thomson and Krasner 1989; Krasner 1995; Hood 2003; Campbell 2003).

Paradoxically, the process of bureaucratization and judicialization of states that I identify above could be interpreted as the *strengthening* of political authorities, for this has increased states' autonomy to make decisions independently of exogenous pressures. The shift of authority over trade measures from Congress to the executive, for example, has reduced

[4] For helpful formulations of the globalization debate, see Weiss 1997; Held et al. 1999; Hobson and Ramesh 2002.

the influence over decision making of *both* protectionists and internationalists and increased the influence of state officials. While state officials are now less exposed to direct political pressures, however, bureaucratization also means the inability of states, due to the exclusion of alternative voices and hence lack of effective opposition, to resist *structural* constraints.[5] This means that "globalists" are correct in their assertion that the state's capacity to manage or resist capital has weakened. In contrast to their analysis, however, this has been the outcome of the political weakening of the opposition, *itself a result of institutional transformations*, rather than a direct or automatic outcome of capital's economic manifestations of power.

We are then experiencing not the "weakening" of the state as much as the "weakening" or loosening of its democratic elements and deliberative potential.[6] The structural transformation of the state altered its democratic nature and weakened the political influence of those political actors, like U.S. protectionist industries and workers, whose resources depend on mobilization and popular support.

The Decline of State Sovereignty and U.S. Hegemonic Power?

Possibly, the ability of states to regulate their markets has been undermined not only because of decreased bargaining leverage vis-à-vis capital but also because of decreased sovereignty vis-à-vis other states or international organizations. This, it should be mentioned, is not a common view. Most scholars of globalization adhere to the neorealist analytical framework and see international organizations as powerless or, alternatively, view them as merely reflecting the interests of the participating parties (Moravcsik 1993; Weiss 1999, 70–71). In either case, it is still considered impossible for international organizations to force a state to act against its perceived interests. Others, however, have argued that the state's monopoly over policymaking, which had never been complete, was now even more seriously threatened.

---

[5] Fred Block (1977b) has convincingly argued that the state would be able to resist structural constraints in the presence of effective opposition. While Block refers to working-class mobilization, opposition can come also from within the marginalized sectors of the capitalist class.

[6] Gritsch reaches a similar conclusion, though via a different analytical reasoning. According to Gritsch, globalization led to states' "increased autonomy" and "diminished democracy" because a globalized process of production reduced capital's and state's dependence on domestic labor for accumulation purposes (Gritsch 2005, 18).

They argue that governments now share authority with a wide range of private bodies, such as insurance companies, big accounting firms, organized crime, and private arbitration companies (Strange 1996; Dezalay and Garth 1996; Sassen 1998; Slaughter 2004). They also share authority with competing public authorities, including international organizations (Cox 1987; Robinson 1996; Jessop 1997; Shaw 2000).

The evidence this book provides is in line with the latter position. The same way that the bureaucratization and judicialization of the U.S. state has led to the weakening of the political leverage of domestic interest groups, judicialization has also weakened the influence of member-states over the WTO at the international level. While member-states maintain the power to formulate the legal texts, they have delegated the authority to interpret them to a third party; while member-states are the ones who retaliate, the current procedures make it almost impossible to oppose retaliation that has been approved by WTO panelists. WTO officials and panelists have become active and significant players in the game. In the judicial proceedings, decisions reflect the internal logic of the WTO more than the interests of those with the most economic resources. As a result, neoliberal goals, which are compatible with the organization's agenda, can be successfully achieved, but protectionist goals have been effectively sidelined.

While the institutionalization of the WTO suggests a decline in the overall influence of member-states, the United States might be an exception. If the WTO is controlled by and hence reflects the interests of the United States (Gowan 1999, 128–29), increased insulation of the WTO from member-states in effect *increases* U.S. influence. But is the international organization merely an instrument in the hands of the United States? The WTO's adherence to a proliberal model is, undoubtedly, an outcome of the years-long direct influence of the United States over the institution and over the content of multilateral agreements. In addition, the WTO has been constrained by its dependence on the cooperation and activity of developed countries and is hence vulnerable to their demands. And, yet, judicialization exactly means the loosening of those direct (situational) and structural influences. The reliance on formal legal rules provides less room for political considerations and hence less opportunity for rich countries to influence the outcome. In chapter 6 I showed that it has become more difficult for the U.S. government, in spite of its economic resources, to pursue goals inconsistent with WTO's bureaucratic and legal logic. The United States continues to successfully challenge protectionist measures of others but it can no longer effectively maintain its own protectionist policies. The liberal orientation of the WTO, in short, should no longer be viewed as an imposition from above by the United States. The WTO is a carrier of the globalization project in its own right.

An argument that relies on negative WTO decisions to show the weakening influence of the United States must confront claims that compliance with negative decisions is supported by the U.S. government because it is seen as an effective way to discard unwanted protectionist measures. These arguments, however, problematically view "U.S. interests" as coherent and unitary in supporting globalization. Instead, I have shown that state agencies differ in their perception of what "U.S. interests" are, with some (for example, the State Department) advancing an internationalist orientation and others (for example, the Commerce Department or Congress) a more domestic one. To address these conflicting sentiments, the U.S. administration would generally be interested in imposing trade liberalization on other countries, in order to improve the access of its internationally competitive industries to foreign markets, while at the same time preserving policies that protect its own declining industries from international competition. The legalization of the WTO weakened the ability of the U.S. government to balance these conflicting interests by combining liberal measures with protectionist ones. Notably, rather than viewing U.S. interests as liberal and explaining WTO activities as reflecting those interests, I argue that it is exactly because of the structural transformation of the WTO and its effect on the institutional arrangements of the U.S. government that the balance in the U.S. government between liberal and protectionist interests tilted further in favor of the former.

In short, the formal constraints of the legalized system made it difficult for the United States to pursue protectionist goals. Its declining ability to utilize economic and political resources to violate WTO agreements is particularly notable given the recent unilateralism and militarism of the U.S. government in other realms of international politics.[7] While this suggests that we should not generalize the U.S. position at the WTO to describe its influence in other international regimes or organizations, it reinforces the argument that the political leverage of member-states, including a hegemon, might vary depending on the institutional arrangements—such as the degree of legalization—that are in place, and that the globalization project is better "served" with the depoliticization of the participants, including those generally supportive of the project.

[7] On U.S. imperialism, see Bacevich 2002; Mann 2003; Harvey 2003.

Further Research on Politics and Globalization

This book contends that our understanding of the current era of globalization, including its emergence, contemporary features, and future developments, cannot be reduced to economic or technological factors. Rather, the political dimension is fundamental for the scope and shape that cross-national interactions take at the economic level, but also, no doubt, at the legal and cultural levels as well. In particular, this book has shown that political struggles, as they shape and are reshaped by institutions, determine the policies that enable (or constrain) future economic trends.

The study of trade policy formation in the United States allowed for a detailed investigation, in the tradition of historical sociology (Skocpol 1985; Calhoun 1996; Calhoun 1998), of globalization's moments of emergence and transformations over time. At the same time, focusing on one policy realm in one country prevents insights that studies of other countries and other policies, especially in a comparative framework, could bring to the surface. A larger research agenda for the study of the politics of globalization, therefore, could include the following.

First, and most obviously, the type of investigation utilized in this book could be usefully applied for other (non-U.S., non-trade) cases. Comparative analyses of how globalizing institutions have come about would allow not only for generalizations based on similarities, but also a sharpened understanding of the possibility of variation. Under what domestic and/or international conditions do advocates of globalization win political struggles? Under what conditions do they lose? Under what conditions would these struggles focus on institutional changes? Also, what types of institutions, other than bureaucratic or judicial ones, enable economic openness? What conditions determine the types of institutions chosen?

While the questions above would require comparative studies of nation-states, insights into the historical and current political developments of globalization can also come from comparative analyses of international organizations. The study of legalization and bureaucratization of international organizations has been so far dominated by rational choice institutionalists that assume that efficiency is the motivating force behind the establishment of and compliance with international regulations and rulings. While I agree with many of their insights, there is clearly a need for additional research that would incorporate political struggles and power into the analysis. Although methodologically challenging, comparative analyses of international organizations would provide great insights into the institutional and political conditions under which international organizations support or oppose the globalization project, and the conditions under which they are able to impose their preferences on member-states.

In addition, the focus on the United States has biased this study in favor of domestic factors over international ones, given the dominance the United States has in diplomatic negotiations. Other countries, particularly poor ones, would have a different balance of domestic and international pressures. There is an increasingly sophisticated literature on how to analytically navigate the balance and interplay between domestic and international factors (Gourevitch 1978; Putnam 1988; Milner 1997; Clark 1999), but these studies have yet to be utilized by those studying international organizations and their capacity to impose rules on sovereign states. One of the implications of this book is that this would depend, inter alia, on the institutional arrangements both at the domestic level *and* the international level, but this insight could benefit from further study.

Finally, the historical institutionalist account of the origins of globalization can also be applied to a study of the present. A central message of this book has been that globalization is an *ongoing* institutional project, and it is vulnerable to ongoing adaptive or outright challenging political strategies. The institutional changes that brought globalization about were the outcome of struggles among conflicting social interests, in which supporters of trade liberalization prevailed. Yet these victories were never complete, and subsequent struggles led to modifications of existing arrangements. These adaptive politics imposed limits on the globalization project: policy outcomes have not been one-sidedly globally oriented, and significant protectionist concessions have been permitted and implemented during the regimes of selective and conditional protectionism. The current regime of trade liberalization, legalized multilateralism, is also vulnerable to adaptive strategies that would permit new exceptions and curb its effects, but with two significant differences. First, with decision-making authority relocated to the WTO, critics of free-trade arrangements shifted their struggles from the domestic to the international level; second, today, the most effective critics of trade liberalization are not uncompetitive industries of developed countries but developing countries and reform-minded nongovernmental organizations (NGOs). Since the collapse of the Seattle Ministerial meeting in December 1999 (McMichael 2000; Wilkinson 2001; Jawara and Kwa 2003), developing countries time and again proved their ability, and willingness, to disrupt negotiations. In addition to substantive demands, such as liberalization of textiles and agricultural subsidies or derestricting of access to drugs, they have also embraced institutional strategies, trying to improve their position and to receive a more effective voice both in diplomatic negotiations and at the judicial proceedings (Oxfam 2000; McMichael 2000, 467).

While to date changes have been modest and have not resulted in significant institutional alternations, and even less so in significant substantive changes, it is possible that the political strategies used by opponents of the globalization project would counterbalance the most recent stage of globalization by at least partially repoliticizing the process of decision making. It is also possible, however, that supporters of the globalization project would react by introducing yet another set of institutional arrangements, creating a new regime of trade policy formation and implementation further biased in favor of their own interests. Precisely because it is not merely economically determined but also politically shaped, the globalization project can be intensified, but it can also be reversed or restrained.

References

Abbott, Kenneth W., and Duncan Snidal. 2001. "Hard and Soft Law in International Governance." *International Organization* 54: 421–56.

Abdelal, Rawi. 2006. "Writing the Rules of Global Finance: France, Europe, and Capital Liberalization." *Review of International Political Economy* 13: 1–27.

——. 2007. *Capital Rules: The Construction of Global Finance*. Cambridge: Harvard University Press.

Aggarwal, Vinod. 1985. *Liberal Protectionism: The International Politics of Organized Textile Trade*. Berkeley: University of California Press.

Albrow, Martin. 1996. *The Global Age*. Cambridge: Polity.

Alter, Karen J. 2001. *Establishing the Supremacy of European Law: The Making of an International Rule of Law in Europe*. Oxford: Oxford University Press.

Alter, Karen J., and Sophie Meunier-Aitsahalia. 1994. "Judicial Politics in the European Community: European Integration and the Pathbreaking *Cassis de Dijon* Decision." *Comparative Political Studies* 26: 535–61.

Amin, Ash. 1994. "Post-Fordism: Models, Fantasies, and Phantoms of Transition." In *Post-Fordism: A Reader*, edited by A. Amin, 1–39. Cambridge: Blackwell.

Anderson, James E. 1992. "Domino Dumping, I: Competitive Exporters." *American Economic Review* 82: 65–83.

Archibugi, Daniele, ed. 2003. *Debating Cosmopolitics*. London: Verso.

Arrighi, Giovanni. 1994. *The Long Twentieth Century: Money, Power, and the Origins of Our Times*. London: Verso.

Babb, Sarah. 2001. *Managing Mexico: Economists from Nationalism to Neoliberalism.* Princeton: Princeton University Press.

Babb, Sarah, and Ariel Buira. 2005. "Mission Creep, Mission Push, and Discretion: The Case of IMF Conditionality." In *The IMF and the World Bank at Sixty*, edited by A. Buira, 59–84. London: Anthem Press.

Bacevich, Andrew. 2002. *American Empire: The Realities and Consequences of U.S. Diplomacy.* Cambridge: Harvard University Press.

Bachrach, Peter, and Morton S. Baratz. 1962. "The Two Faces of Power." *American Political Science Review* 56: 947–52.

———. 1970. *Power and Poverty: Theory and Practice.* New York: Oxford University Press.

Bailey, Michael, Judith Goldstein, and Barry Weingast. 1997. "The Institutional Roots of American Trade Policy: Politics, Coalitions, and International Trade." *World Politics* 49: 309–38.

Baldwin, David, ed. 1993. *Neorealism and Neoliberalism.* New York: Columbia University Press.

Baldwin, Robert E. 1984. "The Changing Nature of U.S. Trade Policy since WWII." In *The Structure and Evolution of Recent U.S. Trade Policy*, edited by R. E. Baldwin and A. O. Krueger, 5–32. Chicago: University of Chicago Press.

———. 1985. *The Political Economy of U.S. Import Policy.* Cambridge: MIT Press.

Baldwin, Robert E., and Jeffrey W. Steagall. 1993. "An Analysis of Factors Influencing ITC Decisions in Antidumping, Countervailing Duty, and Safeguard Cases." Working Paper No. 4282, National Bureau of Economic Research. http://www.nber.org/papers/w4282.pdf.

Barnett, Michael N. 2002. "Historical Sociology and Constructivism: An Estranged Past, A Federated Future?" In *Historical Sociology of International Relations*, edited by S. Hobden and J. M. Hobson, 99–119. Cambridge: Cambridge University Press.

Barnett, Michael N., and Martha Finnemore. 1999. "The Politics, Power, and Pathologies of International Organizations." *International Organization* 53: 699–732.

———. 2004. *Rules for the World: International Organizations in Global Politics.* Ithaca: Cornell University Press.

Bauer, Raymond A., De Sola Pool, and Lewis A. Dexter. 1972. *American Business and Public Policy: The Politics of Foreign Trade.* Chicago: Aldine Atherton.

Bayard, Thomas O., and Kimberley Ann Elliott. 1994. *Reciprocity and Retaliation in United States Trade Policy.* Washington, DC: Institute for International Economics.

Bello, Judith H., and Alan F. Holmer. 1990. "The Heart of the 1988 Trade Act: A Legislative History of the Amendments to Section 301." In *Aggressive Unilateralism: America's 301 Trade Policy and the World Trading System*, edited by J. N. Bhagwati and H. T. Patrick, 49–89. Ann Arbor: University of Michigan Press.

Bergsten, C. Fred. 1971. "Crisis in U.S. Trade Policy." *Foreign Affairs* 49: 619–35.

Bhagwati, Jagdish. 1988. *Protectionism.* Cambridge: MIT Press.

Block Fred. 1977a. *The Origins of International Economic Disorder.* Berkeley: University of California Press.

———. 1977b. "The Ruling Class Does Not Rule: Notes on the Marxist Theory of the State." *Socialist Revolution 33*: 6–28.

———. 1980a. "Beyond Relative Autonomy: State Managers as Historical Subjects." *Socialist Register,* 227–42.

———. 1980b. "Trilateralism and Inter-Capitalist Conflict." In *Trilateralism: The Trilateral Commission and Elite Planning for World Management,* edited by H. Sklar, 519–32. Boston: South End Press.

———. 1996. *The Vampire State and Other Stories.* New York: New Press.

Bonacich, Edna, Lucie Cheng, Norma Chinchilla, Nora Hamilton, and Paul Ong, eds. 1994. *Global Production: The Apparel Industry in the Pacific Rim.* Philadelphia: Temple University Press.

Borrus, Michael. 1983. "The Politics of Competitive Erosion in the U.S. Steel Industry." In *American Industry in International Competition: Government Policies and Corporate Strategies,* edited by J. Zysman and L. Tyson, 60–105. Ithaca: Cornell University Press.

Bown, Chad P. 2004. "Developing Countries as Plaintiffs and Defendants in GATT/WTO Trade Disputes." *World Economy 27*: 59–80.

Bown, Chad P., and Bernard M. Hoekman. 2005. "WTO Dispute Settlement and the Missing Developing Country Cases: Engaging the Private Sector." *Journal of International Economic Law 8*: 861–90.

Brenner, Neil. 2004. *New State Spaces: Urban Governance and the Rescaling of Statehood.* Oxford: Oxford University Press.

Brenner, Robert. 1998. "The Economics of Global Turbulence." *New Left Review 229.*

Busch, Marc, and Eric Reinhardt. 2002. "Testing International Trade Law: Empirical Studies of GATT/WTO Dispute Settlement." In *The Political Economy of International Trade Law: Essays in Honor of Robert Hudec,* edited by D. M. Kennedy and J. D. Southwick, 457–81. New York and Cambridge: Cambridge University Press.

———. 2003a. "Developing Countries and General Agreement on Tariffs and Trade / World Trade Organization Dispute Settlement." *Journal of World Trade 37*: 719.

———. 2003b. "Transatlantic Trade Conflicts and GATT/WTO Dispute Settlement." In *Transatlantic Economic Disputes: The EU, the US, and the WTO,* edited by E.-U. Petersmann and M. A. Pollack, 465–85. Oxford: Oxford University Press.

———. 2003c. "The Evolution of GATT/WTO Dispute Settlement." In *Trade Policy Research,* edited by J. M. Curtis and D. Ciuriak, 143–83. Ottawa: Department of Foreign Affairs and International Trade.

Calhoun, Craig. 1996. "The Rise and Domestication of Historical Sociology." In *The Historic Turn in the Human Sciences,* edited by T. J. McDonald, 305–38. Ann Arbor: University of Michigan Press.

———. 1998. "Explanation in Historical Sociology: Narrative, General Theory, and Historically Specific Theory." *American Journal of Sociology 104*: 846–71.

Camilleri, Joseph, and Jim Falk. 1992. *The End of Sovereignty? The Politics of Shrinking and Fragmenting World.* Brookfield, Vt.: Edward Edgar.

Campbell, John L. 2003. "States, Politics, and Globalization: Why Institutions Still Matter." In *The Nation-State in Question,* edited by T. V. Paul, G. J. Ikenberry, and J. A. Hall, 234–59. Princeton: Princeton University Press.

Carruthers, Bruce, Sarah Babb, and Terrence Halliday. 2001. "Institutionalizing Markets, or the Market for Institutions? Central Banks, Bankruptcy Law, and the Globalization of Financial Markets." In *The Rise of Neoliberalism and Institutional Analysis*, edited by J. Campbell and O. Pederson, 94–125. Princeton: Princeton University Press.

Castells, Manuel. 1996. *The Rise of the Network Society*. Cambridge: Blackwell.

Cerny, Philip G. 1997. "Paradoxes of the Competition State: The Dynamics of Political Globalization." *Government and Opposition* 32: 249–74.

Charnovitz, Steve. 2002. "Judicial Independence in the World Trade Organization." In *International Organizations and International Dispute Settlement: Trends and Prospects*, edited by L. B. De Chazournes, C. Romano, and R. Mackenzie, 219–40. Ardsley: Transnational Publishers.

Chase-Dunn, Christopher, Yukio Kawano, and Benjamin D. Brewer. 2000. "Trade Globalization since 1795: Waves of Integration in the World-System." *American Sociological Review* 65: 77–95.

Chorev, Nitsan. 2005a. "Making and Remaking State Institutional Arrangements: The Case of U.S. Trade Policy in the 1970s." *Journal of Historical Sociology* 18: 3–36.

——. 2005b. "The Institutional Project of Neo-Liberal Globalism: The Case of the WTO." *Theory and Society* 34: 317–55.

Clark, Ian. 1998. "Beyond the Great Divide: Globalization and the Theory of International Relations." *Review of International Studies* 24: 479–98.

——. 1999. *Globalization and International Relations Theory*. Oxford: Oxford University Press.

Clemens, Elisabeth S. 1993. "Organizational Repertoires and Institutional Change: Women's Groups and the Transformation of US Politics, 1890–1920." *American Journal of Sociology* 98: 755–98.

——. 2003. "Rereading Skowronek: A Precocious Theory of Institutional Change." *Social Science History* 27: 443–53.

Clemens, Elisabeth S., and James M. Cook. 1999. "Politics and Institutionalism: Explaining Durability and Change." *Annual Review of Sociology* 25: 441–66.

Cline, William R. 1983. "Introduction and Summary." In *Trade Policy in the 1980s*, edited by W. R. Cline. Washington, DC: Institute for International Economics.

——. 1990. *The Future of World Trade in Textiles and Apparel*. Rev. ed. Washington, DC: Institute for International Economics.

Cohen, Stephen D. 1988. *The Making of United States International Economic Policy*. 3rd ed. London: Praeger.

Congressional Budget Office (CBO). 1994. "How the GATT Affects U.S. Antidumping and Countervailing-Duty Policy." Washington, DC: Congressional Budget Office.

Congressional Research Service (CRS). 2002. "NAFTA Labor Side Agreement: Lessons for the Worker Rights and Fast-Track Debate." The Library of Congress: Congressional Research Service.

Cox, Robert W. 1987. *Production, Power, and World Order: Social Forces in the Making of History*. New York: Columbia University Press.

———. 1992. "Global Perestroika." *Socialist Register*, 26–43.

———. 1996. *Approaches to World Order*. Cambridge: Cambridge University Press.

Cronin, Thomas E. 1980. "A Resurgent Congress and the Imperial Presidency." *Political Science Quarterly* 95: 209–37.

Cupitt, Richard, Rodney Whitlock, and Lynn Whitlock. 1997. "The (Im)mortality of International Governmental Organizations." In *The Politics of Global Governance: International Organizations in Interdependent World*, edited by P. F. Diehl, 7–23. Boulder: Lynne Rienner.

Curzon, Gerard, and Victoria Curzon. 1973. *Hidden Barriers to International Trade*. London: Trade Policy Research Centre.

Daedalus. 1995. Special edition: "What Future for the State?" 124.

Dahl, Robert. 1961. *Who Governs? Democracy and Power in an American City*. New Haven: Yale University Press.

Destler, I. M. 1980. *Making Foreign Economic Policy*. Washington, DC: Brookings Institution.

———. 1986. *American Trade Politics: System under Stress*. Washington, DC: Institute for International Economics.

———. 1992. *American Trade Politics*. 2nd ed. Washington, DC: Institute for International Economics.

———. 1995. *American Trade Politics*. 3rd ed. Washington, DC: Institute for International Economics.

———. 1997. *Renewing Fast-Track Legislation*. Washington, DC: Institute for International Economics.

———. 2005. *American Trade Politics*. 4th ed. Washington, DC: Institute for International Economics.

Destler, I. M., and Peter J. Balint. 1999. *The New Politics of American Trade: Trade, Labor, and the Environment*. Washington DC: Institute for International Economics.

Destler, I. M., Haruhiro Fukui, and Hideo Sato. 1979. *The Textile Wrangle: Conflict in Japanese-American Relations, 1969–71*. Ithaca: Cornell University Press.

Destler, I. M., and John S. Odell. 1987. *Anti-Protection: Changing Forces in United States Trade Politics*. Washington DC: Institute for International Economics.

Dezalay, Yves, and Bryant G. Garth. 2002. *The Internationalization of Palace Wars: Lawyers, Economists, and the Contest to Transform Latin American States*. Chicago: University of Chicago Press.

Dicken, Peter. 1998. *Global Shift: Transforming the World Economy*. 3rd ed. New York: Guilford Press.

Diebold, William, Jr. 1952. *The End of the I.T.O.* Essays in International Finance, no. 16. Princeton University.

———. 1972. *The United States and the Industrial World: American Foreign Economic Policy in the 1970s*. New York: Praeger Publishers.

———. 1974. "U.S. Trade Policy: The New Political Dimensions." *Foreign Affairs* 52: 472–96.

Dillon, Sara. 1999. "Fuji-Kodak, the WTO, and the Death of Domestic Political Constituencies." *Minnesota Journal of Global Trade* 8: 197.

Domhoff, William G. 1990. *The Power Elite and the State: How Policy Is Made in America*. New York: Aldine de Gruyter.

Drahos, Peter, and John Braithwaite. 2003. *Information Feudalism*. New York: Free Press.

Drake, William J., and Kalypso Nicolaidis. 1992. "Ideas, Interests, and Institutionalization: 'Trade in Services' and the Uruguay Round." *International Organization* 46: 37–100.

Dryden, Steve. 1995. *Trade Warrior: USTR and the American Crusade for Free Trade*. Oxford: Oxford University Press.

Duina, Francesco, and Frank Blithe. 1999. "Nation-States and Common Markets: The Institutional Conditions for Acceptance." *Review of International Political Economy* 6: 494–530.

Dunkley, Graham. 2000. *The Free Trade Adventure*. New York: Zed Books.

Eichengreen, Barry. 1989. "The Political Economy of the Smoot-Hawley Tariff." *Research in Economic History* 12: 1–43. Ekiert, Grzegorz. 2003. "The State after State Socialism: Poland in Comparative Perspective." In *The Nation-State in Question*, edited by T. V. Paul, G. J. Ikenberry, and J. A. Hall, 291–320. Princeton: Princeton University Press.

Esser, Josef, and Joachim Hirsch. 1994. "The Crisis of Fordism and the Dimensions of a 'Post-Fordist' Regional and Urban Structure." In *Post-Fordism: A Reader*, edited by A. Amin, 71–97. Cambridge: Blackwell.

Evans, Peter. 1995. *Embedded Autonomy: States and Industrial Transformation*. Princeton: Princeton University Press.

———. 1997. "The Eclipse of the State? Reflections on Stateness in an Era of Globalization." *World Politics* 50: 62–87.

Evans, Peter, Dietich Rueschemeyer, and Theda Skocpol, eds. 1985. *Bringing the State Back In*. New York: Cambridge University Press.

Falk, Richard. 1997. "State of Siege: Will Globalization Win Out?" *International Affairs* 73: 123–36.

Feketekuty, Geza. 1990. "U.S. Policy on 301 and Super 301." In *Aggressive Unilateralism: America's 301 Trade Policy and the World Trading System*, edited by J. N. Bhagwati and H. T. Patrick, 91–103. Ann Arbor: University of Michigan Press.

Ferguson, Thomas, and Joel Rogers, eds. 1981. *The Hidden Election: Politics and Economics in the 1980 Presidential Campaign*. New York: Pantheon Books.

Finger, J. Michael, H. Keith Hall, and Douglas Nelson. 1982. "The Political Economy of Administered Protection." *American Economic Review* 72: 452–66.

Finger, J. Michael, and Julio J. Nogues. 2002. "The Unbalanced Uruguay Round Outcome: The New Areas in Future WTO Negotiations." *World Economy* 25: 321–40.

Finlayson, Jack, and Mark Zacher. 1981. "The GATT and the Regulation of Trade Barriers: Regime Dynamics and Functions." *International Organization* 35: 561–602.

Fordham, Benjamin O., and Timothy J. McKeown. 2003. "Selection and Influence: Interest Groups and Congressional Voting on Trade Policy." *International Organization* 57: 519–49.

Franck, Thomas M., and Edward Weisband. 1979. *Foreign Policy by Congress.* New York: Oxford University Press.

Frieden, Jeff. 1988. "Sectoral Conflict and Foreign Economic Policy, 1914–1940." *International Organization* 42: 59–90.

Friedman, Lawrence M. 2001. "Erewhon: The Coming Global Legal Order." *Stanford Journal of International Law* 37: 347.

Gardner, Richard N. 1980. *Sterling-Dollar Diplomacy in Current Perspective.* New York: Columbia University Press.

Garrett, Geoffrey. 1995. "Capital Mobility, Trade, and the Domestic Politics of Economic Policy." *International Organization* 49: 657–87.

Garrett, Geoffrey, R. Daniel Kelemen, and Heiner Schulz. 1998. "The European Court of Justice, National Governments, and Legal Integration in the European Union." *International Organization* 52: 149–76.

Garrett, Geoffrey, and James McCall Smith. 2002. "The Politics of WTO Dispute Settlement." Paper presented at the annual meeting of the American Political Science Association, July 2002. Available at http://www.international.ucla.edu/cms/files/july02io.pdf.

Garrett, Geoffrey, and George Tsebelis. 1996. "An Institutional Critique of Intergovernmentalism." *International Organization* 49: 171–81.

Gelb, Leslie H., and Anthony Lake. 1973. "Washington Dateline: Watergate and Foreign Policy." *Foreign Policy* 12: 176–88.

General Accounting Office (GAO). June 2000. "World Trade Organization: U.S. Experience to Date in Dispute Settlement System." Washington, DC.

———. August 2000. "World Trade Organization: Issues in Dispute Settlement." Report to the Chairman, Committee on Ways and Means, House of Representatives. Washington, DC.

———. July 2003. "World Trade Organization: Standard of Review and Impact of Trade Remedy Rulings." Washington, DC.

Gill, Stephen. 1992. "Economic Globalization and the Internationalization of Authority: Limits and Contradictions." *Geoforum* 23: 269–83.

Gilligan, Michael. 1997. *Empowering Exporters: Reciprocity, Delegation, and Collective Action in American Trade Policy.* Ann Arbor: University of Michigan Press.

Gilpin, Robert. 1971. "The Politics of Transnational Economic Relations." *International Organization* 25: 398–419.

———. 1975. *U.S. Power and the Multinational Corporation: The Political Economy of Foreign Direct Investment.* New York: Basic Books.

———. 1981. *War and Change in World Politics.* Cambridge: Cambridge University Press.

Goldstein, Judith. 1986. "The Political Economy of Trade." *American Political Science Review* 80: 161–84.

———. 1993. *Ideas, Interests, and American Trade Policy.* Ithaca: Cornell University Press.

———. 1996. "International Law and Domestic Institutions: Reconciling North American "Unfair" Trade Laws." *International Organization* 50: 541–64.

———. 2002. "International Forces and Domestic Politics: Trade Policy and Institution Building in the United States." In *Shaped by War and Trade: International Influences on American Political Development*, edited by I. Katznelson and M. Shefter, 211–35. Princeton: Princeton University Press.

Goldstein, Judith, Miles Kahler, Robert Keohane, and Anne-Marie Slaughter. 2000. "Introduction: Legalization and World Politics." *International Organization* 54: 385–99.

Goldstein, Judith, and Stefanie Lenway. 1989. "Interests or Institutions: An Inquiry into Congressional-ITC Relations." *International Studies Quarterly* 33: 303–27.

Goldstein, Judith, and Lisa L. Martin. 2000. "Legalization, Trade Liberalization, and Domestic Politics: A Cautionary Note." *International Organization* 54: 603–32.

Gourevitch, Peter A. 1977. "International Trade, Coalitions, and Liberty: Comparative Responses to the Crisis of 1873–1896." *Journal of Interdisciplinary History* 8: 281–313.

———. 1978. "The Second Image Reversed: The International Sources of Domestic Politics." *International Organization* 32: 881–912.

———. 1999. "The Governance Problem in International Relations." In *Strategic Choice and International Relations*, edited by D. A. Lake and R. Powell, 137–64. Princeton: Princeton University Press.

Gowa, Joanne. 1983. *Closing the Gold Window: Domestic Politics and the End of Bretton Woods*. Ithaca: Cornell University Press.

Gowan, Peter. 1999. *The Global Gamble: Washington's Faustian Bid for World Dominance*. London: Verso.

Graz, Jean-Christope. 1999. "The Political Economy of International Trade: The Relevance of the International Trade Organization Project." *Journal of International Relations and Development* 2: 288–306.

Greider, William. 1997. *One World, Ready or Not: The Manic Logic of Global Capitalism*. New York: Touchstone.

Grieco, Joseph M. 1990. *Cooperation among Nations: Europe, America, and Nontariff Barriers to Trade*. Ithaca: Cornell University Press.

Gritsch, Maria. 2005. "The Nation-State and Economic Globalization: Soft Geo-Politics and Increased State Autonomy?" *Review of International Political Economy* 12: 1–25.

Grzymala-Busse, Anna, and Pauline Jones Luong. 2002. "Reconceptualizing the State: Lessons from Post-Communism." *Politics and Society* 30: 529–54.

Guthrie, Doug. 2001. *Dragon in a Three-Piece Suit: The Emergence of Capitalism in China*. Princeton: Princeton University Press.

Haggard, Stephan. 1988. "The Institutional Foundations of Hegemony: Explaining the Reciprocal Trade Agreements Act of 1934." *International Organization* 42: 91–119.

Hagy, David W. 1993. "Hegemonic Decline: Great Britain, the United States, and Steel." Ph.D. diss., Tulane University, New Orleans.

Hall, Christopher G. L. 1997. *Steel Phoenix: The Fall and the Rise of the U.S. Steel Industry*. New York: St. Martin's Press.

Hall, Peter A. 1986. *Governing the Economy: The Politics of State Intervention in Britain and France*. Oxford: Polity.

Hall, Peter A., and Rosemary C. R. Taylor. 1996. "Political Science and the Three New Institutionalisms." *Political Studies* 44: 936–57.

Hansen, John Mark. 1991. *Gaining Access: Congress and the Farm Lobby, 1919–81.* Chicago: University of Chicago Press.

Hansen, Wendy L. 1990. "International Trade Commission and the Politics of Protectionism." *American Political Science Review* 84: 21–46.

Hansen, Wendy L., and Thomas J. Prusa. 1997. "The Role of the Medial Legislator in U.S. Trade Policy: A Historical Analysis." *Economic Inquiry* 35: 97–107.

Hanson, Brian T. 1998. "What Happened to Fortress Europe? External Trade Policy Liberalization in the European Union." *International Organization* 52: 55–85.

Harrison, Bennett. 1994. *Lean and Mean: Why Large Corporations Will Continue to Dominate the Global Economy.* New York: Guilford Press.

Harrison, Bennett, and Barry Bluestone. 1988. *The Great U-turn: Corporate Restructuring and the Polarizing of America.* New York: Basic Books.

Harvey, David. 2003. *The New Imperialism.* Oxford: Oxford University Press.

Hattam, Victoria. 1992. "Institutions and Political Change: Working-Class Formation in England and the United States, 1820–96." In *Structuring Politics: Historical Institutionalism in Comparative Analysis,* edited by S. Steinmo, K. Thelen, and F. Longstreth, 155–87. Cambridge: Cambridge University Press.

Hay, Colin, and Daniel Wincott. 1998. "Structure, Agency, and Historical Institutionalism." *Political Studies* 46: 951–57.

Held, David. 1996. *Democracy and the Global Order: From the Modern State to Cosmopolitan Governance.* Stanford: Stanford University Press.

Held, David, Anthony McGrew, David Goldblatt, and Jonathan Perraton. 1999. *Global Transformations: Politics, Economics, and Culture.* Stanford: Stanford University Press.

Helfer, Laurence R., and Anne-Marie Slaughter. 1997. "Toward a Theory of Effective Supranational Adjudication." *Yale Law Journal* 107: 273–391.

Helleiner, Eric. 1994. *States and the Reemergence of Global Finance.* Ithaca: Cornell University Press.

Henisz, Witold, Bennet A. Zelner, and Mauro F. Guillén. 2005. "The Worldwide Diffusion of Market-Oriented Infrastructure Reform, 1977–99." *American Sociological Review* 70: 871–97.

Hersh, Seymour M. 1983. *The Price of Power.* New York: Summit Books

Hirst, Paul. 1994. *Associative Democracy: New Forms of Economic and Social Governance.* Cambridge: Polity Press.

Hirst, Paul, and Grahame Thompson. 1999. *Globalization in Question: The International Economy and the Possibilities of Governance.* 2nd ed. Malden: Polity Press.

Hiscox, Michael J. 1997. "The Trade War at Home: Factor Mobility, International Trade, and Political Coalitions in Democracies." Ph.D. diss., Harvard University, Cambridge.

——. 1999. "The Magic Bullet? The RTAA, Institutional Reform, and Trade Liberalization." *International Organization* 53: 669–98.

——. 2002. *International Trade and Political Conflict: Commerce, Coalitions, and Mobility.* Princeton: Princeton University Press.

Hobden, Stephen, and John M. Hobson, eds. 2002. *Historical Sociology of International Relations*. Cambridge: Cambridge University Press.

Hobson, John M. 1997. *The Wealth of States: A Comparative Study of International Economic and Political Change*. Cambridge: Cambridge University Press.

Hobson, John M., and M. Ramesh. 2002. "Globalisation Makes of States What States Make of It: Between Agency and Structure in the State/Globalisation Debate." *New Political Economy* 7: 5–22.

Hodin, Michael. 1987. *A National Policy for Organized Free Trade: The Case of U.S. Foreign Trade Policy for Steel 1976–78*. New York: Garland.

Holmes, Peter, Jim Rollo, and Alasdair R. Young. 2003. "Emerging Trends in WTO Dispute Settlement: Back to the GATT?" World Bank: Policy Research Working Paper 3133.

Hood, Christopher. 2003. "The Tax State in the Information Age." In *The Nation-State in Question*, edited by T. V. Paul, G. J. Ikenberry, and J. A. Hall, 213–33. Princeton: Princeton University Press.

Hoogvelt, Ankie. 1997. *Globalization and the Postcolonial World*. Basingstoke: Macmillan.

Horlick, Gary N., and Geoffrey D. Oliver. 1989. "Antidumping and Countervailing Duty Law Provisions of the Omnibus Trade and Competitiveness Act of 1988." *Journal of World Trade* 23: 5–49.

Horn, Henrik, Hakan Nordstrom, and Petros C. Mavroidis. 1999. "Is the Use of the WTO Dispute Settlement System Biased?" CEPR Discussion Paper 2340, Centre for Economic Policy Research.

Hudec, Robert E. 1975. *The GATT Legal System and World Trade Diplomacy*. New York: Praeger Publishers.

——. 1980. "GATT Dispute Settlement after the Tokyo Round: An Unfinished Business." *Cornell International Law Journal* 13: 145–203.

——. 1993. *Enforcing International Trade Law: The Evolution of the Modern GATT Legal System*. Salem, NH: Butterworth.

——. 1999. "The New WTO Dispute Settlement Procedure: An Overview of the First Three Years." *Minnesota Journal of Global Trade* 8: 1–53.

Hufbauer, Gary C., Diane T. Berliner, and Kimberly A. Elliott. 1986. *Trade Protection in the United States: 31 Case Studies*. Washington, DC: Institute for International Economics.

Iida, Keisuke. 2004. "Is WTO Dispute Settlement Effective?" *Global Governance* 10: 207–25.

Ikenberry, G. John. 1988. "Conclusion: An Institutional Approach to American Foreign Economic Policy." *International Organization* 42: 219–43.

——. 2001. *After Victory: Institutions, Strategic Restraint, and the Rebuilding of Order after Major Wars*. Princeton: Princeton University Press.

Ikenberry, G. John, David A. Lake, and Michael Mastanduno. 1988. "Introduction: Approaches to Explaining American Foreign Economic Policy." *International Organization* 42: 1–14.

Immergut, Ellen M. 1992. "The Rules of the Game: The Logic of Health Policy-making in France, Switzerland, and Sweden." In *Structuring Politics: Historical*

Institutionalism in Comparative Analysis, edited by S. Steinmo, K. Thelen, and F. Longstreth, 57–89. Cambridge: Cambridge University Press.

——. 1997. "The Normative Roots of the New Institutionalism: Historical Institutionalism and Comparative Policy Studies." In *Theorieentwicklung in der Politikwissenschaft: Eine Zwischenbilanz,* edited by A. Benz and W. Seibel, 325–55. Baden-Baden, Germany: Nomos Verlagsgesellschaft.

——. 1998. "The Theoretical Core of the New Institutionalism." *Politics and Society* 26: 5–34.

Irwin, Douglas A. 1998. "From Smoot-Hawley to Reciprocal Trade Agreements: Changing the Course of U.S. Trade Policy in the 1930s." In *The Defining Moment: The Great Depression and the American Economy in the Twentieth Century,* edited by M. D. Bordo, C. Goldin, and E. N. White, 325–52. Chicago: University of Chicago Press.

Irwin, Douglas A., and Randall S. Kroszner. 1999. "Interests, Institutions, and Ideology in Securing Policy Change: The Republican Conversion to Trade Liberalization After Smoot-Hawley." *Journal of Law and Economics* 42: 643–73.

Jackson, John H. 1967. "The General Agreement on Tariffs and Trade in U.S. Domestic Law." *Michigan Law Review* 66: 249.

——. 1969. *World Trade and the Law of GATT.* Indianapolis: Bobbs-Merrill.

——. 1984. "United States Law and Implementation of the Tokyo Round Negotiation." In *Implementing the Tokyo Round: National Constitutions and International Economic Rules,* edited by J. H. Jackson, J.-V. Louis, and M. Matsusita, 139–97. Ann Arbor: The University of Michigan Press.

——. 1997. *The World Trading System: Law and Policy of International Economic Relations.* 2nd ed. Cambridge: MIT Press.

——. 1998. *The World Trading System: Law and Policy of International Economic Relations.* 2nd ed. Cambridge: MIT Press.

——. 2000. "The Role and Effectiveness of the WTO Dispute Settlement Mechanism." *Brookings Trade Forum* 179.

Jawara, Fatoumata, and Aileen Kwa. 2003. *Behind the Scenes at the WTO.* London: Zed.

Jensen, Nathan, and Hilary Mertaugh. 2005. "Reducing Political Risks through Regulation: The Relationship between Independent Regulatory Agencies and Electricity Infrastructure Investments." Paper presented at The Political Economy of Regulating Multinational Corporations and Foreign Direct Investment Conference, Penn State 2005.

Jessop, Bob. 1990. *State Theory: Putting the Capitalist States in their Place.* University Park: Pennsylvania State University Press.

——. 1997. "Capitalism and Its Future: Remarks on Regulation, Government, and Governance." *Review of International Political Economy* 4: 561–81.

——. 2001. "Institutional Re(turns) and the Strategic-Relational Approach." *Environment and Planning A* 33: 1213–35.

——. 2002. *The Future of the Capitalist State.* Cambridge: Polity Press.

Judis, John B. 2000. *The Paradox of American Democracy: Elites, Special Interests, and the Betrayal of Public Trust.* New York: Pantheon Books.

Kahler, Miles. 2001. "Conclusion: The Causes and Consequences of Legalization." *International Organization* 54: 661–83.

Kahler, Miles, and David A. Lake, eds. 2003. *Governance in a Global Economy: Political Authority in Transition.* Princeton: Princeton University Press.

Kapstein, Ethan B. 1994. *Governing the Global Economy: International Finance and the State.* Cambridge: Harvard University Press.

Keck, Margaret E., and Kathryn Sikkink. 1998. *Activists beyond Borders: Advocacy Networks in International Politics.* Ithaca: Cornell University Press.

Keech, William R., and Kyoungsan Pak. 1995. "Partisanship, Institutions, and Change in American Trade Politics." *Journal of Politics* 57: 1130–42.

Keohane, Robert. 1984. *After Hegemony.* Princeton: Princeton University Press.

———. 1986. "Reciprocity in International Relations." *International Organization* 40: 1–27.

———. 2002. *Power and Governance in a Partially Globalized World.* London: Routledge.

Keohane, Robert, and Helen V. Milner, eds. 1996. *Internationalization and Domestic Politics.* Cambridge: Cambridge University Press.

Keohane, Robert, Andrew Moravcsik, and Anne-Marie Slaughter. 2000. "Legalized Dispute Resolution: Interstate and Transnational." *International Organization* 54: 457–88.

Keohane, Robert, Joseph Nye, and Stanley Hoffman. 1993. *After the Cold War: International Institutions and State Strategies in Europe, 1989–91.* Cambridge: Harvard University Press.

Kerremans, Bart. 1996. "Non-institutionalism, Neo-institutionalism, and the Logic of Common Decision-making in the European Union." *Governance* 9: 217–40.

Kindleberger, Charles. 1973. *The World in Depression, 1929–39.* London: Allen Lane.

Knight, Jack. 1992. *Institutions and Social Conflict.* New York: Cambridge University Press.

Kochavi, Noam. 2005. "Insights Abandoned, Flexibility Lost: Kissinger, Soviet Jewish Emigration, and the Demise of Détente." *Diplomatic History* 29: 503–30.

Kock, Karin. 1969. *International Trade Policy and the GATT 1947–1967.* Stockholm: Almqvist and Wiksell.

Koremenos, Barbara, Charles Lipson, and Duncan Snidal. 2001. "The Rational Design of International Institutions." *International Organization* 55: 761–99.

Krajewski, Marcus. 2004. "Disciplining Governments: The GATS 'Constitution' and Public Interest Regulation." Paper presented at the annual meeting of the British International Studies Association, December 2004.

Krasner, Stephen D. 1976. "State Power and the Structure of International Trade." *World Politics* 28: 317–47.

Krasner, Stephen D., ed. 1983. *International Regimes.* Ithaca: Cornell University Press.

———. 1984. "Approaches to the State: Alternative Conceptions and Historical Dynamics." *Comparative Politics* 16: 223–46.

——. 1995. "Power Politics, Institutions, and Transnational Relations." In *Bringing Transnational Relations Back in*, edited by T. Risse-Kappen, 257–79. Cambridge: Cambridge University Press.

Krauss, Melvyn B. 1978. *The New Protectionism: The Welfare State and International Trade*. New York: New York University Press.

Krippner, Greta. 2003. "The Fictitious Economy: Financialization, the State, and Contemporary Capitalism." Ph.D. diss., University of Wisconsin, Madison.

——. 2005. "The Financialization of the American Economy." *Socio-Economic Review* 3: 173–208.

Lake, David. 1988. *Power, Protection, and Free Trade: International Sources of U.S. Commercial Strategy, 1887–1939*. Ithaca: Cornell University Press.

Leitner, Kara, and Simon Lester. 2004. "WTO Dispute Settlement 1995–2003: A Statistic Analysis." *Journal of International Economic Law* 7: 169–81.

Levi, Margaret. 1988. *Of Rule and Revenue*. Berkeley: University of California Press.

Lipson, Charles. 1982. "The Transformation of Trade: The Sources and Effects of Regime Chance." *International Organization* 36: 417–55.

Lohmann, Susanne, and Sharyn O'Halloran. 1994. "Divided Government and U.S. Trade Policy: Theory and Evidence." *International Organization* 48: 595–632.

Loungnarath, Vilaysoun, and Celine Stehly. 2000. "The General Dispute Settlement Mechanism in the North American Free Trade Agreement and the World Trade Organization System." *Journal of World Trade* 34: 39–71.

Luong, Pauline Jones. 2000. "After the Break-up: Institutional Design in Transitional States." *Comparative Political Studies* 33: 563–92.

Lusztig, Michael. 1998. "The Limits of Rent Seeking: Why Protectionist Become Free Traders." *Review of International Political Economy* 5: 38–63.

Mahoney, James. 2000. "Path Dependence in Historical Sociology." *Theory and Society* 29: 507–48.

Manley, John F. 1983. "Neo-Pluralism: A Class Analysis of Pluralism I and Pluralism II." *American Political Science Review* 77: 368–83.

Mann, Michael. 1997. "Has Globalization Ended the Rise and Rise of the Nation-State?" *Review of International Political Economy* 4: 472–96.

——. 2003. *Incoherent Empire*. London: Verso.

Marks, Matthew. 1978. "Remedies to 'Unfair' Trade: American Action against Steel Imports." *World Economy* 1: 223–29.

Martin, Cathie Jo. 1994. "Business and the New Economic Activism: The Growth of Corporate Lobbies in the Sixties." *Polity* 27: 49–76.

Marx, Karl. 1978 [1859]. "Marx on the History of His Opinions." In *The Marx-Engels Reader*, edited by R. Tucker, 3–6. New York: W. W. Norton.

Marx, Karl, and Friedrich Engels, "The German Ideology." In *The Marx-Engels Reader*, edited by R. Tucker, 146–200. New York: W. W. Norton.

Mastanduno, Michael, David A. Lake, and G. John Ikenberry. 1989. "Toward a Realist Theory of State Action." *International Studies Quarterly* 33: 457–74.

Mattli, Walter, and Anne-Marie Slaughter. 1995. "Law and Politics in the European Union: A Reply to Garrett." *International Organization* 49: 183–90.

———. 1998. "*Revisiting the European Court of Justice.*" *International Organization* 52: 177–209.

Mayer, Frederick W. 1998. *Interpreting NAFTA: The Science and Art of Political Analysis*. New York: Columbia University Press.

McGillivray, Fiona. 2000. *Democratizing the World Trade Organization*. Stanford, CA: Hoover Institution.

McMichael, Philip. 1996. "Globalization: Myths and Realities." *Rural Sociology* 61: 25–55.

———. 2000. "Sleepless since Seattle: What Is the WTO About?" *Review of International Political Economy* 7: 466–74.

———. 2001. "Revisiting the Question of the Transnational State: A Comment on William Robinson's 'Social Theory and Globalization.' " *Theory and Society* 30: 201–10.

———. 2003. *Development and Social Change: A Global Perspective*. 3rd ed. Thousand Oaks, CA: Pine Forge Press.

McRae, D. M., and J. C. Thomas. 1983. "The GATT and Multilateral Treaty Making: The Tokyo Round." *American Journal of International Law* 77: 51–83.

Meunier, Sophie. 2000. "What Single Voice? European Institutions and EU-U.S. Trade Negotiations." *International Organizations* 54: 103–35.

———. 2005. *Trading Voices: The European Union in International Commercial Negotiations*. Princeton: Princeton University Press.

Michalopoulos, Constantin. 2001. *Developing Countries in the WTO*. New York: Palgrave.

Migdal, Joel. 1988. *Strong States and Weak Societies: State-Society Relations and State Capabilities in the Third World*. Princeton: Princeton University Press.

Miliband, Ralph. 1969. *The State in Capitalist Society*. London: Quartet Books.

Mills, C. Wright. 1956. *The Power Elite*. Oxford: Oxford University Press.

Milner, Helen V. 1988. *Resisting Protectionism: Global Industries and the Politics of International Trade*. Princeton: Princeton University Press.

———. 1990. "The Political Economy of U.S. Trade Policy: A Study of the Super 301 Provision." In *Aggressive Unilateralism: America's 301 Trade Policy and the World Trading System*, edited by J. N. Bhagwati and H. T. Patrick, 163–80. Ann Arbor: University of Michigan Press.

———. 1997. *Interests, Institutions, and Information: Domestic Politics and International Relations*. Princeton: Princeton University Press.

Milner, Helen, and Robert Keohane. 1996. "Internationalization and Domestic Politics: An Introduction." In *Internationalization and Domestic Politics*, edited by R. Keohane and H. Milner, 3–24. Cambridge: Cambridge University Press.

Milner, Helen V., and Peter Rosendorff. 1996. "Trade Negotiations, Information, and Domestic Politics: The Role of Domestic Groups." *Economics and Politics* 8: 145–89.

———. 1997. "Democratic Politics and International Trade Negotiations: Elections and Divided Government as Constraints on Trade Liberalization." *Journal of Conflict Resolution* 41: 117–46.

Milner, Helen V., and David B. Yoffie. 1989. "Between Free Trade and Protectionism: Strategic Trade Policy and a Theory of Corporate Trade Demands." *International Organization* 43: 239–72.

Moravcsik, Andrew. 1993. "Preferences and Power in the European Community." *Journal of Common Market Studies* 31: 473–524.

Narlikar, Amrita. 2004. "WTO Institutional Reform: A Role for G20 Leaders?" Paper presented at the Breaking the Deadlock in Agricultural Trade Reform and Development Conference, Oxford. Available at http://www.cigionline.ca/v.2/conf_docs/g20.oxford.narlikar.pdf.

Nivola, Pietro S. 1986. "The New Protectionism: U.S. Trade Policy in Historical Perspective." *Political Science Quarterly* 101: 577–600.

———. 1993. *Regulating Unfair Trade.* Washington, DC: Brookings Institution.

Noland, Marcus. 1997. "Chasing Phantoms: The Political Economy of USTR." *International Organization* 51: 365–87.

Nollen, Stanley D., and Dennis P. Quinn. 1994. "Free Trade, Fair Trade, Strategic Trade, and Protectionism in the U.S. Congress, 1987–88." *International Organization* 48 (3): 491–525.

North, Douglas C. 1990. *Institutions, Institutional Change, and Economic Performance.* New York: Cambridge University Press.

Odell, John S. 1982 *International Monetary Policy: Markets, Power, and Ideas as Sources of Change.* Princeton: Princeton University Press.

Offe, Claus. 1974. "Structural Problems of the Capitalist State: Class Rule and the Political System. On the Selectiveness of Political Institutions." *German Political Studies* 1: 31–57.

O'Halloran, Sharyn. 1994. *Politics, Pressures, and the Tariff: A Study of Free Private Enterprise in Pressure Politics, as Shown in the 1929–1930 Revision of the Tariff.* Englewood Cliffs, NJ: Prentice-Hall.

Ohmae, Kenichi. 1990. *The Borderless World.* London: William Collins.

———. 1995. *The End of the Nation State.* New York: Free Press.

O'Riain, Sean. 2000. "The Flexible Developmental State: Globalization, Information Technology, and the 'Celtic Tiger.' " *Politics and Society* 28: 157–93.

Orren, Karen, and Stephen Skowronek. 2002. "The Study of American Political Development." In *Political Science: The State of the Discipline,* edited by I. Katznelson and H. V. Milner, 722–54. New York: W. W. Norton.

Oxfam. 2000. "Institutional Reform of the WTO." Oxfam GB Discussion Paper. Available at http://www.oxfam.org.uk/what_we_do/issues/trade/downloads/wto_reform.rtf.

Panitch, Leo. 1994. "Globalization and the State." In *Socialist Register 1994,* edited by R. Miliband and L. Panitch, 60–93. London: Merlin Press.

———. 1996. "Rethinking the Role of the State." In *Globalization: Critical Reflections,* edited by J. H. Mittelman, 83–113. Boulder, CO: Lynne Rienner.

Pastor, Robert A. 1980. *Congress and the Politics of U.S. Foreign Economic Policy, 1929–1976.* Berkeley: University of California Press.

Paul, T. V., G. John Ikenberry, and John A. Hall. 2003. *The Nation-State in Question.* Princeton: Princeton University Press.

Pearson, Charles S. 1990. "Free Trade, Fair Trade? The Reagan Record." In *The Direction of Trade Policy*, edited by C. Pearson and J. Riedel, 24–59. Cambridge: Basil Blackwell.

Pearson, Charles, and James Riedel. 1990. "United States Trade Policy: From Multilateralism to Bilateralism?" In *The New Protectionist Wave*, edited by E. Grilli and E. Sassoon, 100–119. New York: New York University Press.

Petersmann, Ernst-Ulrich. 1994. "The Dispute Settlement System of the World Trade Organization and the Evolution of the GATT Dispute Settlement System since 1948." *Common Market Law Review* 31: 1157–1244.

Pier, Carol. 2006. "Workers' Rights Provisions in Fast Track Authority, 1974–2007: An Historical Perspective and Current Analysis." *Indiana Journal of Global Legal Studies* 13: 77–103.

Pierre, Jon, and B. Guy Peters. 2000. *Governance, Politics, and the State*. New York: St. Martin's Press.

Pierson, Paul. 1996. "The Path to European Integration: A Historical Institutional Analysis." *Comparative Political Studies* 29: 123–63.

——. 2000a. "The Limits of Design: Explaining Institutional Origins and Change." *Governance* 13: 475–99.

——. 2000b. "Increasing Returns, Path Dependence, and the Study of Politics." *American Political Science Review* 94: 251–68.

Pierson, Paul, and Theda Skocpol. 2002. "Historical Institutionalism in Contemporary Political Science." In *Political Science: The State of the Discipline*, edited by I. Katznelson and H. V. Milner, 693–721. New York: W. W. Norton.

Pincus, Jonathan J. 1975. "Pressure Groups and the Pattern of Tariffs." *Journal of Political Economy* 83: 757–78.

Polanyi, Karl. 1957 [1944]. *The Great Transformation: The Political and Economic Origins of Our Time*. Boston: Beacon Press.

Polillo, Simone, and Mauro F. Guillén. 2005. "Globalization Pressures and the State: The Worldwide Spread of Central Bank Independence." *American Journal of Sociology* 110: 1764–1802.

Pollack, Mark A. 1997. "Delegation, Agency, and Agenda Setting in the European Community." *International Organization* 51: 99–134.

Pontusson, Jonas. 1995. "From Comparative Public Policy to Political Economy: Putting Political Institutions in Their Place and Taking Interests Seriously. Review Essay." *Comparative Political Studies* 28: 117–47.

Prechel, Harland. 1990. "Steel and the State: Industry Politics and Business Policy Formation, 1940–1989." *American Sociological Review* 55: 648–68.

Preeg, Ernest H. 1995. *Traders in a Brave New World: The Uruguay Round and the Future of the International Trading System*. Chicago: University of Chicago Press.

Prusa, Thomas J. 1996. "The Trade Effects of U.S. Antidumping Actions." Working Paper No. 5440, National Bureau of Economic Research. Available at http://www.nber.org/papers/w5440.pdf.

Putnam, Robert. 1988. "Diplomacy and Domestic Politics: The Logic of Two-Level Games." *International Organization* 42: 427–60.

Raghavan, Chakravarthi. 2000. *The World Trade Organization and Its Dispute Settlement System: Tilting the Balance against the South.* Malaysia: Third World Network.

Reich, Robert. 1992. *The Work of Nations.* New York: Vintage.

Reinhardt, Eric R. 1996. *Posturing Parliaments: Ratification, Uncertainty, and International Bargaining.* Ph.D. diss., Columbia University, New York.

Reisman, Simon. 1996. "ITO and GATT." In *The Bretton Woods-GATT System. Retrospect and Prospect After Fifty Years,* edited by O. Kirshner, 82–86. New York: Sharpe.

Rhodes, Carolyn. 1993. *Reciprocity, U.S. Trade Policy, and the GATT Regime.* Ithaca: Cornell University Press.

Robinson, William I. 1996. *Promoting Polyarchy: Globalization, U.S. Intervention, and Hegemony.* Cambridge: Cambridge University Press.

———. 2001. "Social Theory and Globalization: The Rise of a Transnational State." *Theory and Society* 30: 157–200.

Rodrik, Dani. 2000. "How Far Will International Economic Integration Go?" *Journal of Economic Perspectives* 14: 177–86.

Rogowski, Ronald. 2002. "Trade and Representation: How Diminishing Geographic Concentration Augments Protectionist Pressures in the U.S. House of Representatives." In *Shaped by War and Trade: International Influences on American Political Development,* edited by I. Katznelson and M. Shefter, 181–210. Princeton: Princeton University Press.

Romano, Cesare. 1999. "The Proliferation of International Judicial Bodies: The Pieces of the Puzzle." *New York University Journal of International Law and Politics* 31: 709–51.

Rosenau, James N. 1980. *The Study of Global Interdependence.* London: Pinter.

Rosendorff, B. Peter, and Helen V. Milner. 2001. "The Optimal Design of International Trade Institutions: Uncertainty and Escape." *International Organization* 55: 29–857.

Rosenthal, Paul C., and Robert T. C. Vermylen. 2000. "The WTO Antidumping and Subsidies Agreements: Did the United States Achieve Its Objectives during the Uruguay Round?" *Law and Policy in International Business* 31: 871.

Rothstein, Bo. 1992. "Labor Market Institutions and Working-Class Strength." In *Structuring Politics: Historical Institutionalism in Comparative Analysis,* edited by S. Steinmo, K. Thelen, and F. Longstreth, 33–56. Cambridge: Cambridge University Press.

Ruggie, John G. 1982. "International Regimes, Transactions, and Change: Embedded Liberalism in the Post-War Economic Order." *International Organization* 36: 397–415.

———. 1998. *Constructing the World Policy.* London: Routledge.

Rupert, Mark. 2000. *Ideologies of Globalization: Contending Visions of a New World Order.* London: Routledge.

Ryan, Michael. 1995. *Playing by the Rules: American Trade Power and Diplomacy in the Pacific.* Washington, DC: Georgetown University Press.

Sabel, Charles F. 1994. "Flexible Specialization and the Re-emergence of Regional Economies." In *Post-Fordism: A Reader,* edited by A. Amin, 101–56. Cambridge: Blackwell.

Safire, William. 1975. *Before the Fall: An Inside View of the Pre-Watergate White House*. New York: Da Capo.

Sassen, Saskia. 1996. *Losing Control? Sovereignty in an Age of Globalization*. New York: Columbia University Press.

———. 1998. *Globalization and Its Discontents: Essays on the New Mobility of People and Money*. New York: New Press.

Sassoon, Enrico. 1990. "Protectionism and International Trade Negotiations during the 1980s." In *The New Protectionist Wave*, edited by E. Grilli and E. Sassoon. New York: New York University Press.

Schattschneider, E. E. 1935. *Politics, Pressure, and the Tariff*. New York: Prentice-Hall.

———. 1960. *The Semi-Sovereign People: A Realist's View of Democracy in America*. New York: Holt, Rinehart and Winston.

Schickler, Eric. 2001. *Disjointed Pluralism: Institutional Innovation and the Development of the US Congress*. Princeton: Princeton University Press.

Schmidt, Susanne K. 2000. "Only an Agenda Setter? The European Commission's Power over the Council of Ministers." *European Union Politics* 1: 37–61.

Schneider, Gerald. 1995. "The Limits of Self-reform: Institution-building in the European Union." *European Journal of International Relations* 1: 59–86.

Schnietz, Karen E. 2000. "The Institutional Foundation of U.S. Trade Policy: Revisiting Explanations for the 1934 Reciprocal Trade Agreements Act." *Journal of Policy History* 12: 417–44.

———. 2003. "The Reaction of Private Interests to the 1934 Reciprocal Trade Agreements Act." *International Organization* 57: 213–33.

Schwab, Susan C. 1994. *Trade-Offs: Negotiating the Omnibus Trade and Competitiveness Act*. Cambridge: Harvard Business School Press.

Secchi, Carlo. 1997. "The Political Economy of the Uruguay Round: Groups, Strategies, Interests, and Results." In *Multilateralism and Regionalism after the Uruguay Round*, edited by R. Faini and E. Grilli, 61–111. London: Macmillan Press.

Sell, Susan. 2003. *Private Power, Public Law: The Globalization of Intellectual Property*. Cambridge: Cambridge University Press.

Shapiro, Martin. 1993. "The Globalization of Law." *Global Legal Studies Journal* 1:37–64.

Shaw, Martin. 2000. *Theory of the Global State: Globality as an Unfinished Revolution*. Cambridge: Cambridge University Press.

Shepsle, Kenneth A. 1989. "Studying Institutions: Some Lessons from the Rational Choice Approach." *Journal of Theoretical Politics* 1: 131–47.

Shoch, James. 2000. "Contesting Globalization: Organized Labor, NAFTA, and the 1997 and 1998 Fast-Track Fights." *Politics and Society* 28: 119–50.

———. 2001. *Trading Blows: Party Competition and U.S. Trade Policy in a Globalizing Era*. Chapel Hill: University of North Carolina Press.

Silk, Leonard. 1972. *Nixonomics*. New York: Praeger.

Simmons, Beth A., Frank Dobbin, and Geoffrey Garrett. 2006. "Introduction: The International Diffusion of Liberalism." *International Organization* 60: 781–810.

Sklair, Leslie. 1991. *Sociology of the Global System: Social Change in Global Perspective*. Baltimore: Johns Hopkins University Press.

Skocpol, Theda. 1985. "Sociology's Historical Imagination." In *Vision and Method in Historical Sociology*, edited by T. Skocpol, 1–21. New York: Cambridge University Press.

———. 1992. *Protecting Soldiers and Mothers: The Political Origins of Social Policy in the United States*. Cambridge: Harvard University Press.

Skocpol, Theda, and Ken Finegold. 1982. "State Capacity and Economic Intervention in the Early New Deal." *Political Science Quarterly* 97: 255–78.

Slaughter, Anne-Marie. 2004. *A New World Order*. Princeton: Princeton University Press.

Slaughter, Anne-Marie, Alec Stone Sweet, and Joseph H. H. Weiler, eds. 1998. *The European Court and National Courts—Doctrine and Jurisprudence: Legal Change in Its Social Context*. Oxford: Hart Publishing.

Smith, James. 2003. "WTO Dispute Settlement: The Politics of Procedure in Appellate Body Rulings." *World Trade Review* 2: 65–100.

———. 2004. "Inequality in International Trade? Developing Countries and Institutional Change in WTO Dispute Settlement." *Review of International Political Economy* 11: 542–73.

Smith, Martin J. 1994. *Pressure, Power, and Policy: State Autonomy and Policy Networks in Britain and the United States*. Pittsburgh: University of Pittsburgh Press.

Sokolovsky, John. 1998. "The Making of National Health Insurance in Britain and Canada: Institutional Analysis and Its Limits." *Journal of Historical Sociology* 11: 247–80.

Solomon, Robert. 1977. *The International Monetary System, 1945–1976: An Insider's View*. New York: Harper and Row.

Stark, David, and László Bruszt. 1998. *Postsocialist Pathways: Transforming Politics and Property in East Central Europe*. New York: Cambridge University Press.

Steinberg, Richard H. 2002. "In the Shadow of Law or Power? Consensus-Based Bargaining and Outcomes in the GATT/WTO." *International Organization* 56: 339–74.

Steinmo, Sven. 1993. *Taxation and Democracy: Swedish, British, and American Approaches to Financing the Modern State*. New Haven: Yale University Press.

Stern, Paula. 1979. *Water's Edge: Domestic Politics and the Marking of American Foreign Policy*. Westport, CT: Greenwood Press.

Stone Sweet, Alec. 1998. "Constructing a Supranational Constitution: Dispute Resolution and Governance in the European Community." *American Political Science Review* 92: 63–80.

Strange, Susan. 1979. "The Management of Surplus Capacity: Or How Does Theory Stand Up to Protectionism 1970s Style?" *International Organization* 33: 303–34.

———. 1996. *The Retreat of the State: The Diffusion of Power in the World Economy*. Cambridge: Cambridge University Press.

Swank, Duane. 2002. *Global Capital, Political Institutions, and Policy Change in Developed Welfare States*. Cambridge: Cambridge University Press.

———. 2003. "Withering Welfare? Globalisation, Political Economic Institutions, and Contemporary Welfare States," in *States in the Global Economy: Bringing*

Domestic Institutions Back In, edited by L. Weiss, 58–82. Cambridge: Cambridge University Press.

Takacs, Wendy E. 1981. "Pressures for Protectionism: An Empirical Analysis." *Economic Inquiry* 1: 687–93.

Taussig, Frank William. 1964. *The Tariff History of the United States*. New York: Augustus M. Kelley Publishers.

Thelen, Kathleen. 1991. *Union of Parts: Labor Politics in Postwar Germany*. Ithaca: Cornell University Press.

———. 1999. "Historical Institutionalism in Comparative Politics." *Annual Review of Political Science* 2: 369–404.

———. 2003. "How Institutions Evolve: Insights from Comparative Historical Analysis." In *Comparative Historical Analysis in the Social Sciences*, edited by J. Mahoney and D. Rueschemeyer, 208–40. New York: Cambridge University Press.

———. 2004. *How Institutions Evolve: The Political Economy of Skills in Germany, Britain, the United States, and Japan*. Cambridge: Cambridge University Press.

Thelen, Kathleen, and Sven Steinmo. 1992. "Historical Institutionalism in Comparative Politics." In *Structuring Politics: Historical Institutionalism in Comparative Analysis*, edited by S. Steinmo, K. Thelen, and F. Longstreth, 1–32. Cambridge: Cambridge University Press.

Thomson, Janice E., and Stephen D. Krasner. 1989. "Global Transactions and the Consolidation of Sovereignty." In *Global Changes and Theoretical Challenges*, edited by E.-O. Czempiel and J. N. Rosenau, 195–219. Lexington, MA: Lexington Books.

Trubek, David M., Yves Dezalay, Ruth Buchanan, and John R. Davis. 1994. "Global Restructuring and the Law: Studies of the Internationalization of Legal Fields and the Creation of Transnational Arenas." *Case Western Reserve Law Review* 44: 407.

Tumlir, Jan. 1985. *Protectionism: Trade Policy in Democratic Societies*. Washington, DC: American Enterprise Institute.

Twiggs, Joan E. 1987. *The Tokyo Round of Multilateral Trade Negotiations: A Case Study in Building Domestic Support for Diplomacy*. New York: University Press of America.

Verdier, Daniel. 1994. *Democracy and International Trade: Britain, France, and the United States, 1860–1990*. Princeton: Princeton University Press.

Vernon, Raymond. 1954. "America's Foreign Trade Policy and the GATT." Essays in International Finance, no. 21. International Finance Section, Department of Economics and Sociology, Princeton University.

Vogel, Steven. 1996. *Freer Markets, More Rules*. Ithaca: Cornell University Press.

Waldner, David. 1999. *State Building and Late Development*. Ithaca: Cornell University Press.

Waltz, Kenneth N. 1979. *Theory of International Politics*. New York: McGraw-Hill.

Watson, Richard A. 1956. "The Tariff Revolution: A Study of Shifting Party Attitudes." *Journal of Politics* 18: 691–92.

Weber, Max. 1968 [1922]. *Economy and Society*. Translated and edited by G. Roth and C. Wittich. New York: Bedminster Press.

Weiler, Joseph H. H. 1994. "A Quiet Revolution: The European Court of Justice and Its Interlocutors." *Comparative Political Studies* 26: 510–34.

Weir, Margaret. 1992a. *Politics and Jobs: The Boundaries of Employment Policy in the United States*. Princeton: Princeton University Press.

———. 1992b. "Ideas and the Politics of Bounded Innovation." In *Structuring Politics: Historical Institutionalism in Comparative Analysis*, edited by S. Steinmo, K. Thelen, and F. Longstreth, 188–216. Cambridge: Cambridge University Press.

Weiss, Linda. 1997. "Globalization and the Myth of the Powerless State." *New Left Review* 225: 3–27.

———. 1998. *The Myth of the Powerless State*. Ithaca: Cornell University Press.

———. 1999. "Globalization and National Governance: Antinomy or Interdependence?" *Review of International Studies* 25: 59–88.

———, ed. 2003. *States in the Global Economy: Bringing Domestic Institutions Back In*. Cambridge: Cambridge University Press.

Wendt, Alexadner. 1999. *Social Theory of International Politics*. Cambridge: Cambridge University Press.

Wilkinson, Rorden. 2000. *Multilateralism and the World Trade Organization: The Architecture and Extension of International Trade Regulation*. London: Routledge.

———. 2001. "The WTO in Crisis: Exploring the Dimensions of Institutional Inertia." *Journal of World Trade* 35: 397–419.

Winham, Gilbert R. 1986. *International Trade and the Tokyo Round Negotiation*. Princeton: Princeton University Press.

Woodruff, David. 1999. *Money Unmade: Barter and the Fate of Russian Capitalism*. Ithaca: Cornell University Press.

Woods, Tim. 2003. "Capitalist Class Relations, the State, and New Deal Foreign Trade Policy." *Critical Sociology* 29: 393–418.

World Trade Organization (WTO). July 2001. "Overview of the State-of-Play of WTO Disputes." WTO, Geneva.

Yoffie, David B. 1983. *Power and Protectionism: Strategies of the Newly Industrializing Countries*. New York: Columbia University Press.

Young, Iris M. 2000. *Inclusion and Democracy*. Oxford: Oxford University Press.

Zeiler, Thomas W. 1992. *American Trade and Power in the 1960s*. New York: Columbia University Press.

———. 1998. "Managing Protectionism: American Trade Policy in the Early Cold War." *Diplomatic History* 22: 337.

Zysman, John. 1994. "How Institutions Create Historically Rooted Trajectories of Growth." *Industrial and Corporate Change* 3: 243–83.

———. 1996. "The Myth of the 'Global' Economy: Enduring National Foundations and Emerging Regional Realities." *New Political Economy* 1: 157–84.

Index